T0301517

Innovation in Public Sector Services

Für Marie

The editors would like to acknowledge the importance of funding within the project 'Innovation in the Public Sector (PUBLIN)', under the EU Programme for Research, Technological Development and Demonstration on 'Improving the human research potential and the socio-economic knowledge base, 1998–2002' under the EU Fifth Framework Programme. Work contained in a number of the book chapters was funded by the PUBLIN project.

Innovation in Public Sector Services

Entrepreneurship, Creativity and
Management

Edited by

Paul Windrum

*Reader in Innovation Management, Manchester Metropolitan
University Business School, UK. Visiting Professor at Max
Planck Institute for Economics, Jena, Germany*

Per Koch

*Assistant Director, NIFU STEP Studies in Innovation
Research and Education, Norway*

Edward Elgar
Cheltenham, UK • Northampton, MA, USA

Published by
Edward Elgar Publishing Limited
The Lypiatts
15 Lansdown Road
Cheltenham
Glos GL50 2JA
UK

Edward Elgar Publishing, Inc.
William Pratt House
9 Dewey Court
Northampton
Massachusetts 01060
USA

Reprinted 2015, 2016

A catalogue record for this book
is available from the British Library

Library of Congress Control Number: 2008926585

ISBN 978 1 84542 631 6

Printed and bound in Great Britain by the CPI Group (UK) Ltd

Contents

Figures

Tables

Contributors

Faridah Djellal	University François Rabelais of Tours, France.
Faïz Gallouj	Clersé, University of Lille 1 and Ifrési-CNRS, France.
Manuel García-Goñi	Universidad Complutense de Madrid, Spain.
Helge Godø	NIFU STEP, Studies of Innovation, Research and Education, Norway.
Mark Hall	University of Bristol, UK.
Robin Holt	University of Liverpool, UK.
Per Koch	Assistant Director, NIFU STEP, Studies in Innovation Research and Education, Norway.
L'udmila Malíková	Comenius University, Slovakia.
Andrés Maroto	University of Alcalá and Servilab, Spain.
Andrea Mina	University of Cambridge, UK.
Richard R. Nelson	Columbia University, USA.
Ronnie Ramlogan	University of Manchester, UK.
Luis Rubalcaba	University of Alcalá and Servilab, Spain.
Katarina Staroňová	Comenius University, Slovakia.
Paul Windrum	Reader in Innovation Management, Manchester Metropolitan University Business School, UK.

Foreword

The broad topic addressed in this book – innovation in public services – is extremely important and little studied. Most of the research on innovation has been focused on innovation by private for-profit firms, and the innovations studied have tended to be physical products or the technological processes used to produce them. Recent research, for example, that concerned with innovation in medicine or in education has widened the scope somewhat, bringing organizations like hospitals and schools into the picture and new professional practices. There is a small literature on innovations in organizational forms and styles of management. There is some on the development of new government policies and programmes. But this literature is not extensive.

This is not to say that there has been little research on public services. There is a vast literature in political science and some in economics on the mechanisms and factors that determine the government policies and programmes that are in place at any time. Many government programmes, and the services that they provide, have been subjected to searching cost–benefit analyses. There is an extensive literature on how public agencies are organized, on the nature of public bureaucracies and on public administration. There are many sophisticated normative writings concerned with how to do good policy analysis and the canons of good administration. But very little of this literature has been concerned self-consciously with innovation in public services.

It must be understood that innovation is a term of art. In the general orientation of research concerned with innovation, innovating is seen as a purposive act or set of acts aiming to do something better, to meet a new need or respond to new circumstances. The conception of trying something new, and not simply making a different choice among prevailing and well perceived alternatives, is an essential part of the innovation concept. While the objective of doing things differently so as to improve performance is very much part of the literature on the evaluation of public programmes and organizational and managerial reform of government agencies, most of that literature sees the issue as making better decisions, as contrasted with trying something new and different.

This book is built around the concept of improving public services through innovation in the sense of trying something new and different rather than through better analysis and decision making. The latter draws one's attention to doing careful cost–benefit studies of perceived alternatives, and following the canons of good organizational structure and management. The focus on innovation draws one's attention to the ability of those involved in public programmes to be creative, entrepreneurial, risk taking, and capable of learning from experience how to improve new programmes. This is very much what this book is about.

This perspective on how to improve public programmes is much needed and, as I have said, unfortunately relatively rare. Up until relatively recently, the writing and teaching about how to improve the performance of business firms was largely focused on doing better analysis and making better decisions. Over the past decade, however, the importance of being able to innovate effectively, and of entrepreneurship, has come to the fore both in business schools and the press. This book may start the ball rolling in the same direction regarding how to improve the provision of public services.

Richard R. Nelson
June, 2007

PART I

Issues in public sector innovation and entrepreneurship

1. Innovation and entrepreneurship in public services

Paul Windrum

1.1 INTRODUCTION

Service sectors now make up the majority of economic activities in the USA, Europe and Japan. Yet the contribution of services faces a major challenge: advancing productivity growth, employment and welfare require a strengthening of the innovative performance in services. In Europe, the Lisbon 2000 strategy identified the need to enhance performance in services activities. This led to the definition of a new strategy for the internal market for services, and to the adoption of a corresponding framework directive in 2006, among other service-related actions. The contribution of services to economic growth, employment and welfare will not be possible without a major role for innovation in services.

This book addresses a fundamental knowledge gap: it seeks to understand and explain the dynamics of public sector services innovation.[1] Public sector innovation is a key contributor to national growth, and to the welfare of individual citizens, yet precious little research has been conducted on public sector innovation.[2] In part, this is a legacy of the old view that held that manufacturing is the sole source of productivity growth and economic wealth, while services are unproductive and technologically backward. This old view has been successfully challenged in recent years by research on services innovation in the private sector. Now is the time to critically evaluate the contributions of innovative public sector service providers. The lack of prior research on public sector innovation is also, in part, a consequence of disciplinary myopia. Innovation studies have overwhelmingly focused on innovation in private sector manufacturing and private sector service firms. Meanwhile, political science considers change in the public sector – in the form of 'policy change' and 'reform' – but fails to address innovation. Yet innovation certainly exists in public sector services. On a daily basis, novel ideas and technologies are developed in public health and medicine, in universities and general education, and in social services.

The chapters in this book highlight the importance of entrepreneurship, creativity and management within the public sector. They challenge and break open the Weberian view of public sector organizations as static bureaucracies in which new ideas are stifled. In its place, we find innovation champions – 'policy entrepreneurs' and 'service entrepreneurs' – who are willing to experiment and take risks in applying, for the first time, radical new ideas. These are either ideas which they have developed themselves, or else are the first application of ideas developed elsewhere. Of course, the environment within which public sector entrepreneurs operate is very different to that of private sector markets. Social responsibility and accountability, plus the very different networks found in the public sector, give rise to a very different set of barriers and enablers for the diffusion of innovations. This book investigates the range of social, technical, and political management skills and knowledge that are employed by public sector entrepreneurs on a daily basis.

As noted, recent research on private sector services has moved our understanding of innovation beyond manufacturing. Yet the current state-of-the-art research provides, at best, a partial understanding of the drivers, dynamics and impacts of services because it does not address the role of public sector organizations within the innovation process. What is needed is a systematic research programme on innovation within the public sector, and the interactions between public and private sector organizations within the innovation process. This book represents a first step for this new, challenging research agenda. It addresses seven core questions:

1. Do public services innovate?
2. If so, under what conditions do public service organizations innovate?
3. What form does this innovation take?
4. When and how does innovation occur?
5. What role does entrepreneurship and management reform play in the innovation process?
6. How does an evolving policy context influence innovation?
7. What is the link between public sector innovation and private sector innovation?

Together, the chapters in this book contribute to our understanding of the factors that stimulate and shape new service innovations, leading to new variety in services, and the complex set of factors that determine what service innovations are to be taken up and diffused. In particular, this book addresses the role of entrepreneurship, management and creativity in the generation of innovations within the pubic sector.

Some readers may be surprised to read that entrepreneurship, management and creativity exist in the public sector. Despite the fact that public sector entrepreneurship has been discussed since the 1960s and 1970s, it is a common (mis)conception, in many developed countries, that the public sector is not entrepreneurial and does not innovate. Public sector institutions are considered conservative, bureaucratic and slow moving, and to whatever extent they do change, this is primarily a consequence of changes that occur outside public institutions, that is, as a result of the innovative activities of non-governmental organizations (NGOs) or private sector firms. Innovations developed elsewhere are belatedly adopted by the public sector. This view is frequently tied to the 'public versus private sector debate' (Rubalcaba, 2007). In this debate public and private services are presented as a discrete choice, that is, either public or private service provision. Given the supposed superior innovative potential of the private sector, policy should focus on the privatization of public services, thereby ensuring increasing productivity growth and employment, as well as superior quality of service provision. This has been the predominant view in Europe and the USA since the 1980s. The consequence has been an outsourcing/competitive tendering of basic services, the adoption of management practices originally developed in the private sector (notably under the New Public Management rubric), and public–private funding initiatives.

This view has (however unconsciously) spilled over into a bias within innovation literature towards private sector service organizations. Notable examples are the Baumol (1967) debate regarding the implications of the services economy for national productivity and growth, the assimilation–demarcation–synthesis debate regarding the nature of service innovation and manufacturing innovation, and the role of business services as essential intermediate inputs for economic growth. There is a sad irony here. The objective of innovation studies is to understand the processes that drive innovation and the link between innovation and social and economic change. Yet, by neglecting public sector innovation, the innovation literature has omitted important dimensions of the innovation process, and failed to address the impact of public sector innovation on productivity growth and employment.

1.2 INNOVATION IN THE PUBLIC SECTOR

The public sector comprises a system of public institutions that affect peoples' everyday lives in a myriad of ways. These institutions include the political institutions and structures that determine and implement laws. They provide basic social and public services, such as social welfare services, education and health. These institutions are essential to our modern understanding of a capitalist democracy. Public sector services can account for a significant part of all economic activity. In most developed nations the public sector accounts for around 20 per cent of employment and around 15 per cent of national GNP. The public sector can also play a dominant role in the employment of highly educated people. Indeed, parts of the public sector are among the most knowledge-intensive in the economy, and play a central role in the creation and distribution of knowledge in society. In the UK, for example, the public sector accounts for around 40 per cent of GNP, some 20 per cent of total employment and 30 per cent of all professional level employment.

Given the importance of the public sector, public sector innovation is of central concern in discussions of social welfare, productivity growth and long-term employment. As noted, there are very few studies that have taken into account innovation in both the public and private sectors. One notable exception is Earl (2002, 2004). Her work draws on a sample of public and private Canadian organizations for the period 1998–2000. Around 80 per cent of public sector organizations within the sample had introduced significantly improved organizational structures or management techniques. By contrast, just 38 per cent of private organizations had introduced such innovations within the same period. Perhaps even more striking are the reported levels of technological change. Some 44 per cent of private sector organizations reported the introduction of significantly improved technologies. However, some 85 per cent of public sector organizations reported the introduction of significantly improved technologies for the same period. As Earl notes, part of this difference is explained by organization size. Small private sector firms have low adoption rates, while for larger firms (with 100 or more employees) the adoption rates are similar for the private and public sector organizations. This, however, does not alter the finding that public sector organizations are at least as innovative as private sector organizations.

The range of public sector organizations is diverse, as are the role(s) that they play in the innovation process. Public organizations may be important users of new innovations, determining whether they develop and the shape that they subsequently take. There is an important role for public procurement and the public sector can be a key partner in user–producer development. Public sector organizations may also play an active role in the development of new technologies. They are frequently the suppliers of complementary services and infrastructures that are essential to the effective use of private sector goods and services. Public and private sector organizations interact in the vast majority of service sectors in Europe and the USA. Social and personal services, including health and education, are amongst the most obvious examples. It is the same case for bio pharmaceuticals and medical technologies. Public–private provision is also essential in network services and business services, such as transport and information and communication technologies (ICTs). In fact, looking across the EU member states, there is a large variety of ways in which private and public organizations interact in service provision. Take, for example, the car. Policy makers and public institutions at all levels (local, regional and national) are involved in the effective running of a series of services that support the private car sector. The efficient running of a car-based transport 'system' requires the coordination of traffic flow and parking space. The former includes support services, such as road lighting, road maintenance, traffic signals and signs, repair garages and breakdown services. These are provided by a mix of private and public sector providers.

The public sector can also play an essential role as a regulator. In the case of the car, a complicated regulation system is present in nearly all countries, with a combination of national and local government regulatory bodies responsible for the formulation and delivery of urban and environmental planning programmes covering road construction, urban development and traffic control. Public bodies are additionally involved in the provision of safety-related functions, such as proficiency tests for drivers, regular mechanical tests for car safety, road police, and accident and emergency services. Finally, a system of taxation operates to levy car users in order to fund the publicly provided services that are essential to the smooth functioning of the car-based transport system.

The public sector can be an innovator in its own right. Public sector organizations have played a significant role in the development of many of the technologies that surround us today, ranging from the internet and the World Wide Web to biotechnology. The importance of publicly funded university science for social and economic development has been recognized since Vannevar Bush's report to President Roosevelt (Bush, 1945). This report formed the basis of the post-war consensus on the need for active government support and funding for science in the USA and Europe. Of course, the public sector is made up of more than just universities, and many public organizations have contributed to radical technological innovation and development. The military have actively championed key technologies that have later spilled over into civilian use. The most obvious recent example is the internet, which has its origins in the secure US military network, the ARPANET. There are many other examples, such as lasers, logistics and process technologies. The health sector has played a pivotal role in new medical technologies, instruments, drugs and treatments. Large public organizations have championed and supported the development of successive generations of new ICTs. Public transport has championed the development of high speed trains, civil aircraft and infrastructures. Public education has developed knowledge infrastructures.

Telecommunications companies (though now largely privatized in Europe and the USA since the 1980s) were essential to the development of satellite communications, mobile telephony and the internet.

1.3   CORE RESEARCH THEMES AND ISSUES

The chapters of this book mark an important step towards a general and consistent basis for the understanding of innovation in public sector services. First, there is the identification and discussion of different types of innovation. Second, research is conducted on key factors that affect the timing, nature and success of public sector innovations. Section 1.3.1 presents a taxonomy of public service innovation. This is based on the empirical and theoretical research findings of this book. Section 1.3.2 then discusses six general factors that are found to shape and direct innovation.

1.3.1   Taxonomy of Public Sector Innovation

In order to develop a clear understanding of 'what' types of innovation are found in the public sector a taxonomy of public service innovation is presented that draws on the research contained in this book. The taxonomy comprises six types of innovation:

1. service innovation
2. service delivery innovation
3. administrative and organizational innovation
4. conceptual innovation
5. policy innovation, and
6. systemic innovation.

   Service innovation is the introduction of a new service product or an improvement in the quality of an existing service product. This includes all innovations involving changes in the characteristics of service products and the design of services. This is directly comparable with product innovations in manufactured goods, and is the traditional focus of innovation studies of manufacturing innovation. Service delivery innovation involves new or altered ways of delivering to clients, or otherwise interacting with them, for the purpose of supplying specific public services. Administrative and organizational innovation changes the organizational structures and routines by which front office staff produce services in a particular way and/or back office staff support front office services. Over the last 20 years, the introduction of New Public Management (NPM) has been a major force for organizational reforms in the public sector. The organizational principles of NPM are not necessarily new, but NPM has ushered in new methods for the organization of public sector services.

The first three categories – service, service delivery and organizational innovation – have been examined in studies of private sector innovation. Extending the analysis to product, service and organizational innovations in the public sector is important in order to test what (we think) we know about innovation. The objective of innovation research is to establish a consistent and general basis for understanding innovation and its socio-economic impact. It is paradoxical that the innovation literature has hitherto neglected the public sector – a major provider of services in all developed economies. What is needed, and what this book starts to do, is to reopen and extend the demarcation–assimilation–synthesis debate.[3] Just as research on private sector services and service organizations tested and challenged theories and concepts originally developed in studies of manufacturing, so we need to extend the domain of research to the public sector and retest our theories and concepts. This process of critical reappraisal is likely to throw up new insights in its own right. In addition, the research presented in this book adds three categories of innovation that have hitherto been largely ignored – conceptual innovation, policy innovation and systemic innovation. Past research on private sector innovation has 'black boxed' these forms of innovation, possibly as a means of simplification. This is not an option when studying public sector innovation. In opening up and developing research on these three additional types of innovation, researchers may in the future consider their importance for explanations of innovation in private sector organizations. Such a change would mark a major shift in innovation research.

Conceptual innovation is the development of new world views that challenge assumptions that underpin existing service products, processes and organizational forms. It can occur at all levels and involve the introduction of new missions, new world views, objectives, strategies and rationales. Conceptual innovations are particularly important to institutions operating under social or public objectives because they establish a link between the social economic objectives of a public organization and its operational rationale. One of the most important examples of a radical conceptual innovation in recent history is the 'minimalist state'. This was prompted in the late 1970s by a perceived crisis in a post-war consensus based on the interventionist state support of private sector capital. One consequence was the creation of large-scale public sector service provision. The conceptual shift to the minimalist state has led to an ongoing reassessment of who (public or private) should produce what, how, at what time, using what type of relationship structures, what management practices, and under what contractual obligations. The result has been the replacement of public sector provision by private sector firms, as part of an agenda for a 'rolling back of the state', and the introduction of NPM private sector styles of organization.

Policy innovations change the thought or behavioural intentions associated with a policy belief system (Sabatier, 1987, 1999). The chapters in this book carefully examine the learning processes underlying policy development in public sector bureaucracies. At the ministerial level, we find policy innovation comes in two forms: incremental innovation, based on policy learning by the government, and radical innovation, sparked by conceptual innovation. Policy innovations are associated with three types of learning (Glasbergen, 1994). First, there is learning of how policy instruments can be improved to achieve a set of goals. Second, there is conceptual learning that follows changes in shared understanding of a problem and appropriate courses of action, that is, follows conceptual innovations. Examples include the development of new policy concepts, such as integrated environmental policy and the re-evaluation of existing policy values. Third, there is social learning based on shared understanding of the appropriate roles of policy actors and the rules for interaction change based on new ideas about social interaction and governance.

Policy instrument learning tends to be incremental in nature and is based on single-loop learning. Single-loop learning does not question the fundamental design, goals and activities of an organization. By contrast, conceptual and social learning tend to be radical in nature and involve double-loop learning. It requires a rethink or a change of the theories in use. Double-loop learning tends to be prompted by a crisis or revolution (Argyris and Schon, 1978). These alter the conceptual/belief frames that are used to define the problem to be addressed, the information that must be collected, and the dimensions that must be evaluated. Such frames focus attention and simplify analysis. There is a clear link with policy innovations and conceptual innovations. Changing frames direct attention to different options and can lead to different preferences.

Systemic innovation involves new or improved ways of interacting with other organizations and knowledge bases. These interactions have changed dramatically over the last 20 years, partly as a consequence of deregulation and increasing competition, partly as the result of budgetary constraints in public administration and the increasing role of service outsourcing, and partly as a result of increasing sophistication by consumers. Privatization, and the contracting-out of public services, has resulted in new relations with private sector firms and non-governmental organizations, and fundamentally changed the public welfare system. The emergence of public–private partnerships in the EU agenda during the 1990s is a clear example of this. The transition to market economies by Central and Eastern European countries was another key factor. Interest in public–private innovation

interactions may even be more relevant than in Western EU countries
because transition economies require a new definition of the role of the
public sector and new forms of services provision in which public and private
may complement each other.

1.3.2 Factors Affecting the Timing, Direction and Success of Innovation

The research contained in this book identifies a number of common factors
that determine when and how innovation occurs, and whether innovation
is successful. Six generic factors are identified:

- incentive structures
- public sector entrepreneurs
- bottom-up and top-down innovation
- impact of New Public Management (NPM) on innovation
- implications of consumerism.

1.3.2.1 Incentive structures
In order to understand the key drivers and incentive structures of public
sector innovation we need to consider the fundamental dilemma that exists
within the 'minimalist state' paradigm. On the one hand, there is a need to
address citizens' insatiable desire for more and better quality public services. On the other hand, there is the belief that overall public expenditure
and taxation should not increase. Indeed, public expenditure and taxation
should ideally fall over time. As noted already, one means of addressing this
fundamental dilemma is the privatization of services. Developed Western
countries have explored this avenue to a greater or lesser extent. However,
there are social, economic and cultural limits to the privatization of public
services. Where this is the case, the 'solution' is public sector innovation.

The empirical case studies in this book highlight the problem-driven
focus of innovation in public services. Underlying innovation drivers that
one commonly meets are changing demographics (notably falling birth
rates and population ageing), social changes such as the breakdown of the
nuclear family, and health and social problems arising from new types of
work (for example, sedentary white collar jobs) and new lifestyles. It is clear
that many innovations in public health and social services sectors are a
response to one or more of these underlying pressures. In addition to these
aggregate drivers, innovations may be driven by more specific (local) problems. Examples include the need to reduce waiting lists and the duration of
treatment within specific hospitals.

The empirical research also highlights a number of important facilitators
for innovation. Facilitators are factors that aid the uptake, development

and dissemination of innovation within and across public sector organizations. These facilitators may operate at the aggregate (national) level or
at the local level. Of particular importance are incentive structures and
support mechanisms that allocate resources (finance and other forms of
support) to promote creativity. Allied to supported creativity, there need to
be structures and systems that promote, stimulate and disseminate the
outputs of this creativity – that is, innovations.[4] In addition to an organizational environment that encourages creativity and innovation, there
needs to be a surrounding environment that supports competence building.

1.3.2.2   Public sector entrepreneurs

As noted already, it is still rather uncommon to see discussions about public
sector entrepreneurship. However, discussion of public entrepreneurship
within political science and public administration dates back to the 1960s
and 1970s; notably Ostrom (1964), Wagner (1966), Frohlich et al. (1971)
and Jones (1978). In recent years the concept of public entrepreneurship
has also appeared within mainstream entrepreneurship literature.

Entrepreneurs are found to be essential in all of the innovation case
studies presented in this book. The link between innovation and entrepreneurship dates back to Schumpeter (1934). In Schumpeter's classic description the entrepreneur is the driving force that initiates the development of
a novel innovation and successfully manages the diffusion of the innovation. Public sector entrepreneurs seek to change the world around them.
They are creative individuals who can develop new ideas that challenge the
status quo. What is more, they are risk takers who are well connected within
social networks. They use these connections to draw upon the social
and financial resources necessary to develop radically new innovations.
Network connections are important because no single individual will have
all the competences and financial resources necessary to carry out an innovation by themself. Hence, an existing set of connections and skills in
developing new contacts are essential qualities for successful entrepreneurs.
Another essential quality discussed by Schumpeter is determination. An
entrepreneur maintains their belief in the innovation, even in the face of
severe setbacks and unforeseen events that threaten its success. Such determination is vital to the successful diffusion of the innovation.

Public and private sector entrepreneurs do, of course, differ with respect
to their basic motivation, although in the end these may be differences in
degree rather than absolutes. The simple distinction that can be drawn is
that private sector entrepreneurs are motivated by profit while public sector
entrepreneurs are motivated by social welfare. Politicians, for example, are
driven by a desire to change society in order to improve the quality of life
of citizens. Yet one should guard against overly simplistic distinctions.

Schumpeter (1934) observed that private sector entrepreneurs are not only driven by the quest for profits. They also have personal and social motivations. These include the development of products that improve the quality of life of their customers, and personal status and meaning within their professional community and society at large. In some cases, this can extend to the desire for personal fame and to be remembered in history. Such motivations can lead to private philanthropy, the setting up of foundations and investment in museums and other civic buildings. They go well beyond the quest for immediate profit.

One can also find this complex range of motivations among politicians and other leading public figures. Politicians, for example, share many of the personal qualities attributed to entrepreneurs. They are driven by a desire to change the way society works. In part this is motivated by altruism, in part by private goal seeking. They wish to leave their mark on history. An important aspect in achieving success lies in altering the timing, quality and delivery of public services. This requires determination and resourcefulness. Politicians must have strong powers of rhetoric and persuasion, and be able to mobilize social and financial support. It is, therefore, important to guard against simplistic distinctions between altruism and selfishness in the public and private sectors. Understanding the richness of individual motivations is essential if we are to understand the drives of public/private sector entrepreneurs.

1.3.2.3 Top-down and bottom-up innovation

Public sector entrepreneurs, and the innovations they develop, can be found at different hierarchal levels. This is reflected in discussions about bottom-up and top-down innovations. 'Top-down' indicates that the process was initiated high in the hierarchy, for example, by ministers, while 'bottom-up' indicates the process was initiated lower down in the hierarchy, for example, by public employees or by mid-level policy makers. Top-down innovations tend to be initiated with changes in governance frameworks and regulation. They may be oriented towards achieving greater efficiency in the supply of existing services. By contrast, bottom-up innovations may be more focused on an expansion of the quality of supplied services or the development of a new service.

Top-down innovations are the most commonly reported type in the media. These are championed by politicians, who are also sometimes the original source of these ideas. Top-down innovations tend to be general in nature, taking the form of generic political goals rather than detailed changes in specific services. Implementation tends to be handed over to the institution concerned.[5] In the top-down perspective, implementation is a passive process at the end of a chain of processes (Pressman and Wildavsky,

1973; van Meter and van Horn, 1975). This is very much in line with Max Weber's concept of the 'ideal bureaucracy' in which a clear demarcation exists between a political leadership and bureaucrats. Politicians are charged with decision making while public employees deliver the public services that are defined by politicians.

The existence of bottom-up innovation challenges and overturns the Weberian idealization. Far from being subordinate to a political leadership, public sector managers and service personnel can be entrepreneurs in their own right. They play an important role in the formation of political agendas and in decision making. As a consequence, innovation is an ongoing process within the public sector (Elmore, 1980; Barrett and Hill, 1984). Far from being conservative, public sector managers may champion very radical changes in public services. Radical changes can provide an opportunity for service entrepreneurs to make their mark (as they do for politicians). The innovation potential of service entrepreneurs may be higher than that of political entrepreneurs because service entrepreneurs are specialists with a deep knowledge of their field, usually with professional training and qualifications. The public sectors in developed countries employ a large number of university trained personnel. Politicians, by contrast, are generalists who must have some knowledge of many areas of policy and government. Politicians rarely have the training or the opportunity to develop in-depth understanding of specific fields.

There are two important issues associated with bottom-up innovation. The first is under-reporting. Far less attention is paid to bottom-up innovations. This has ramifications for incentivizing and rewarding local initiatives. It also has serious implications for measuring public sector innovation and its contribution to aggregate productivity growth and welfare. The second important issue is policy. If service entrepreneurs play an important role in the creation and development of new innovations, then policy should recognize these actors, their role, and confer on them the necessary resources and responsibilities.

Finally, one needs to recognize the possibility of conflict between political and service entrepreneurs. In part, conflicts may reflect the different viewpoints and perspectives of agents that operate at different hierarchal levels. For example, political entrepreneurs may seek efficiency gains through organizational restructuring. Service level staff may perceive this reorganization as largely disruptive and oppose it, preferring instead to focus on service level innovations in order to improve service quality as well as efficiency. Conflicts will be resolved in varying ways under different regimes. Regimes, therefore, influence the direction and types of innovation that are encouraged. It is to the New Public Management regime that we next turn.

1.3.2.4 Impact of New Public Management on innovation

The impact of New Public Management (NPM) on innovation is specifically considered by Hall and Holt in Chapter 2, and is also discussed in a number of the case studies. NPM is driven by the belief that acquiring and developing private sector management skills and practices is necessary in order to deal with the fundamental dilemma of the public sector – that of ever increasing demands for better quality public services and the need to control public expenditure. By defining the basic dilemma of the 'minimal state' in this way, the focus of NPM becomes one of cost efficiency. What is more, consumer satisfaction becomes central to the definition and measurement of cost efficiency. The logic follows that, since private sector managers are well versed in addressing consumers, it makes sense for public sector managers to adopt private sector managerial principles and practices.

With regards to NPM and innovation, it is important to first dispel the idea (popularized by some NPM advocates) that innovation did not occur in the public sector prior to NPM. It is hoped that the earlier discussion of the role of the public sector in innovation systems has convinced the reader that this idea is unsupportable. What is correct, however, is the proposition that NPM has inspired changes that have transformed the public sector and the focus of innovation within it. Individual public organizations are charged with meeting measurable 'performance targets' for customer satisfaction, efficiency and expenditure. State monies are now distributed within a performance-based transfer system that rewards organizations that meet the established performance targets and withholds funds from those organizations that fail to meet these targets.

The NPM regime is an important factor shaping the direction of innovation in the public sector. Its logic favours the development of certain types of innovation while discouraging the development of others. This holds across each of the six types of innovation contained in our taxonomy, that is, certain types of service, service delivery, administrative and organizational, conceptual, policy and systemic innovations are selected while others are rejected. Notably, NPM favours innovations that support the decentralization, privatization and contracting-out of services; promotes competition between public providers and private firms/not-for-profit organizations; develops consumerism; and separates political and administrative decision making from service production.

1.3.2.5 Implications of consumerism

As noted, NPM replaces democratic controls (that is, rules and regulations) to govern the production and distribution of services with market-type controls that are based on consumer satisfaction. 'Consumerization' raises a number of issues. First, there is the replacement of citizens by customers. The rights and responsibilities of citizens, and the relationship between citizens and the state, are very different to that of customers. Although the debate has not yet begun, there is a need to readdress the basis of our understanding of civil society and the role played by the public sector within civil society.

Second, consumer sovereignty requires knowledge, information, choice and effective relationships between buyers and sellers. We need to recognize the differences that exist between customers of different types of services. In knowledge-intensive services, such as health, it is not obvious whether individuals will possess the information and knowledge necessary to make informed diagnoses of their illness and, hence, independent choices about alternative treatments. Analogies between customers of health services and consumers of domestic household goods can quickly break down. Decisions about which brands of goods to purchase, and the long-term impact of such decisions, are very different to making informed health decisions. What is more, the scale of commitment required to become an informed user also differs according to the service being considered. As discussed in the health case studies, it is far harder to become an empowered, independent health customer, and to fundamentally change one's lifestyle, than it is to purchase a packet of cornflakes, a new car or a package summer holiday.

An important part of the rationale for creating informed, empowered customers is that this will produce a change in individual behaviour that leads to greater efficiency and/or cost savings. For example, environmentally aware consumers will be concerned about the pollution they create (their 'carbon footprint'). More recycling leads to savings in refuse collection and processing, and reduces the demand for landfill. Reducing the quantity of household waste reduces the cost of service collection and enables governments to meet their green policy commitments. In health, empowered customers will take greater care of their own health, reducing the financial burden they place on the health system.

Consumerization may yet prove a double-edged sword. There is no consensus about the appropriate balance between individual and social responsibility. Consumers may demand that governments, as service providers to whom they pay money in the form of taxes, take responsibility for solving customers' problems. If this occurs, then consumerization will place an even greater burden on the state. Take, as an example, the case of health and tobacco smoking. Smokers know their behaviour is bad for their health but are extremely loathe to change their lifestyle. In part, this is due to the highly addictive nature of nicotine. Are smokers as individuals entirely responsible for any ill health that may (statistically) be linked to smoking?

Alternatively, is ill health the responsibility of a health service that is charged with the ongoing servicing and maintaining of individuals' health? To draw an analogy with the servicing of a car, the legal responsibility lies with the service provider, not the owner.

Confusion on the issue of societal and individual responsibility pervades current health policy. In the late 1990s it was proposed that smokers should be refused cancer treatment unless they quit smoking prior to treatment. The result was a public outcry that ensured the proposal was never put into practice. Yet recent bans on smoking in public places in a number of European countries have been accepted by the public. What is interesting is the rationale. The justification of the policy is that secondary smoking harms others, and so bans are protecting the health of non-smokers. It is not a measure designed to force individual smokers to do something, that is, to give up cigarettes. If it were, then the policy would force one group of individuals to cede choice and to accept greater intervention in their personal lives. Clearly, a 'consumerisation' of public services is not a panacea. Rather, it raises some fundamental issues regarding individual responsibility and the responsibility of the state, and the relationship between the individual and society.

1.4   OVERVIEW OF THE BOOK

The research presented in this book provides a host of new theoretical and empirical insights into innovation and entrepreneurship in the public sector. Theory is grounded in new empirical research that is conducted at the macro, meso and micro levels. The book is organized into two parts. Chapters 1 to 4 develop key themes that motivate research in this area. Chapter 2 is a critical analysis of the theory and practice of New Public Management. Chapter 3 explores the heterogeneity of welfare state models that exist in Europe, and the variety of different approaches and methods that have been used to modernize public services. It examines the empirical link between the size and performance of the public sector in different EU countries and economic growth. Chapter 4 provides a detailed case study of a health service innovation. The case study raises and contextualizes a set of key issues for health sector innovation and for innovation in many public sector services: the problem of scarce resources, the encouragement of competition between alternative providers, social/cultural barriers and enablers of innovation, and the impact of performance measurement.

A series of detailed case studies of public health and social services innovations are presented in Chapters 5 to 10. The health and social service sectors are significant due to their direct contribution to social welfare, and because innovation is central to meeting the challenges posed by changing demographics (population ageing and falling birth rates), the breakdown of the nuclear family, and the health and social problems associated with the growth of sedentary white collar jobs. These services are politically sensitive and attract intense media attention. Politicians are actively engaged in developing policies and programmes which promote innovations that improve service quality and delivery while keeping costs under control.

The case studies highlight connections between the six types of innovation that are described in our taxonomy. Service, service delivery, organizational, conceptual, policy and systemic innovations do not occur in isolation. Instead, connections between them mean that multiple types of interconnected innovations need to be implemented in order for change to occur. The case studies indicate the existence of common trends and patterns in innovation across Europe. Yet, at the same time, there is variety in the way that public sector entrepreneurs tackle problems in different national or regional settings.

In addition to the important role played by public sector entrepreneurs and NPM, attention is drawn to consumerization – changing the relationship between clients and service providers through customer empowerment and the personalization of public services. The case studies investigate the implications and impact of NPM and consumerization on innovation opportunities, and how they affect the innovation opportunities of public sector entrepreneurs.

Chapter 11, the final chapter of the book, brings together the findings of the research and uses them to further develop the discussion of innovation and entrepreneurship outlined in the current chapter. First, it uses the collective findings to address the seven core research questions identified in this chapter, that is: Do public services innovate? If so, under what conditions do public service organizations innovate? What form does this innovation take? When and how does innovation occur? What role does entrepreneurship and management reform play in the innovation process? How does an evolving policy context influence innovation? What is the link between public sector innovation and private sector innovation?

As well as summarizing and reflecting on the research findings, Chapter 11 uses these research findings to develop and extend the taxonomy of innovation introduced in this chapter. Moreover, the findings form the basis of a model of public sector entrepreneurship.

NOTES

1. The origins of the book lie in the research project 'Innovation in the Public Sector' (PUBLIN). The project was funded under the EU Fifth Framework Programme (contract

HPSE-CT-2002-00142) and ran between 2003 and 2006. It sought to gain a better under-standing of innovation and policy. A number of the chapters contained within this book are based on research conducted within this project.
2. This is also the case for National Systems of Innovation (NSI) research. While this research draws attention to the important roles played by public institutions in support-ing the creation and distribution of new knowledge in society, little or no attention is given to the innovation process within the public sector.
3. See Windrum (2007) for an overview of the demarcation–assimilation–synthesis debate.
4. Also see Hauknes (2005) on the need for an alignment between the goals/objectives of a public organization and its incentive structures for innovation.
5. This may be due to the need for more detailed competence on special issues, or it may be part of a strategy to involve those who work in the relevant public sector, since reforms are seen to be more successful when the relevant actors are involved in the process (Brunsson and Olsen, 1993).

REFERENCES

Argyris, C. and D. Schon (1978), *Organizational Learning: A Theory of Action Perspective*, Reading, MA: Addison-Wesley.
Barrett, S. and M. Hill (1984), 'Policy, bargaining and structure in implementation theory: towards an integrated perspective', *Policy and Politics*, **12**(3), 219–40.
Baumol, W. (1967), 'Macroeconomics of unbalanced growth', *American Economic Review*, **2**, 415–26.
Brunsson, N. and J.P. Olsen (1993), *The Reforming Organization*, London: Routledge.
Bush, Vannevar (1945), *Science The Endless Frontier*, report to the President by Vannevar Bush, Director of Scientific Research and Development, Washington, DC: United States Government Printing Office, accessed May 2007 at www.nsf.gov/od/lpa/nsf50/vbush1945.htm.
Earl, L. (2002), *Innovation and Change in the Public Sector: A Seeming Oxymoron. Survey of Electronic Commerce and Technology, 2000*, cat. no.88F0006XIE02001, Ottawa: Statistics Canada (Science, Innovation and Electronic Information Division).
Earl, L. (2004), *An Historical Comparison of Technological Change, 1998–2000 and 2000–2002, in the Private and Public Sectors*, cat. no.88F0006XIE200407, Ottawa: Statistics Canada (Science, Innovation and Electronic Information Division).
Elmore, R. (1980), 'Backward mapping: implementation research and policy deci-sions', *Political Science Quarterly*, **94**(3), 601–16.
Frohlich, N., J.A. Oppenheimer and O.A. Young (1971), *Political Leadership and Collective Goods*, Princeton, NJ: Princeton University Press.
Glasbergen, P. (ed.) (1994), *Managing Environmental Disputes. Network Management As an Alternative*, Deventer, Netherlands: Kluwer.
Hauknes, J. (2005), 'Some thoughts about innovation in the public and private sector compared,' in T. Halvorsen, J. Hauknes, I. Miles and R. Røste (eds), 'On the differences between public and private sector innovation', *Publin Report No. D9*, accessed May 2007 at www.step.no/publin.
Jones, P. (1978), 'The appeal of the political entrepreneur', *British Journal of Political Science*, **8**(4), 498–504.

van Meter, D.S. and C.E. van Horn (1975), 'The policy implementation process: a conceptual framework', *Administration and Society*, **6**(4), 445–88.
Ostrom, E. (1964), 'Public entrepreneurship: a case study in ground water basic management', dissertation for University of California at Los Angeles.
Pressman, J.L. and A. Wildavsky (1973), *Implementation*, Berkeley, CA: California University Press.
Rubalcaba, L. (2007), *The Services Economy: Challenges and Policy Implications for Europe*, Cheltenham, UK and Northampton, MA, USA: Edward Elgar.
Sabatier, P.A. (1987), 'Knowledge, policy-oriented learning, and policy change', *Knowledge, Creation, Diffusion, Utilization*, **8**, 649–92.
Sabatier, P.A. (ed.) (1999), *Theories of the Policy Process*, Boulder, CO: Westview Press.
Schumpeter, J.A. (1934), *The Theory of Economic Development: An Inquiry Into Profits, Capital, Credit, Interest and Business Cycle*, Cambridge, MA: Harvard University Press.
Wagner, R.E. (1966), 'Pressure groups and political entrepreneurs: a review', *Public Choice*, **1**, 161–70.
Windrum, P. (2007), 'Services innovation', in H. Hanusch and A. Pyka (eds), *The Edward Elgar Companion to Neo-Schumpeterian Economics*, Cheltenham, UK and Northampton, MA, USA: Edward Elgar, Chapter 39.

2. New Public Management and cultural change: the case of UK public sector project sponsors as leaders

Mark Hall and Robin Holt

2.1 INTRODUCTION

Of the many initiatives aimed at improving the innovate nature of public service provision, one of the most significant in the UK has been the introduction of New Public Management. The spirit of this managerial reform is one of accountability in which public servants recognize and embrace responsibility for the direct delivery of service by being answerable to the clients and politicians, and open to competition from other potential providers. The idea is that this operational and limited strategic latitude and results-oriented assessment affords the civil servants institutional space to innovate based on their own insight and experience, relatively free from the shackles of daily political interference. Hood and Scott (2000) describe this as a bargain, where civil servants give up their right to anonymity and permanent positions and in exchange politicians give up their right to interfere in the managerial space of service provision. The hope is that in being free to act and innovate and having responsibility for the outcomes, improved service provision will result. What we investigate in this chapter is an empirical case of New Public Management in operation; specifically the cultural conditions by which the innovative aspirations of New Public Management might take root. We identify those experiences in which innovation was inhibited in some way (notably in the persistence of political influence, albeit in more formal, arm's-length guises) and where, given the space, civil servants were able to innovate.

2.2 NEW PUBLIC MANAGEMENT

Throughout the 1990s, many governments embarked on reforms of one sort or another to the provision of public services. These were prompted by related demands for accountability, responsive, targeted and quality provision, and spending efficiencies. Some governments tried to implement discrete changes, while others attempted wholesale reforms (Lane, 2000) including decentralization, deregulation, privatization, the introduction of executive agencies and internal markets and tendering schemes (Ferlie et al., 1996). The upshot would be a government able to deliver high quality goods and services, be responsive to customers, empower clients and be entrepreneurial (Osborne and Gaebler, 1992) whilst maintaining expected levels of public service integrity (Brerton and Temple, 1999).

A term that seeks to encompass all these reform movements is New Public Management or NPM (Hood, 1998). Essentially, NPM can be seen as the growing awareness within the public sector of a need to acquire and develop management skills and attitudes more traditionally associated with the corporate and production sectors of the economy. The resultant endeavour is characterized by a drive to bring public sector management reporting and accounting procedures closer to (a particular perception of) business methods, rooted in 'management thought' on 'best' practice through the adoption of a set of different (sometimes conflicting) reforms and initiatives. NPM describes a controlled, seeping deregulation, occurring within public management, designed to foster sensitivity to market pressures expressed, primarily, as a responsibility for outputs, using objectives rather than procedure as a performance measure (Naschold, 1996; Carter et al., 1992).

NPM originated in the UK, spawning from a shift in managerial focus in public administration that can be traced back in the UK to documents such as the Fulton Report of 1968 (Bromwich and Lapsley, 1997). It has spread to other countries using Anglo-Saxon forms of government (for example, the USA, Australia and New Zealand), to Scandinavian countries and further to Continental Europe (Lane, 2000).

NPM has been variously described as a doctrine, philosophy, movement and paradigm (Keraudren and van Mierlo, 1998). Whatever its description, it is a concept that is underpinned by two theories: public choice theory and neo-Taylorism. These are supplemented by the additional concept of 'public entrepreneurship' (Osborne and Gaebler, 1992).

Public choice theory is concerned with inconsistencies in the classical model of representative democracy. Its proponents contend that the chief problem with the classical model is that, by continuously expanding their budgets, bureaucrats seek to please politicians and also gain individual benefits (utility) in terms of power and prestige from the same budgetary growth. The general result is progressively rising levels of public spending together with progressively falling levels of public service because it is the interests of bureaucrats and politicians rather than those of the wider public that are being served. Niskanen (1971), proposed four key activities to counteract the effects of bureaucratic monopoly:

1. More competition in the delivery of public services.
2. Privatization or contracting-out in order to reduce waste.
3. More and better information about the availability of alternatives to public services.
4. Stricter controls on bureaucrats through the executive and legislature, taking the form of checks and balances.

Where public choice theory concentrates on the relationships between organizations (both public and private), advocates of neo-Taylorism 'hone in' on the internal aspects of organizing by which those organizations are created and sustained. The argument is that the managerial methods and techniques found in private sector firms are efficient ways of controlling bureaucracy that can be usefully adopted within the public sector. What proponents of neo-Taylorism in the public sector frequently fail to acknowledge is that the managerial methods and techniques advocated have only proved successful in certain situations, under certain conditions and are rarely complete panaceas (Pollitt and Bouckaert, 2004). Nevertheless, what seems to prove attractive is that despite the difficulties in generalizing from one context to the next, the spirit and attitudes typically associated with the private generation of material wealth remain sufficiently attractive to warrant the effort; the public sector is ripe for entrepreneurial improvement (Osbourne and Gaebler, 1992).

2.3   THE PUBLIC SECTOR PROJECT SPONSOR AS LEADER – A CULTURAL PERSPECTIVE

To investigate the ways in which UK public sector managers respond to the conditions imposed by NPM we chose to focus on a specific role, namely the 'project sponsor'. During 2002–03 we conducted 12 face-to-face interviews, each lasting two hours, with sponsors working for 12 separate UK government departments or agencies (Hall and Holt, 2002). Project sponsors are described within UK government documentation (HM Treasury 1999a, 1999b) as the public client's (department or agency) representative acting as a single focal point for day-to-day management of the public client's interests, typically in a given construction capital works project. Those we interviewed were involved in managing the construction of hospitals, prisons, roads, office buildings, courts and military installations. Under the auspices of NPM, project sponsors are being asked to take senior political and financial responsibilities while also becoming increasingly immersed in the detailed delivery of projects. One of the goals of aggregating many different obligations in one role (that is, the project sponsor) is to establish a 'one-stop shop', reducing the layers of hierarchy and interaction and so improving communications and removing transaction costs. Another effect of removing departmental hierarchies is the removal of committees. Decision making should, thus, become more decisive and immediate, meaning suppliers to the project receive a clearer 'voice' from the client. In becoming more open, however, the project sponsor is also becoming exposed to demands from many different stakeholders, and it is in managing such demands that the sponsor has to become adept.

Holt and Rowe (2000), in their cross-sectoral analysis of the construction industry and the role of the project sponsor, established that the problems posed by different stakeholder views were both technical (the provision of expert advice, knowledge and systems) and the more nebulous, but equally crucial, managerial (understanding different values, legitimating or excluding different interests, liaising and communicating between parties and within organizational structures). This blend suggested that there was no value equilibrium or 'right' solution. The project sponsor was there to explore divergent issues as much as to harmonize interests, and to realize satisfactory solutions given constraints and varying points of view (Simon, 1990). Given this, the role of the project sponsor was hypothesized as being one of leadership (Heifetz and Laurie, 1997); a quality that not only clearly conveyed the formal, strategic needs for service delivery, but also a sense of faith in the capacity of the project stakeholders (specifically the project team) to innovate solutions to deliver to those needs. In other words, the kind of leadership being envisaged is what Goffee and Jones (2004) call 'being yourself, with skill'. Where leaders often fail, they argue, is in presuming leadership to be about hierarchy, objective vision, personal traits and isolation, when in fact it is a relational, non-hierarchical engagement with others and their different views. In other words, good leaders are people who recognize that others will only be led if they have an interest in being led to the extent that their experiences are significant (endowed with purpose and recognition), identity confirming (a sense of belonging), exciting, and authentic (taken seriously by others).

So the kind of leaders being envisaged here are ones able to engage in, and encourage others to engage in, mechanisms of dialogue and consultation. To do this in ways that respect the different and sometimes divergent views of others, these mechanisms would no longer be solely directed at departmental hierarchies and auditors, and increasingly at other stakeholders (taxpayers, local community groups, private suppliers) (McSwite, 1997). Any such consultation would inevitably expose the public management process to latitude that would be difficult to coordinate in traditional ways (it may result in replication, oversights or incoherence). However, the way in which consultation is conducted at the level of implementation, settled through individual client voices as opposed to that of strategic policy, means that it would be a negotiable exposure (Peters, 1998). The upshot would be a blend of pluralist administration and a willingness to embrace the contradictions inherent in the public management role.

However, this 'ideal' positioning for project sponsors is contingent on the cultural environments of those project sponsors. Given the multiple pulls of NPM, a culture that validates and verifies the position and role of the project sponsor acting as a leader is required. If we assume culture to be 'the common sense way things are done or viewed in a specific organization or group', the research question becomes how can a culture be created that allows project sponsors to thrive as the kind of leaders described by Goffee and Jones (2004)? This is a particularly pressing question when one goes on to consider the differences between public and private managerial activity from the perspective of their relative environments, the relationships between these environments and organizations, and the organizations themselves. Public managers have to deal with a socio-political environment rather than a purely economic one, they have a wider range of norms (often conflicting) to absorb when attempting to bring about and evaluate their 'outputs', and their organizations are structured according to manifest historical patterns very distinct from those characterizing a modern corporation. Given these differences it is not surprising that NPM has attracted criticism for being too managerialist in its ideals. The skills to innovate and encourage innovation in others associated with leadership in the public sector are distinct from private sector ones. The scope of the environment, the complexity of the relations and the histories of the organizations suggest a culture that is far from clear and unitary, and hence a mode of leadership formed much more on consensus and longer-term perspectives.

2.4 THE 12 PROJECT SPONSORS

The above considerations were fed into our semi-structured interview schedules with the investigative aim of exploring two issues:

- Understanding whether a 'dominant' cultural environment existed within which public sector projects were undertaken, and if so its nature.

- Understanding whether there were multiple and complex pulls and constraints within this NPM initiatives, and if so how this affected the opportunity for innovative decision making.

From our enquiry, a series of different cultural themes emerged that, woven together, formed the overall culture within which the project sponsors spoke and acted. These were grouped as follows:

1. Political environment
2. End-user and third party concerns
3. Accountability
4. Public sector–private sector conflict
5. Inter-departmental pull.

2.4.1 Political Environment

This theme concerns the political environment, changes in that environment over time and how these changes have impacted on the project sponsor's ability to deliver on the project aims or on progress. In the sense of our analysis, 'politics' refers to the goals and aims of a specific, public-sector organization (department or agency). Where the political environment was found to be an important factor in the ways project sponsors engaged in dialogue, it appeared to be related to the relatively long nature of many capital works projects. The concerns of project sponsors were twofold. First, there are the changes in departmental structure, imposed by central government and generally reflecting a shift in policy as a result of developments in the political landscape. These changes frequently lead to changes in the aims of the department and the manner in which they are expected to achieve those aims. The project sponsor is then expected to incorporate these changes part way through a project, although that project was originally conceived within a set of different, possibly conflicting, political aims. The consequences of switching emphasis in such a manner can be very disruptive. In one example the project sponsor attributed changes in the political environment of the project as having an important influence on the timely delivery of the project.

> The original project conception included [work] on both the Welsh and English sides. . . . Ultimately, the Welsh Office procured [work] on the Welsh side, and [we] procured the English side. This decision was taken relatively late through the planning stage and was influenced by political opportunity to use private finance.

The changing political preference towards private finance instigated a dual-decision structure within a purported unitary project, prompting all manner of complications and significant delays due to communication barriers and system incompatibility.

Second, there are conflicts between the political aims of government and the goals of the project sponsor and their department. The classic example of this is an accounting practice called 'annuality'. This entails departments being allocated budgets which they are required to use within an accounting year. However, many projects last for more than one year and annual budgets can create major problems in the allocation of funds for project completion, leading to uncertainty for the project sponsor and project suppliers. Interestingly, the project sponsors felt that annuality was not simply an administrative convenience, but was actively used to control their activity insofar as it enabled politicians to control the speed and length of funding. So whilst there was no direct interference with daily decision making, project sponsor decisions were being regulated by the prospect of 'lumpy' and uncertain funding regimes.

In response to this annuality problem there was a move by the UK Government's Office of Government Commerce to shift to a more neutral and managerial resource accounting system. This suggests that the political problem has, at least, been recognized. However, evidence from the project sponsors indicated that, despite the introduction of resource accounting, annuality remained in place and continued to impose constraints on the possibility to consistently finance innovative service solutions.

2.4.2 End-user and Third Party Concerns

A recurrent theme for project sponsors was the impact of end-users and third parties on assessing relative project success. Their influence could, in particular, have serious implications for the timely delivery of projects along with the scope for innovation. This meant that the project might be performing well in terms of innovative inputs but, because of multiplying third party and end-user needs and requirements, is not 'closed out', having a negative impact on the outcomes. This factor created problems for project sponsors trying to maintain a technically innovative focus on the operational demands of project life whilst remaining sensitive to wider social concerns. In one case a project sponsor mentioned how she tried to 'manage' the impact of end-users by constraining their opportunity to impact the project.

> A long lead-time was found to be unfavourable as it gave stakeholders an opportunity to engage in protracted discussion and stopped us getting on with the job. While user consultation was important, it had to be managed, structured, so that it didn't block the process. All too often it is built into the critical path [programme] of the project. It should not be on the critical path but informing it.

So here we have project sponsors looking to engage others but having to manage and control user expectations at the onset, rather than continually elicit user involvement through the project life. A number of the sponsors were experiencing too heavy a weighting towards front-end consultation; a process catalysed by the ethic of user choice across the UK public sector. There were suspicions as to the value of extending such choice ad infinitum, particularly in instances where it began to impact upon the interests of other stakeholders in the project and so undermine effort at instilling cross-organizational trust.

2.4.3   Accountability

While accountability was not considered to be of paramount importance, it was an underlying factor. In almost every case it centred on one issue, best described by a project sponsor:

> Anyone who works for a government client knows that they have to be accountable and that they have to show value for money. The value for money issue has been a key topic for some time now but the problem is how to move that forward – lowest cost does not always mean best value. . . . There may be many soft issues that make something other than lowest cost equate to best value but unless you can prove it in financial terms, it is very hard to argue in a way that deals with accountability. You're most aware of it on tender evaluations. We evaluate tenders on all sorts of issues other than cost and the difficulty is in combining the quality of service with price to identify best value, which is quite a hard process to do objectively.

Thus, the difficulty in 'proving' value for money was seen as a potential barrier in allowing the delivery of, in particular, appropriate levels of quality. The scope to innovate was restricted insofar as it was inherently less certain, and hence less easy to demonstrate 'on paper'. The default setting becomes one of satisfying the accountability requirements in terms of cost, whilst accepting only a basic minimum in terms of quality and innovation. Of particular interest was the language used by some project sponsors: words such as 'fearful', 'accused' and 'criticized' all appeared to represent a pervading sense of accountability and a dominant underlying concern. Another project sponsor described how demands to demonstrate 'value for money' (economic viability) could constrain him from delivering innovation.

> I think the economics drive the process and what we can do in terms of environmental benefit and social benefit and, even, what we can do in terms of standards of protection are driven by that. That gives it a slightly different angle. We're not looking at the best or optimum solution to solve the problem, we're looking at the optimum solution to get best return on capital.

So it was the dictates of return on capital rather than the delivery of long-term, innovative and quality service that pervaded and informed project activity. The language of economics dominated other forms of discourse, thereby foreclosing the project sponsor's opportunity to operate innovatively. Some project sponsors attempted to create a tender review procedure that mitigated the 'lowest cost' mentality while retaining a robust approach to accountability, but these were in the minority, so that at the beginning stages of a project it was the language of cost that tended to dominate discussions, and into which subsequent discussions about other interests had to be fitted.

2.4.4 Public Sector–Private Sector Conflict

This theme concerns the tension between the public sector as a client for projects and the private sector in the form of suppliers of products and services. It was of overwhelming importance to project sponsors' experiences of their projects because it was these organizations that dominated the day-to-day affairs. It transpired that successfully overcoming the almost inevitable tensions between the public client and the private contractors, sub-contractors and consultants of the project team lay with the perceptions regarding the clarity, openness and fairness of the tendering and procurement procedures. Another significant factor was the personal relationship between the project sponsor and the individuals representing private suppliers and consultants. Where these are poorly implemented, project success can be impacted negatively. Private sector and public sector tension frequently led to contractual conflict and resulted in wasteful and protracted negotiation of claims. It occurred for a variety of reasons and in a number of ways, as the examples illustrate:

- Lack of awareness and inexperience of procurement implications.

   Overall, although the project was generally a success, in that it was completed and handed over on time and within budget, the defects were a nightmare and snagging was still ongoing fully two years after the contractor had finished on site. Although the contractor had an attitude of getting in and finishing the job and getting out as quickly as possible, this was to the detriment of quality; there was absolutely no right-first-time/zero defects attitude in evidence.

- The relative isolation of the project sponsor from organizational and project teams.

   On the project, we had the contractors battling with us from one side and each department having a go at us from the other side.

- The confrontational and mistrustful nature of the UK construction industry.

  There were certain lines the contractor spun us from time to time that were less than true. Unless you get to the situation of commercial openness and honesty then you get to a situation where you know he is spinning you a line and you doubt anything else he tells you.

- The fragmented nature of the construction industry, giving rise to inter-organizational bickering and commercial positioning to the detriment of the public interest.

  There was a problem with an adversarial culture because the contractor bid below cost and was engaged on the lowest price as a single criterion. The contract was let at £63m against a pre-tender estimate of £70–£80m. The financial settlement is still being finalized [three years later]. Procurement strategy was poor and a better strategy could have considerably improved the outcome.

- Personality clashes on specific projects.

  I think if people have empathy for each others' work then you are halfway there. If there were more attention to individuals getting together at an early stage that would certainly be helpful because people get very nervous: they don't want to give information away.

- Emphasis upon contractual terms and responsibilities.

  The responsibility for getting things right firmly lies with the contractor and the designer – it's the designer's responsibility to instruct the contractor if something has gone wrong (the designer is supported by his quality inspectors).

2.4.5   Inter-departmental Pull

This theme refers to conflicting needs and goals within the public sector client agency or department and how these can act to the detriment of the project. It manifested itself in the need for project sponsors to continually defer to authorities within their own department or agency. It was found to be more of a concern for some project sponsors than others, depending on the nature of the specific agency or department. Where it was a problem, it led to difficulties for the project sponsor as they had insufficient authority and decision making power. The consequence of this was delays in decisions regarding site issues that led to frustration for the project team. One project sponsor remarked:

As often happens, we had to go through a [internal departmental] consultation process and this was one of the reasons why the design was delayed. The consultation process dragged on rather because we didn't get the speedy response from the [internal department] groups that we were expecting, and I had to keep pushing them to get their responses and observations back.

Making sure that people felt 'part of the programme' was a constant endeavour, requiring the sponsor to lay out and reiterate the project decisions and the rationale for them to their peers and line managers in ways that elicited their interest and continued support.

2.5 THE PROBLEMS WITH NEW PUBLIC MANAGEMENT

The above themes were experienced as a weave rather than isolate threads, and their separation was reached by way of academic analysis rather than explicit comment from the sponsors themselves. Understood as themes, though, they reveal a cultural environment characterized by complexity and tension of the kind suggested by critics of NPM and as reasons why managerialist reforms are not the innovatory panacea they are made out to be. We found that the often divergent demands of public probity and equity, performance-driven public accountability and private sector gain, all set within a context of political change and uncertainty, meant the simple idea of NPM (creating accountable and operationally independent policy providers to foster innovation and efficiency) was lost in translation. The result was project sponsors who, whilst they might be aware of an atmosphere of changing expectations labelled NPM, found it difficult to lead and innovate in such an atmosphere because of a lack of consistency and coherence in the culture (or cultures) within which public service was enacted. The result tended to be feelings of frustration and isolation, such as in attempting to lead one set of interests others felt ignored or threatened.

At one cultural level the isolation is inevitable. The project sponsor is generally a civil servant removed from the group structure with which they are familiar for a specific project. They are detached, for a time, from their department or agency with its familiar set of norms and values and placed within an often unfamiliar environment with what would seem to be contradictory norms and values. Kahn et al. (1966) referred to this situation as role conflict and ambiguity (see also Biddle, 1979). Yet this ambiguity can be compounded by NPM reforms. Once in this position, the project sponsor can form close connections with elements of the industry – the private sector advisors, expert consultants and contractors – finding a specific 'economic' reality coming to dominate and impregnate other realities more familiar to public service. The project sponsors can easily be exposed to the pervading blame culture and internecine strife prevalent in the environment of capital works projects (see, for example, Loosemore, 1998), where the relationships formed by the private contractors are temporary and each is likely to be pursuing short-term financial gain rather than forming long-term, mutually beneficial relationships. The civil servant charged with delivering the project is left bereft of the support of a familiar group of like-minded individuals concerned for the provision of public service. This fosters an attitude that Hood (1998) refers to as 'fatalism'. The fatalist approach to public management is epitomized by 'conditions where cooperation is rejected, distrust widespread and apathy reigns' (Hood, 1998, p. 9). Leadership remains an ideal that cannot be acted upon in such situations because choices are felt to be limited or absent and alliances are tenuous at best, emphasized by a lack of group coherence (Jensen, 1998). Unpredictability and unintended effects became commonplace. In such situations, the project sponsors tended to respond in an ad hoc fashion to events after they had occurred. Rather than participating in and controlling events from different perspectives, the mindset became one of 'survival' for the project duration. The result was a deficit in opportunities for entrepreneurship, 'pro-activity' and innovation described as characterizing NPM by Osborne and Gaebler (1992).

So the goals of NPM are not realized. The risk is that civil servants, like project sponsors, quickly revert to a mode of 'skilled incompetence' (Agyris, 1990), focusing on the adoption of defensive routines that protect themselves and their agency or department from the difficulties imposed by the fragmented private sector climate and relative sense of distance from 'core' civil service activity. The different demands of the project stakeholders are only imperfectly aired, often with one or a minority being accorded influence, and the possibility of leadership, earlier discussed, foreclosed as being just too troublesome to contemplate. Public duty is seen as being fulfilled (the rules have been followed) but the different voices left are smothered. Even where professional project managers are employed as project sponsors by agencies and departments, the same problems can be encountered.

We did find, however, occasions when individual project sponsors felt sufficiently confident to 'go it alone', and this frequently resulted in more successful projects. Certainly, there is a loose correlation between project sponsors prepared to operate on their own initiative and successful project outcomes. This characteristic meant that it was possible for project sponsors to speak and act within the bind of *different* cultural threads and hence outside of a single, dominating set of cultural patterns. The lack of holistic direction and aim, however, led to what Hood calls an individualist pattern to their cultural condition (Hood, 1998, p. 9); one dominated by ad hoc negotiation oriented to common denominators, as opposed to the explicit delivery of value for money backed by professionalized development of the project sponsor role.

2.6 USING BENCHMARKING TO CREATE AN INNOVATIVE CULTURE

In essence, it would seem that one area in which NPM in the UK has failed to deliver on its intention is its lack of attention to how multiple cultural influences and tensions impact upon efforts by civil servants to exercise independent and innovatory judgement. One way of resolving the tensions discussed here is to employ some of the tools of NPM in an imaginative way. One of these tools, for example, is the use of in-project benchmarking, which we investigated in a related study (Hall and Holt, 2003).

'In-project' benchmarking systems measure delivery *during* projects as well as outcomes at the end of projects. By developing in-project measures, the process of benchmarking need not be seen with distrust, but as a tool for the strategic and operational management of projects because the learning aspect is removed from one of retrospective analysis and reporting to forward-looking, team-based problem solving. Without this real-time presence, benchmarking risks losing the potentially valuable input from those in a position to identify problems and effect and manage solutions or resolutions. This emphasis upon learning has been found to lead to a significant shift in the reception and use of benchmarking because it allows members of the project team to invest in the rigour of the method without feeling unduly restricted by the resultant judgements. It is intended as a flexible tool, free from any specific idea about what an organization or its environment of operation (public or private) should look like. Instead, it insists upon the correct application of method within a project. Because in-project benchmarking relies upon practitioners to impart their understandings of process and products, it relies less upon dictating rigid patterns of activity than establishing clear communication channels that encourage self-motivation to pursue improvement (Walgenbach and Hegele, 2001).

By undertaking in-project benchmarking, public sector project sponsors can potentially benefit from:

1. The ability to design a performance plan linked to examples of good practice and identify organizational strategy from multiple parties. In addition, it might be anticipated that changes in policy and operation made by these parties in light of changes in operational experience made under the performance plan, could be assessed and monitored.

2. The ability to identify, respond to and even pre-empt project-related risks so as to target resources more effectively. In-project benchmarking is, in effect, to be treated as an extensive risk management process where problems, solutions and resolutions are identified and pursued by the team at project team level.
3. The ability to define value for money and 'best' value and so secure the requirements of serving the long-term public interest and sustained accountability. By using in-project benchmarking clients should be able to assess themselves using multiple criteria (in addition to cost and time; for example, a client might understand performance in terms of sustainability, respect for people and stakeholder inclusion).

Once understood in terms of these potential benefits, in-project benchmarking also has to concern itself with the contingency issues of relevance and application (Beretta et al., 1998). The in-project benchmarking template has to be sufficiently robust to fulfil the above aims while remaining sufficiently flexible and succinct that it is usable on an in-project basis by the multiple parties involved without itself becoming a burdensome task.

Our study of in-project benchmarking began with a different cohort of nine project sponsors interviewed from projects that previous research (Graves and Rowe, 1999) had identified as being particularly successful in terms of budget and time outcomes or as failures. The interviews concentrated on factors that they felt had made the project work or not. Areas impacting upon poor performance included: poor supply chain coordination; heightened contractual visibility and wrangling; procedural bureaucracy; poor focus on health and safety; a lack of end-user consultation; inappropriate investments in IT; and a lack of risk management schedules. Following these interviews we designed, along with project teams from three pilot construction projects with a major UK Government Department, in-project benchmarks covering each of the above areas. An interview with the project sponsor along with a focus group with the project team was conducted for each of the projects, both of which focused on the experiences of designing and using in-project benchmarking systems. We found that where these systems were invested in (that is, they were used to frame daily decision making and to assist with project reviews) and were driven by participants themselves, there were major advantages in terms of realizing the kind of innovatory leadership necessary to the delivery of long-term value for money projects. Specifically, we found that in order for in-project benchmarking to deliver on its aims and create an innovatory environment across different organizations, four activities were being undertaken:

1. Common language
2. Risk and knowledge management
3. Contractual influences
4. Complexity and breadth of data templates.

2.6.1 Common Language

One common complaint from project sponsors, suppliers and even wider stakeholders was the plethora of often conflicting initiatives being piloted within UK industry and UK government, with an often interchangeable and confusing use of terminology. A starting point, then, was to agree on the definitions to be used in performance measurement and the reasons why they were important for the project. This meant defining:

- performance indicators (an area in which performance is considered important enough to measure)
- measures (means of measuring each area)
- benchmarks (target to be aimed for).

By bringing this activity into the open, the different perspectives and concerns of the various project parties (central government, department/agency processes, end-user groups, suppliers, personal and group ethics) were made apparent and their relevance discussed. Other definitional issues concern agreement as to the meaning of apparently obvious concepts, such as 'budget', 'programme' and 'margin'. The aim of the process was, in part, to establish a meaningful series of measures that could be used to compare performance both from project to project and across government agencies and departments and, in due course, between government sectors in different countries. Definitional problems would create serious problems in ensuring the validity of such comparisons. This linked to a more basic aim of using this discussion of terminology to broach the different cultural themes we discussed earlier; in-project benchmarking might not produce agreement on all concerns, but it at least enabled actual and emerging problems in communication, expectation and values to be aired and so potentially solved, resolved or dissolved. Without a common language, any performance benefits accruing from innovations and costs savings may go unrecognized, or even be challenged as incompatible with one or other set of interests at play within the project (Schein, 1993).

2.6.2 Risk and Knowledge Management

One of the goals of in-project benchmarking was to encourage project sponsors to gain an understanding of the potential benefits that can be gained from appropriate risk apportionment within projects, including a more comprehensive view of risk. While a series of risk types can be considered, including financial, political/economic, design, operational and legal aspects, of equal importance to risk type, especially to public clients, is the distinction between 'perception' risk and 'technical' risk. The traditional focus is on how risk is managed and apportioned and how this relates to project outcomes. Risks divide into three categories:

- Technical risks associated with such entities as financing vehicles, contracts or physical products.
- Behavioural risks associated with human frailties, interests and bias.
- Systems risks associated with inherent complexities of systems integration.

In the past the approach has been to approach risk management somewhat as a technical exercise. However, in NPM, with the introduction of private sector supply chains in service delivery – and the need to account for the personalities and corporate cultures within such chains – all three forms of risk demand equal attention and need contingencies to be set in place. Thus, while management of risk is seen as key, a problem lies in the traditional, procedural approach to its management; it is more than simply an exercise in consulting scientific experts.

From the interviews and focus groups we found that where risk management was more successfully used, it included technical risks but also looked at interfaces with stakeholders and suppliers more generally and how these might be managed. It also seemed to be important that the risk management process occurred within a team environment so that everyone had a 'buy-in' and contributed to the consideration of the risks being considered and their potential solutions.

2.6.3   Contractual Influences

The contractual influence is a potential block to the innovative delivery of good services in that the general 'contractual' nature of private suppliers can interfere with creating and spreading ideas. Having to stipulate in exactitude the contract requirements makes for a rigid process that is not easily adapted to good risk management nor the acceptance of possibly different perspectives on project activity and project strategy.

From the research we found that whilst the construction industry's attitude was frequently experienced as adversarial and overly 'contractual', a solution lay with simply encouraging greater openness about the needs and expectations of all the project parties. Once 'on the table' in the form of indicators, measures and benchmarks, common discussion as to how to best meet them prompted ideas as to their being realized.

2.6.4 Complexity and Breadth of Measurement Systems

The length and breadth of measurement systems is frequently seen as being onerous. While accepting the need to be thorough, it seems that the ambience of the measurement experience is more important than what is being measured. The implication is that performance measurement focuses people upon what they are doing and, more importantly, why they are doing it. This alludes to the learning potential behind measurement.

The difficulty lies in achieving a balance between the need for a template that is sufficiently generic that it is relevant to the wide variety of projects procured by the public sector while remaining relevant to the needs of specific projects. A further issue is to develop a measurement system into an instrument that could be seen as a tool for the management and control of projects as much as a device for reporting on project performance to a third party.

We found that the very act of acquiring appropriate information to complete the benchmarking requirements acted as a catalyst for the project team to operate together more closely; again helping bring together and make more coherent the multiple cultural threads experienced by the project sponsor. It allowed each project team member to reflect upon the relationship between their own views of the risks faced by the project and how these impacted upon project success. Information gathering proved most effective as a management and control tool where the project sponsor engaged directly with their suppliers and consultants to arrive at agreed responses to the areas of performance being measured. This had the effect of accessing multiple perspectives about the way projects were managed and allowing critical and reflective attitudes to prevail towards prescribed activities. Project sponsors were even prepared to challenge accepted modes of control with a view to enhancing the outcomes.

2.7 CONCLUSION

We have argued that while NPM continues to ignore the cultural environment within which civil servants say and do things the aspiration to improve service quality and delivery will remain just that. It is not sufficient simply to change the rules and processes of provision, but to recognize the norms and expectations by which those rules are understood. We have described how one set of civil servants – project sponsors – experienced such changes as they sought to build management teams to lead large-scale capital works projects for the UK government. We identified five broad cultural themes whose influence upon project activity had, in some way, to be negotiated by the project sponsor if everyone involved in the project, and affected by the project, was to be 'brought along' in ways that contributed to a successful outcome. We argued that though these themes were recognized by the sponsors, their active management was often not possible, or even envisaged, meaning that the culture often became a source of frustration, something *against* which the project sponsor had to contend.

We then went on to suggest that one way of managing these cultural influences is to use in-project benchmarking tools. We recounted how, in our experience, those project sponsors who had used these tools most successfully were those who were able to recognize their contribution to: creating a common language across the multiple project parties; structuring a risk management process that accommodated behavioural and structural as well as technical risks; creating a more constructive dialogue between public and private sector interests; and providing common activities for project members in the form of information gathering.

We have suggested that where leadership of the kind envisaged by NPM reforms can occur, within projects at least – when the various parties are able to air both their expectations and aims for the project and the value-structures informing these – benchmarking can play a formative role, providing it is implemented in an appropriate manner; that is, oriented to learning and team-based working rather than third-party scrutiny. In this way it provides project teams with a distinct methodology wherein the various groups and organizations involved in project life are provided with the means to circumvent cultural divisions in the pursuit of learning and communication.

REFERENCES

Agyris, C. (1990), *Overcoming Organizational Defences*, Needham, MA: Allyn and Bacon.

Beretta, S., A. Dossi and H. Grove (1998), 'Methodological strategies for benchmarking accounting processes', *Benchmarking for Quality Management and Technology*, 5(3), 165–83.

Biddle, B.J. (1979), *Role Theory: Expectations, Identities and Behaviors*, New York: Academic Press.

Brerton, M. and M. Temple (1999), 'The new public service ethos: an ethical environment for governance', *Public Administration*, 77(3), 455–74.

Bromwich, M. and I. Lapsley (1997), 'Decentralisation and management accounting in central government: recycling old ideas?', *Financial Accountability and Management*, 13(2), 181–201.

Carter, N., R. Klein and P. Day (1992), *How Organizations Measure Success: The Use of Performance Indicators in Government*, London: Routledge.

Ferlie, E., A. Pettigrew, L. Ashburner and L. Fitzgerald (1996), *The New Public Management in Action*, Oxford: Oxford University Press.

Goffee, R. and G. Jones (2004), 'What makes a leader?', *Business Strategy Review*, **15**(2), 46–50.

Graves, A. and D. Rowe (1999), *Benchmarking the Government Client – Stage Two Study*, HM Treasury report, London: Stationery Office.

Hall, M. and R. Holt (2002), 'UK public sector project management – a cultural perspective', *Public Productivity and Management Review*, **25**(3), 298–312.

Hall, M. and R. Holt (2003), 'Developing a culture of performance learning in UK public sector project management', *Public Performance and Management Review*, **26**(3), 263–75.

Heifetz, R. and D. Laurie (1997), 'The work of leadership', *Harvard Business Review*, **75**(1), 124–34.

HM Treasury (1999a), *The Procurement Group Procurement Guidance. No. 1: Essential Requirements for Construction Procurement*, London: Stationary Office.

HM Treasury (1999b), *The Procurement Group Procurement Guidance: Supplementary Guidance to PG 1 on the Role of the Project Sponsor*, London: Stationary Office.

Holt, R. and D. Rowe (2000), 'Total quality, public management and critical leadership in civil construction projects', *International Journal of Quality and Reliability Management*, **17**(4–5), 541–53.

Hood, C. (1998), *The Art of the State: Culture, Rhetoric and Public Management*, Oxford: Clarendon Press.

Hood, C. and C. Scott (2000), *Regulating Government in a Managerial Age*, report by the Centre for the Analysis of Risk and Regulation, London: London School of Economics.

Jensen, L. (1998), 'Cultural theory and democratizing functional domains. The case of Danish housing', *Public Administration*, **76**(1), 117–39.

Kahn, R., D. Wolfe, R. Quinn, J. Snoek and R. Rosenthal (1966), 'Adjustment to role conflict and ambiguity in organizations', in B. Biddle and E. Thomas (eds), *Role Theory: Concepts and Research*, New York: John Wiley and Sons, pp. 277–82.

Keraudren, P. and H. van Mierlo (1998), 'Theories of public management and their practical implications', in T. Verheijen and D. Coombes (eds), *Innovations in Public Management: Perspectives from East and West Europe*, Cheltenham, UK and Lyme, USA: Edward Elgar, pp. 39–56.

Lane, J-E. (2000), *New Public Management*, London: Routledge.

Loosemore, M. (1998), 'The methodological challenges posed by the confrontational nature of the construction industry', *Engineering, Construction and Architectural Management*, **5**(3), 283–93.

McSwite, O. (1997), *Legitimacy in Public Administration: A Discourse Analysis*, London: Sage.

Naschold, F. (1996), *New Frontiers in Public Sector Management: Trends and Issues in State and Local Government in Europe*, Berlin: de Gruyter.

Niskanen, W.A. (1971), *Bureaucracy and Representative Government*, Chicago, IL: Aldine.

Osborne, D. and T. Gaebler (1992), *Reinventing Government: How the Entrepreneurial Spirit is Transforming the Public Sector*, Wokingham: Addison-Wesley.

Peters, B. (1998), 'Managing horizontal government: the politics of co-ordination', *Public Administration*, **75**(2), 295–311.

Pollitt, C. and G. Bouckaert (2004), *Public Management Reform: A Comparative Analysis*, 2nd edn, Oxford: Oxford University Press.

Schein, E.H. (1993), 'On dialogue, culture and organizational learning', *Organizational Dynamics*, **22**(2), 40–52.

Simon, H. (1990), 'Invariants of human behaviour', *Annual Review of Psychology*, **41**, 1–19.

Walgenbach, P. and C. Hegele (2001), 'What can an apple learn from an orange? Or: what do companies use benchmarking for?', *Organization*, **8**(1), 121–44.

3. Structure, size and reform of the public sector in Europe

Andrés Maroto and Luis Rubalcaba

3.1 INTRODUCTION

Dynamic economic growth requires a modern public sector, whose size and performance fit in with the new global boundaries. A competitive economy needs a competitive public sector where both innovation and reform play a major role. This chapter presents data on the main characteristics of public services in Europe and compares these with the USA. The chapter links the types of reform that are ongoing in Europe with the dimensions behind their performance. A particular focus on knowledge-intensive services is provided, within the ongoing direction towards public sector modernization. The findings highlight the uneven behaviours that result from different public sector structures and sizes, and also identify the common needs of modernization.

In the era of globalization, competitiveness-related challenges dominate the business and policy worlds. In Europe, objectives that include growth, employment and productivity are essential targets for the development of the Lisbon strategy, announced by the European Commission in 2000 and reformulated in late 2004. Recent European Union (EU) reforms play an important role in innovation policies, as these reforms are predicted to deal with the competitiveness challenges and should help close the gap with the USA, which has enjoyed superior productivity growth over the last ten years. In this context, the role of the public sector is twofold: it continues to represent a major economic sector whose size, structure and activity are fundamental to macroeconomic stability and growth; and its performance serves as a social and economic instrument for the provision of improved and more efficient services. These two roles are interrelated. A better performing administration allows public sectors to adjust their size and structure to a better fit. An efficient and modern public sector does not necessarily need to be large in size. Moreover, a smaller public sector may be a better performing one. Having said this, the links between size, structure and performance vary considerably depending on the country. This is particularly true in Europe, where vastly different models, sizes and organizational structures exist.

This chapter presents, on the one hand, the basic statistics and economic dimensions of the public sector in Europe and, on the other, the need and types of reform useful for the achievement of improved performance and efficiency. The chapter complements Chapters 1, 2 and 4 of this book, which, collectively, set the context for the case studies that follow. The study of innovation in the public sector can be introduced by a preliminary analysis of the main data and concerns in Europe. The significance and impact of innovation in public administrations are influenced by differences in their size, dimensions and socio-economic organization. It is necessary to consider the public sector within the social context in which institutions interact, and the relationship between these public institutions and the private sector. In addition, it is necessary to examine the influence of politics, management, evaluation, cultural treatment and entrepreneurship in the public sector on the development of innovative and learning processes. Thus, it is convenient to set up a preliminary analysis of the structure and methods of operating and reforming the European public sector.

The following sections of this chapter explain the role of the public sector within modern economies (Section 3.2); introduce theoretical and empirical data on the growth of the public sector in Europe, highlighting the importance and performance of the public sector in Europe (Section 3.3); discuss the issue of public sector reform and examine alternative approaches and methods for modernizing public administrations, with particular focus on the role of knowledge-intensive services and pro-innovation action (Section 3.4); and, finally, conclusions are given (Section 3.5).

3.2   THE ROLE OF THE PUBLIC SECTOR IN MODERN ECONOMIES

The modern public sector is the subject of a long and ongoing controversy in which alternative organizational models, sizes and profiles have evolved. In all cases, the state is actively present in social and economic life. Economic life constantly depends on the economic decisions of governments. This is readily illustrated by taxes levied on citizens and capital owners; transfer payments; public parks, highways and other publicly provided infrastructure; and, more recently, the role played by public politics in environmental conservation and promoting sustainable development. Contemporary political theories focus on politics as a reflection of society, the political phenomenon being a disaggregated consequence of individual behaviours influenced by subjective facts. However, some recent opinions within political science link the phenomenon with the traditional economic study of institutions. This 'New Institutionalism' focuses on the relative independence of political institutions and emphasizes the need to appreciate their functioning (see, for example, Christensen and Laegreid, 2001). Taken together, the above points indicate that the public sector has great economic and social importance for all market economies. In the EU it is clearly evident and widely recognized. The welfare state economies in Europe have long sought to provide higher social protection levels for poorer citizens and have engaged in income redistribution, accepting that a trade-off may exist between these social goals and economic growth.

In addition to the debate about the welfare state and competitiveness (Rubalcaba, 2002), a number of other debates are shaping discussions on the role of the state. For example, there is the debate on complementarity/substitution between the public and private sectors (see, for example, Frydman et al., 1999; David et al., 2000), and the debate on modernization, entrepreneurship and innovation in the public sector (the core subject of this book). In light of these debates, our discussion of the size and structure of the public sector is of significance, not only for countries within the EU but also for countries in other regions around the world. Reform of the public sector should be based on the best possible balance between market failures to be solved and public failures as collateral effects, the safeguard of public interest and private interest, social protection and economic dynamism – a balance that should be found in each type of state system.

3.3   SIZE AND PERFORMANCE OF PUBLIC SECTOR ACTIVITIES IN EUROPE

Obvious differences between national economic performance led to the question of why some countries are so much wealthier than others, and whether the size, structure and organization of the public sector contributes to cross-country income and growth gaps (Handler et al., 2005). The public sector influences overall economic performance via two channels. First, it produces goods and services and therefore directly impacts on overall output and productivity by its size and efficiency. Second, it affects the way private production takes place. This section considers the first channel.

3.3.1   Measuring the Size of the Public Sector

As public production is difficult to measure with a single statistical indicator, the size and the composition of government activities are gauged

Table 3.1   Public sectors in European countries, 2002

Country	Public employment (percentage of total employment)	Public expenditure (percentage of GDP)	Tax ratio (percentage of GDP)
Austria	12.2	51.3	43.1
Belgium	16.8	50.5	45.9
Denmark	29.0	55.8	48.8
Finland	22.4	50.1	45.0
France	21.2	53.5	43.9
Germany	10.2	48.5	40.5
Greece	11.4	46.8	36.3
Ireland	11.0	33.3	29.9
Italy	14.4	48.0	43.0
Luxembourg	14.9	44.0	41.4
Netherlands	10.7	47.5	39.3
Portugal	17.0	45.9	37.2
Spain	13.0	39.9	36.3
Sweden	30.0	58.3	50.6
UK	17.8	40.7	36.6
EU-15	16.8	47.6	40.8
USA	14.7	35.7	28.5
Japan	8.1	38.2	27.0

Source: Eurostat (2004) and OECD (2004b).

using different indicators, which all cover the supply side of public activities (see, for example, Beeton, 1987; Gemmel, 1993; Karras, 1997; Light, 1999). Consequently, any quantitative evaluation of the magnitude of the public sector must be observed with caution, and the empirical evidence shown in Table 3.1 should be considered with this qualification in mind.

In some EU countries, public sector expenditure accounts for over 50 per cent of GDP. These include the Nordic countries (Finland, Denmark and Sweden), France, Belgium and Austria. By contrast, in countries such as those around the Mediterranean (Spain, Portugal and Greece) public expenditure accounts for 40–47 per cent of GDP, and in Ireland accounts for around one third, of GDP. This is similar to the levels found in Japan and the USA. Some countries, such as Belgium, the Netherlands, UK and Ireland, have substantially decreased the share of public expenditure since the early 1980s. Public sector deficits tend to be counter-cyclical in European countries and are cross-correlated with deficits in other European states. This is not the case in the USA or Japan. Further, the redistribution functions of the public sector size in the EU are far more significant than in the USA or Japan.

In terms of employment, the public sector has remained more or less constant across the EU since 1980, fluctuating at around 17 per cent of total employment. A slight downward trend can be observed from 1992 as a result of individual developments in a number of countries. In contrast to the stationary trend for the EU as a whole, the experience of individual countries is very heterogeneous in level and long-term development. While the Nordic countries and France have the highest figures (more than 20 per cent of total employment in 2002), public employment in Germany and the Netherlands is around 10 per cent. In the Southern EU countries (except Italy) public sector employment increased from very low levels in 1980, while in the UK the share of public employment has declined since 1980.

The tax ratio in the EU countries shown in Table 3.1 reflects a wide range; from just over 35 per cent of GDP (in Ireland and the Mediterranean countries) to more than 50 per cent (in Sweden) and reflects the levels in expenditure ratios. The average tax ratio in the EU steadily increased up to the end of the 1990s, when this indicator experienced a slight downturn (in 2002 it was about 40 per cent). In the USA the ratio remained broadly stable, while the behaviour of the taxation ratio in the Japanese economy has been more variable.

Most of the new member states of the EU are former communist countries. They have experienced transitions from strongly interventionist state economies to market models more typical of Western European countries (Utrilla de la Hoz, 2001). At the present time, almost all new EU member states have levels of tax and public expenditure that are similar to those of the EU, although they are relatively high compared to countries with comparable levels of output (European Commission, 2000).

The structure of public sector expenditures in the EU, Japan and the USA in 2002 is illustrated in Figures 3.1 and 3.2. Social transfer is by far the largest block of public expenditure in EU countries. It accounts for 18.7 per cent of GDP, around three times the amount spent on health and general public services, the next two largest blocks. The largest difference with the USA and Japan is in social protection. EU countries redistribute around 12 per cent of GDP more than the USA, and 8.5 per cent more than Japan. EU countries also, on average, spend more on heath as a percentage of GDP. They spent less than half the share of GDP on defence than the USA. Finally, the USA spent more on education than EU countries and, significantly, Japan in 2002.

The tax mix (Figure 3.2) differs remarkably between the EU, Japan and the USA. Consumption taxes are the major revenue source in the EU (about 29 per cent of total taxes), followed closely by social security contributions

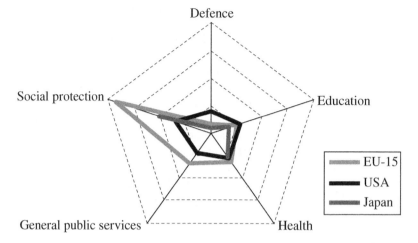

Note: Japanese data on general services are missing.

Source: Eurostat (2004) and OECD (2004b).

Figure 3.1   Public sector expenditures in the EU, USA and Japan, 2002 (as percentage of GDP)

(28 per cent), and personal income taxes (26 per cent). In Japan, social security contributions, as well as taxes on corporate income, have a higher share than in both the EU and the USA. The USA relies heavily on taxes on personal income (42.3 per cent). Finally, a common pattern of social expenditure is observed among European countries. Provisions for retired people is by far the largest category (41 per cent of total spending in 2002), with sickness and healthcare the second largest (28 per cent).

3.3.2   Size/Performance of the Public Sector and Economic Growth

Most empirical studies of public sector performance assess either the relative performance of specific producing units (for example, hospitals) against each other, frequently using frontier analysis, or broad sector aggregates (for example, health, education or administration), assessing performance over time or across countries. Cross-country studies on public sector efficiency frequently rely on indicators, such as the educational achievement of school pupils at a given age, life expectancy or the extent of corruption in a given country, or macroeconomic indicators, such as GDP per head, economic growth or income distribution (see World Economic Forum, 2003; IMD, 2004).

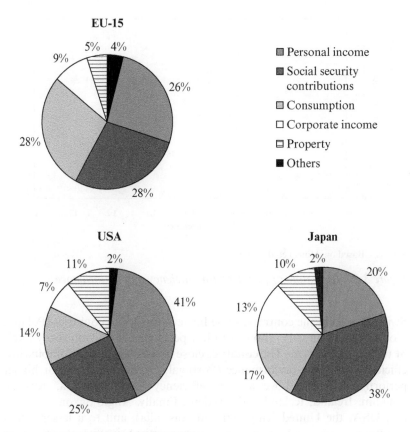

Source: Eurostat (2004) and OECD (2004b).

Figure 3.2 Tax mix by source in the EU, Japan and USA, 2002 (as percentage of total taxes)

Afonso et al. (2003) compute indicators of public sector performance (which describe the outcomes of public sector activity) and public sector efficiency (which relate the outcomes to resource use). To establish indicators for overall public sector performance, selected socio-economic indicators are used for public administration, education, health, infrastructure, income distribution, economic stability and economic performance.

Figure 3.3 shows the relationship between public sector performance and efficiency in EU countries, and some other OECD countries. Both high performance and efficiency levels can be observed in countries such as Luxembourg, the Netherlands, Norway, Finland, Denmark and

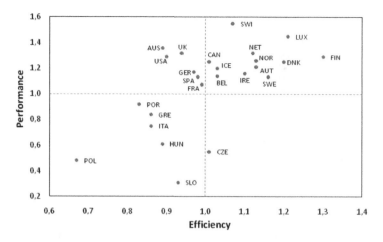

Source: Based on Afonso et al. (2003).

Figure 3.3   Indicators of public sector efficiency and performance

Switzerland. On the contrary, some Eastern European countries (Poland, Slovakia and Hungary) show both low performance and efficiency levels of their public sectors. The countries close to the average line combine low efficiency with low performance (Portugal, Greece and Italy) or higher performance with above average efficiency levels (Canada, Austria, Belgium, Ireland, Iceland and Sweden). Finally, Anglo Saxon countries (the USA, the United Kingdom and Australia), and to a lesser extent Germany, France and Spain, appear to be relatively inefficient in their use of public resources, but they record above-average scores in terms of performance. Afonso et al. (2003) conclude that the higher performance and efficiency scores of small governments suggest that the size of public sector may be too large in many industrialized countries, leading to diminishing marginal productivity.

The performance of the public service sector, in particular, can be measured by the score in four public sector functions (SCP, 2004): stabilization and growth of the economy, distribution of welfare, allocation of public services and the quality of public administration (Table 3.2). Luxembourg and Ireland perform well in terms of stabilization and growth. Of all EU-15 countries, Germany, France and Italy achieve the least satisfying results, mainly because of their rather poor performance on economic growth and budget deficits. The composite score indicating the quality of public administration shows a fairly wide range. Finland again has the highest score, followed by Denmark, Sweden and

Table 3.2   Indicators of public service sector performance

Country	Stabilization and growth of the economy	Distribution of welfare	Allocation of public services	Quality of public administration
Belgium	1.29	1.45	1.33	1.10
Denmark	1.38	1.61	1.32	1.71
Germany	1.13	1.61	1.16	0.93
Greece	1.23	0.89	1.37	0.82
Spain	1.27	1.05	1.32	1.26
France	1.16	1.21	1.33	1.21
Ireland	1.64	0.89	1.56	1.36
Italy	1.13	1.05	1.25	0.87
Luxembourg	1.72	1.53	1.15	1.66
Netherlands	1.33	1.69	1.24	1.31
Austria	1.37	1.53	1.34	1.39
Portugal	1.27	0.81	1.01	1.08
Finland	1.46	1.61	1.52	1.91
Sweden	1.37	1.61	1.34	1.50
UK	1.32	0.97	1.14	1.23
EU-15	1.34	1.30	1.29	1.29
USA	1.23	0.63	1.22	1.38

Source: SCP (2004).

Luxembourg. On the allocation function of the public sector, Ireland and Finland score well above average. In terms of welfare distribution, only the Scandinavian countries, Germany and the Netherlands approach the Lisbon target.[1]

The quest for economic growth is a third target, one that is central in macroeconomic policy. Economists of the Leviathan public choice school tend to support the view that a large public sector is detrimental to economic growth. Yet evidence of a correlation between GDP growth and the government growth rate, and more weakly between GDP growth and government size, have been associated with the argument that there is a strong positive externality between public and private sectors (see, for example, Rodrik, 1998; Fatás and Mihov, 1999). In Europe, due to the creation of a single currency area and the disappearance of national monetary policies, the debate has focused on the role that national fiscal policies can play and the need for a fiscal federation. The permanent limits on budget deficits set by the 'Growth and Stability Pact' have been criticized for not leaving enough room for fiscal policy to smooth GDP fluctuations (Eichengreen and Wyplosz, 1998), although most economists agree with the European

Commission that some kind of pact is necessary to guarantee coherence within a common economic and monetary policy.

3.4   THE NEED FOR REFORM AND AREAS OF REFORM IN THE EUROPEAN PUBLIC SECTOR

After the rapid expansion of the welfare state in the 1950s and 1960s, the public sector has been under considerable pressure over the past few decades. Declining public confidence in government institutions, and growing demands on public finances, have prompted governments to initiate measures that trim the public sector and make it more efficient and effective. This 'new' state will be the outcome of deep reforms; reforms that will enable the state to perform roles that the market is unable to perform. The objective is to build a state that responds to the needs of its citizens – a democratic state in which bureaucrats respond to politicians, and politicians to voters in an accountable way. For this reason, political reforms seek to increase the legitimacy of governments. There has been fiscal adjustment, privatization and deregulation to reduce the size of the state and improve its financial health; and administrative reform that, in addition to improving the financial situation of the state, aims to provide the means of good governance.

Nowadays, although structural adjustment remains a major objective in European countries, the emphasis has changed towards the reform of the state, and particularly towards administrative reform. The central issue is how to rebuild the state and how to redefine a new state in a global world. This change of focus is also taking place in the European Union, where administrative reform has been added to tax reform, as well as social security reform and the elimination of state monopolies. Comprehensive public administration reforms, undertaken in many countries during the 1970s and 1980s, have given way to more targeted reforms. These have often been carried out in response to pressures to limit public spending, to strengthen economic performance or to keep up with the innovations introduced in the private sector, such as the introduction of new information technologies. Country-specific forces are usually at the root of public sector reforms (Knox, 2002).

3.4.1   Types of Reforms

The reform strategies that have been adopted can be catalogued in several ways. Pollitt and Bouckaert (2004) identify four types: maintain, modernize, marketize and minimize. 'Maintain' involves tightening up traditional control mechanisms. 'Modernize' involves organizing alternative structures and processes of government policy making. Here the focus of reform is to improve management (managerial modernization) and/or to foster participation by citizens and user groups (participatory modernization). 'Marketize', the third strategy, involves introducing a private sector focus to the public sector and its values. It does not mean that services are privatized. Techniques common to the private sector are transplanted wholesale to the public sector. 'Minimize' – reducing the public sector – involves privatizing functions that have traditionally been in the domain of the public sector. The railways in the UK are frequently cited as an example of bad privatization, but privatization has been much more successful in other sectors (such as telecommunications) and in most cases the new enterprises and the new markets become much more efficient and perform better.

Following a recent European Commission report, Table 3.3 summarizes three types of reform that enhance efficiency in the public sector: management reform, introduction of information technology, and privatization and outsourcing.

In recent years, people have become increasingly aware that bureaucratic public administration is inconsistent with the demands of civil society in contemporary capitalism. People demand much more than the state can deliver. The reason for this gap is not simply fiscal, as O'Connor (1992) points out, or political, as Huntington (1968) stresses. It is also administrative. Economic and political resources are by definition scarce, but this limitation may be partially overcome by their efficient use by the state. The role of a proficient public administration becomes strategic in reducing the gap between social demands and their fulfilment. There is, however, a broader reason for the interest in reforming the state, and particularly public administration: the increasing relevance of protecting public patrimony (*res publica*) against rent-seeking activities. Certain types of goods, such as the environment, are inherently 'public' goods. Reform of the public sector means less direct provision by the state and more public services provided by society.

3.4.2 The New Public Administration Management and Decentralization

The new Managerial Public Administration[2] (MPA) has some basic characteristics: it is outcome- and citizen-oriented; it assumes that politicians and civil servants are entitled to a limited degree of trust; it uses decentralization and the incentive to creativity and innovation as strategy; and it controls public managers by means of management contracts (March

Table 3.3 Recent public sector reforms

Type of reform	Human resources management	Introduction of ICT	Privatization and outsourcing
Mechanisms	Improvements in the incentive structure (wage differentiation, hiring and firing practices, promotion)	Introduction of ICT, changes in working methods and e-Government practices	Arm's-length agencies, privatization of service providers and public–private partnerships
Critical factors	Reliable output and performance indicators	Quality of information, time savings, speed of response in interaction with citizens and businesses and common standards across public agencies	Increasing efficiency, productivity, profitability and capital investment spending, risk sharing, management skills and employment reductions
Examples	New Public Management and Total Quality Management	e-Europe 2005 Action Plan and US Government 2002 Program	See Bennet et al. (2004), Claessens and Djankov (2002), Frydman et al. (1999), Gonenc et al. (2000), Nicoletti and Scarpetta (2003), Van der Nord (2002), and La Porta and Lopez-de-Silanes (1999)

Source: European Commission (2005b).

and Olsen, 1984). This kind of state structure is usually identified with neoliberal views because managerial techniques were often introduced at the same time as structural adjustment programmes that tried to deal with the fiscal crisis of the state. Despite this, different ideologies move forward in this same way, although with different methods and intensities. A perceived superiority of managerial administration over bureaucratic administration has led governments (with different ideological tendencies) to engage in administrative reform. This has tended to have two objectives: expenditure reduction in the short run and increased efficiency, through greater managerial control (including innovation, to a certain extent) in the mid term.

MPA, as it has been seen, involves a change of management strategy, but this strategy must be put to work in a reformed administrative structure. The general idea is the decentralization of delegation authority (McCue and Pitzer, 2000). Many authors contend that authority or control, especially in government, must be decentralized in order to provide more responsive support to end-users, eliminate bureaucratic obstacles to programme accomplishment, improve inter-departmental coordination and empower service delivery managers to procure what they need without impediment by a centralized organization (Osborne and Gaebler, 1992). It is interesting to point out that this decentralization process in the internal structure of European countries is developing at a time when countries within the EU are engaging in greater transnational integration.

It can be seen that decentralization has many aspects. One is functional decentralization, where resources and powers are developed into semi-autonomous institutions. Then there is territorial decentralization, which increases the role of other government tiers, such as regions and local authorities (SCP, 2004). Decentralization is usually approached from a financial perspective, with a focus on devolving public resources. Regarding the proportion of the government budget spent by local authorities, three groups of countries can be identified in Europe. First, there are the Scandinavian countries, which have a very strong local sector (accounting for one-third of total spending). The second group comprises a number of Western European countries, such as France, ranging from 20 per cent to 30 per cent. Finally, there are several countries with a small local sector, mainly Southern European countries but also Ireland and Belgium (Council of Europe, 1997).

These data provide just a first snapshot. They must always be viewed in the light of the autonomy of local authorities and the distribution of public servants among the different government tiers. If these indicators are analysed, the groups identified above remain largely intact (SCP, 2004). In terms of employment, the data show a shift in staff employed by central government to staff on the payroll of local and regional authorities. The proportion of public servants working in central government is declining, while the proportion of staff working at the local and regional level is on the increase (Pollitt and Bouckaert, 2004).

3.4.3   Changes in Administrative Cultures and Systems

Differences in administrative culture have major impacts both on fundamental choices concerning the structure of the public sector and on the daily functioning of the government apparatus. Administrative culture forms part of a wider political and social culture. Hofstede's dimensions probably provide the best known categorization of administrative cultures (Hofstede, 1980), although other attempts have been made (Mamadouh, 1999). It is clearly no simple matter to group countries on the basis of their administrative culture. Loughlin (1994) groups countries on the basis of broad philosophical and cultural traditions. He distinguishes an Anglo-Saxon (minimal state), a Germanic-organicist and a French Napoleonic state tradition. The Scandinavian type is a mix of the first two. Finally, Hooghe (2002) used four dimensions developed by Page (1995) – cohesion, autonomy from political control, caste-like character and non-permeability of external interest – to construct an index of 'Weberian bureaucratic tradition' (strong, medium, weak). This indicates the degree to which a national administrative culture corresponds to the Weberian model of strong cohesion, large degree of autonomy from political control, strong caste-like character of the bureaucracy and low permeability of external interests.

Each of these categorizations has its own focus and so it is difficult to obtain a clear overview. The categorization of some countries seems fairly coherent, but the absence of clear indicators means it still entails some risk. The Anglo-Saxon tradition differs considerably from the Continental tradition. This is reflected, among other factors, in the fact that many public servants in the UK are generalists, while in Germany they tend to have a legal background. The large number of studies on the cultural differences of European public servants show how important it is to take a more in-depth look at this subject. Obviously, the evolution towards a European Administrative Space will be affected by different views on the role of public administration in society (SCP, 2004).

Policy implementation is supported by administrative processes such as financial management, human resources management and information technology (fundamentally, e-Government). The scope of this section extends to the public sector in general, but the government – and the public administration in particular – is responsible for the quality of financial management, human resources and openness in the public sector.

Various factors have prompted public authorities to modernize their budget cycle through managing the public sector finances. The financial reform agenda consists of three major components: greater financial responsibility, results-based budget and multi-year budget. The New Public Management movement has shifted the focus from traditional a priori control to control in retrospect, and placed greater emphasis on results and the financial responsibility of management. Two indicators of the degree of parliamentary control over the budget and of management freedom are the degree of detail to which the budget is appropriated and the end of year flexibility (see, for example, OECD/World Bank, 2003). Thus, the countries with the highest degree of management freedom in Europe are Denmark, the UK and the Netherlands, while Belgium and Spain are examples of those countries with the least discretionary powers (European Commission, 2005b).

Personnel policy, or 'human resources management', is another horizontal policy area currently experiencing change. Strategic human resources policy, competency management, equal opportunities policy and public service motivation are key concepts in the modernization of human resources management. Personnel planning and the recruitment of young staff by promoting the public sector as a good employer are therefore key objectives of current human resources policy.

Finally, the development of a knowledge-based society also has implications for the services and communications of the public sector. There is a general tendency in the public sector towards automating bureaucratic procedures and processes, and electronic interaction with citizens (European Commission, 2003). Thus, e-Government is one of the newest forms of modernization in the public sector. In this field, benchmarks are frequently used to compare and rank countries (Janssen et al., 2004). Among European countries, the UK and Scandinavian countries have the best average score in almost all of these studies. On the other hand, countries such as Ireland and those of Southern Europe score below average in terms of e-Government. The new EU member states do not score as well as the EU-15, although Estonia, the Czech Republic and Slovenia have progressed furthest in the field of e-Government during recent years.

3.4.4 Other Methods of Public Sector Modernization and the Role of Innovative Services

An important policy debate that is emerging concerns the modernization of public administration through the design and implementation of better governance (OECD, 2002, 2003b, 2004a), better regulation and reduction of red tape (European Commission, 2005a; OECD, 2003a). There are also research and policy actions dealing with the question of employment and human capital in the public sector (OECD, 2001). Besides the issues related to management and organization (the full research line on New Public Management), there is also increasing awareness of the role of public–private partnerships (PPP) (European Commission, 2004a) as a way of improving efficiency in the provision of services of general interest (European Commission, 2004b).

Unfortunately, there exists a significant lack of research and debate on key issues. Notable amongst these are innovation and improved public services. With regards to the interaction between public and private services, it is important to point out the growing role of business services (Knowledge intensive services (KIS) in particular) in the modernization and innovation of public administrations. These services are a source of innovation and effectiveness for all economic activities (Rubalcaba, 1999), which is a crucial point for European public sectors. A successful strategy in modernizing the public sector could lead to direct and indirect positive impacts. On the one hand, there is the opportunity for better services to be delivered to citizens and the more efficient use of resources. On the other hand, there are spillover effects for all organizations dealing with public administrations and less budgetary pressure to cut social rights derived from a barely consolidated welfare state.

Table 3.4 shows seven major functions that services perform in public administrations and identifies major related business services for each function. For many functions, business services constitute a source of innovation, such as technological (for example, ICT services) or organizational (for example, outsourced services). The link between innovation and the modernization of the public sector requires a comprehensive understanding of the relationship between public sector performance and the overall performance of the economy. Business services provide innovative elements to public administration that constitute a strong linkage element in this integration (Rubalcaba, 2004).

From this wider perspective, business, services can contribute to the performance of public administration in four ways. From a horizontal point of view (a possible effect on all public services):

- Any public service can be provided in a more efficient and modern way.
- Outsourcing of business services, knowledge and advanced services in particular (for example, IT services, management consultancy) as a key source of modernization, innovation and linkage to the market services sector.

Table 3.4   Business services useful for the modernization of public administration

Major functions in public administration suitable to be modernized by services	Examples of business services
1. Political strategy, evaluation of users' needs and resources, development of new policies	• Management consultancy; polling opinion and market research; social research and development
2. Administration and control	• Billing, accountancy and auditing; legal services; quality control and quality standards
3. ICT management	• Computer services; internet and intranet services; telecommunication services
4. Personnel	• Selection and provision of personnel; professional training
5. Marketing and communication with users	• Advertising; direct marketing; Web pages services and e-governance services
6. Transport and logistics	• Logistics and transport services; express courier; renting, leasing and real estate
7. Facility management services	• Security services; building cleaning services; catering; environmental services/waste disposal; maintenance and repair of equipment; energy services

From a vertical point of view (only certain public services):

• New, totally or partially privatized services – the use of outsourcing is an example of this, but also state support of private institutions (schools and hospitals), the privatization of state-owned companies (such as railways, telecommunications and electrical plants) and concession systems.
• An alternative to outsourcing – public/private partnerships.

The type of 'culture' that the interaction between private and public services generates boosts both the efficiency and the performance of the public sector. Even if the innovation in public and private services have similarities and dissimilarities and the obstacles to innovation in public sectors are many and various (Mulgan and Albury, 2003), the private/public interaction necessarily reinforces cooperative and pro-innovative strategies.

3.5   CONCLUSION

The modern public sector is a consequence of a long and controversial process in which different organizational models, sizes and profiles have evolved. The structure, size and performance of the public sector is the subject of fiery debate in Europe. The significance and impact of innovation in public administration is affected by differences in size, performance and socio-economic organization. By adopting the Lisbon Agenda (European Commission, 1997), member states of the European Union set themselves, in 2000, the daunting task of making the Union the most competitive economic area in the world. It seems increasingly doubtful whether this ambitious goal can be completed successfully. However, the pattern and performance of the public sector of national economies is a crucial factor in the race to achieve the objectives of the Lisbon Agenda. In addition, growing demands and declining confidence in the public sector have prompted governments to initiate structural policies aimed at trimming the public sector and increasing its efficiency and effectiveness.

Although the role of the size of the public sector in the performance and evolution of the economy is widely discussed in the economics literature, well known difficulties involved in measuring size and the importance of the public sector are readily demonstrated. Still, whether measurements use the level of public expenditure, or any other indicator, some results are consistent. The weight of the public sector in EU countries is at present approximately 48 per cent of current GDP, easily surpassing that of Japan and the USA. Within this, important differences exist amongst EU countries. The relevance of the public sector is smaller in most Southern and Anglo-Saxon European countries. On the other hand, France, Belgium and the Nordic countries (especially Sweden) have higher figures in the public sector. In any case, with some exceptions such as France, the dominant trend in the EU has been, during the 1990s, a decline in the size of the public sector, in contrast with the observed trend in other countries, such as Japan, Switzerland and Norway.

In terms of the performance of the public sector, moderate differences can be found across European countries. Unsurprisingly, countries with small public sectors report the best economic performance while countries with large public sectors show more equal income distribution. When weighting performance by the resources used to achieve it, there are important differences across countries. Thus countries with small public sectors report significantly higher public sector efficiency indicators than countries with medium-sized or large public sectors. All these findings suggest diminishing marginal productivity in higher public spending.

This chapter has identified key areas in which reform and modernization of the public sector are possible. Based on different strategies and ideas

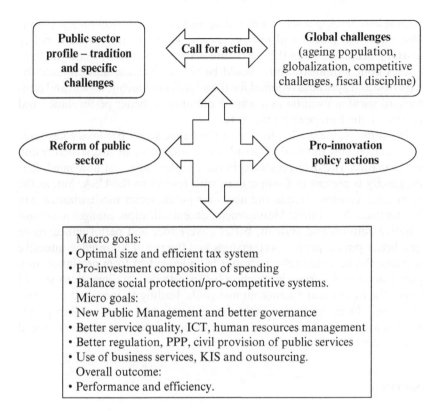

Figure 3.4   Framework for pro-innovation reform in the public sector

coming from the new Managerial Public Administration and New Public Management, various areas for policy action exist. However, recent debates on better governance and improved regulation neglect the role of innovation and the development of new and improved public sector services. There are many ways in which innovation can contribute to higher performance in the public sector. In addition, the interaction of public and private sector services requires far more political attention and research. Here lies the importance of this book.

In line with the research reported in this chapter, Figure 3.4 summarizes key areas for public sector reform when innovative actions are taken from different profiles and traditions in Europe. From existing challenges, both global (for example, an ageing population and the need for welfare state reform, competitive pressures due to globalization and the need for fiscal discipline) and specific (based on the situation of a given country and its public sector tradition), a call for action is invited where public sector reform can develop a set of innovative and pro-innovation policy actions that affect the macro and microeconomic levels. In this context, policy learning accumulated in the use of innovative actions is of major importance. Public administrations should be able to increase and evaluate the expertise and aptitudes required for the adoption of technological and non-technological innovation as a way of obtaining a better performance and reform of the European public sector.

In summary, the modernization of the public sector becomes a key issue when considering the need for an adequate integration of size, structure and performance. The data presented in the chapter show just how much heterogeneity is present in Europe, even with respect to the USA. Yet, at the same time, common trends and needs for public sector modernization can be identified: New Public Management, decentralization, changes in administrative cultures and systems, better governance and performance, more and better public–private partnerships and the use of knowledge-intensive services. Public sector reform cannot be independent from pro-innovation policy actions. A correct interaction between these two dimensions should boost the macro and microeconomic goals, leading to increased performance and efficiency in the public sector. Better and more modern public sectors will lead to higher standards in services provision, increasing social and economic welfare.

NOTES

1. The aim of the Lisbon Agenda is to achieve a poverty rate of 10 per cent.
2. MPA is a concept used by some authors (see, for example, Bresser-Pereira, 2001) to define the way the state organization is managed nowadays in social-liberal countries. In contrast, New Public Management (NPM) is a school or paradigm for design of government (Hood, 1995), but also an international reform movement and a narrative about public sector reform (Roberts, 2000). It is a broad and complex term used to describe the wave of public sector reforms apparent throughout the world since the 1980s. Based on public choice and managerial schools of thought, NPM seeks to enhance the efficiency of the public sector and the control the government has over it (OECD, 1995).

REFERENCES

Afonso, A., L. Schuknecht and V. Tanzi (2003), 'Public sector efficiency: an international comparison', European Central Bank working paper 242.
Beeton, D.J. (1987), 'On the size of public sector', *Applied Economics*, **19**(7), 927–36.
Bennett, J., S. Estrin, J. Maw and G. Urga (2004), 'Privatization methods and economic growth in transition economies', Centre for Economic Policy Research discussion paper 4291.

Bresser-Pereira, L.C. (2001), 'A new management for a new state: liberal, social and republican', the 2001 John L. Manion lecture, Canadian Centre for Management Development, Ottawa, 3 May 2001.

Christensen, T. and P. Laegreid (2001), 'A transformative perspective on administrative reforms', in T. Christensen and P. Laegreid (eds), *New Public Management: The Transformation of Ideas and Practice*, Aldershot and Burlington, VT: Ashgate, Chapter 2.

Claessens, S. and S. Djankov (2002), 'Privatization benefits in Eastern Europe', *Journal of Public Economics*, **83**, 307–24.

Council of Europe (1997), *Local Government Finance*, Strasbourg: Council of Europe.

David, P., B. Hall and A. Toole (2000), 'Is public R&D a complement or substitute for private R&D? A review of the econometric evidence', *Research Policy*, **29**(4–5), 497–529.

Eichengreen, B. and C. Wyplosz (1998), 'The Stability Pact: more than a minor nuisance?', *Economic Policy*, **26**, 65–113.

European Commission (1997), 'Agenda 2000 for a stronger union', *Bulletin of the European Union*, supplement 5/1997, Brussels.

European Comission (2000), *Recent Fiscal Development in the Candidate Countries*, Brussels: European Commission.

European Commission (2003), 'The role of e-Government for Europe's future', COM (2003) 567, September, Brussels.

European Commission (2004a), 'Green Paper on public–private partnerships (PPP)', COM (2004) 312, June, Brussels.

European Commission (2004b), 'White Paper on services of general interest', COM (2004) 347, Brussels.

European Commission (2005a), 'Better regulation for growth and jobs in the European Union', COM (2005), Brussels.

European Commission (2005b), *European Competitiveness Report 2004*, Brussels: European Commission.

Eurostat (2004), New Cronos database, 2004.

Fatás, A. and I. Mihov (1999), 'Government size and automatic stabilizers: international and intranational evidence', Centre for Economic Policy Research discussion paper 2259.

Frydman, R., C. Gray, M. Hessel and A. Rapaczynski (1999), 'When does privatization work? The impact of private ownership on corporate performance in the transition economies', *Quarterly Journal of Economics*, **114**, 1153–91.

Gemmel, N. (1993), *The Growth of the Public Sector: Theories and International Evidence*, Aldershot, UK and Brookfield, USA: Edward Elgar.

Gonenc, R., M. Maher and G. Nicoletti (2000), 'The implementation and the effects of regulatory reform. Past experience and current issues', OECD Economics Department working paper 251.

Handler, H., B. Koebel, P. Reiss and M. Schratzenstaller (2005), 'The size and performance of public sector activities in Europe', Austrian Institute of Economic Research working paper 246.

Hofstede, G. (1980), *Culture's Consequences. International Differences in Work-related Values*, Thousand Oaks, CA: Sage.

Hood, C. (1995), 'The New Public Management in the 1980s: variations on a theme', *Accounting, Organizations and Society*, **20** (2/3), 93–109.

Hooghe, L. (2002), *The European Commission and the Integration of Europe. Images of Governance*, Cambridge: Cambridge University Press.

Huntington, S. (1968), *Political Order in Changing Societies*, New Haven, CT: Yale University Press.

IMD (2004), *World Competitiveness Yearbook*, Geneva: Institute for Management Development.

Janssen, D., S. Rotthier and K. Snijkers (2004), 'If you measure it they will score. An analysis of international e-government benchmarking', paper presented at the 4th European Conference on e-Government, 17–18 June, Dublin Castle, Dublin.

Karras, G. (1997), 'On the optimal government size in Europe: theory and empirical evidence', *Manchester School of Economic and Social Studies*, **65**(3), 280–94.

Knox, C. (2002), 'Public service reform, Northern Ireland exclusive', review of public administration briefing paper 26.

La Porta, R. and F. Lopez-de-Silanes (1999), 'The benefits of privatization. Evidence from Mexico', *Quarterly Journal of Economics*, **114**(4), 1193–242.

Light, P.C. (1999), *The True Size of Government*, Washington, DC: Brookings Institution.

Loughlin, J. (1994), 'Nation, state and region in Western Europe', in L. Bekemans (ed.), *Culture: Building Stone for Europe 2002. Reflections and Perspectives*, Brussels: Peter Lang Publishing.

Mamadouh, V. (1999), 'National political cultures in the European Union', in M. Thompson, G. Grendstad and P. Selle (eds), *Cultural Theory as Political Science*, London: Routledge.

March, J.G. and J.P. Olsen (1984), 'The new institutionalism: organizational factors in political life', *American Political Science Review*, **78**(3), 734–49.

McCue, C.P. and J.T. Pitzer (2000), 'Centralized versus decentralized purchasing: current trends in governmental procurement practices', *Journal of Public Budgeting, Accounting and Financial Management*, **12**(3), 400–20.

Mulgan, G. and D. Albury (2003), 'Innovation in the public sector', Strategy Unit, Cabinet Office, October 2003.

Nicoletti, G. and S. Scarpeta (2003), 'Regulation, productivity and growth: OECD evidence', OECD Economics Department working paper 347, Paris.

O'Connor, J. (1992), *The Fiscal Crisis of the State*, New York: St Martin's Press.

Organisation for Economic Co-operation and Development (OECD) (1995), *Governance in Transition. Public Management Reforms in OECD Countries*, Paris: OECD.

OECD (2001), 'Labour market policies and the public employment service', OECD proceedings, Paris.

OECD (2002), *Regulatory Policies in OECD Countries. From Interventionism to Regulatory Governance*, Paris: OECD.

OECD (2003a): *From Red Tape to Smart Tape. Administrative Simplification in OECD Countries*, Paris: OECD.

OECD (2003b): 'Public sector modernisation', OECD policy brief, October, Paris.

OECD (2004a), 'Public sector modernisation: governing for performance', October 2004, Paris.

OECD (2004b), 'OECD in figures, 2003', Paris.

OECD/World Bank (2003), 'Survey on budget practices', accessed at http://www.oecd.org/gov/budget/database.

Osborne, D. and T. Gaebler (1992), *Reinventing Government*, Reading, MA: Addison Wesley.

Page, E. (1995), 'Administering Europe', in E. Page and E. Hayward (eds), *Governing the New Europe*, Cambridge: Polity Press.
Pollitt, C. and G. Bouckaert (2004), *Public Management Reform. A Comparative Analysis*, Oxford: Oxford University Press.
Roberts, A. (2000), 'The New Public Management. An overview', World Bank staff training course 10 March.
Rodrik, D. (1998), 'Why do more open economies have bigger governments?', *Journal of Political Economy*, **106**, 997–1032.
Rubalcaba, L. (1999), *Business Services in European Economy: Growth, Employment and Competitiveness*, Brussels: European Commission.
Rubalcaba, L. (2002), *Competitividad y Bienestar en la Economía Española*, Madrid: Ediciones Encuentro.
Rubalcaba, L. (2004), 'The role of business services in the modernisation and innovation on public administrations: policy implications for the European Union', *Publin Post Newsletter*, **2/3** (4–5).
Social and Cultural Planning Office (SCP) (2004), *Public Sector Performance. An International Comparison of Education, Health Care, Law and Order and Public Administration*, The Hague: SCP.
Utrilla de la Hoz, A. (2001), *La Economía Pública en Europa* [*Public Economy in Europe*], Madrid: McGraw-Hill.
Van der Noord, P. (2002), 'Managing public expenditure. The UK approach', OECD Economics Department working paper 341, Paris.
World Economic Forum (2003), *Global Competitiveness Report 2003–2004*, Geneva: World Economic Forum.

4. Survey of research on health sector innovation

Faridah Djellal and Faïz Gallouj

4.1 INTRODUCTION

This chapter surveys the literature devoted to innovation in the health sector, with particular focus on public sector hospitals as this is where the vast majority of past research has been conducted. By conducting this survey we appreciate health sector innovation in all its diversity, and the diversity of possible loci of innovation. The chapter provides a general foundation for the six health case studies (Chapters 5 to 10) of the book.

The chapter is divided into seven sections. Section 4.2 discusses the challenges raised by innovation within the health sector hospitals and the key generic drivers of innovation in health. These are resources, competition, social or societal considerations, and performance measurement and 'transparency'.

In Sections 4.3 to 4.6 we focus on the literature on innovation in hospitals, as this is where most research is conducted. This enables us to explore more clearly the four major key drivers of innovation discussed in Section 4.2 and to examine the detailed literature on innovation that exists in this area.

The theoretical and empirical literature on innovation in hospitals contains four very different perspectives about hospitals. The first group includes those studies by traditional economists that view the hospital as a production function. The second group of studies views the hospital as a 'set of technological and biopharmacological capacities', and emphasizes the role of medical innovation, that is, the various types of (tangible and intangible) technological and biopharmacological innovations in the healthcare field. The third group comprises an increasingly large number of studies that consider hospitals as information systems and highlight the importance of new information and communication technologies (ICTs). The fourth group of studies is the most recent and views the hospital as one (albeit it very important) provider within a wider system of healthcare provision. This perspective highlights the complexity of services that need to be integrated and managed, and the particular role played by hospitals as a healthcare system hub. Here, the functional approach, in which hospitals are reduced to their function of healthcare providers, gives way to an approach that is both organizational (hospitals as providers of a multiplicity of diverse services) and network-based (hospitals as parts of larger networks of healthcare provision).

Section 4.7 concludes that 'production function', 'capabilities' and 'information' approaches only provide atomistic and fragmented views of innovation in hospitals. In other words, a 'system' approach is more efficient as far as it seems to be able not only to grasp the diversity of forms of innovation within (and beyond) hospitals but also the diversity of actors involved.

4.2 THE FACTORS DRIVING INNOVATION

The question of innovation cannot be investigated without considering a number of general issues influencing the evolution of healthcare systems. From the point of view of innovation, these issues reflect constraints that have to be taken into account or circumvented – factors that explain the emergence and direction of innovation and goals to be pursued. For several years four major factors, closely correlated with each other, have been shaping trajectories of innovation and change in the health sector. They are resources, competition, social or societal considerations, and performance measurement and 'transparency'.

4.2.1 Resources

In France, as in most OECD countries, health expenditure has been growing continuously for a number of years. Thus, at the beginning of 2002, such expenditure accounted for about 9.5 per cent of GDP (compared with 4.2 per cent in 1960, 5.8 per cent in 1970, 7.6 per cent in 1980 and 9.3 per cent in 1990).

Control of this expenditure has become a major economic and social policy issue in OECD countries. Thus since the end of the 1970s, successive governments in France have sought to put in place methods for administrative control of the healthcare system. The favoured methods have involved limiting the growth in reimbursable costs, freezing public hospital expenditure and controlling the level of healthcare provision (Delaeter, 1991).

Thus resource constraints and regulatory constraints (the two are, of course, closely linked) are at the root of many innovations in hospitals. For most hospitals, after all, the challenge is to plan and implement new development strategies. These strategies generally have five main thrusts: the search for new sources of funding, the expansion of existing activity, the development of new activities, the optimization of processes and the rationalization of procedures (rationalization of logistical and administrative departments through outsourcing and re-engineering), and experimentation with new forms of work organization and working time.

4.2.2   Competition

Recent years have seen a considerable increase in competition (or awareness of competition), whether within the public or private sectors, between the public and private sectors or even with doctors in private practice (Moisdon and Tonneau, 1996). The effects of this competitive pressure are very significantly reinforced by the financial constraints to which hospitals are now subject. They are further aggravated by the emergence of major networks of 'private providers' attracted by a market offering good prospects for the future. Thus, some of the traditional public monopolies, such as those in specialized surgery or complex functional investigations, are now being contested.

This competitive pressure has several consequences for innovation. First, it creates very strong incentives to acquire and make effective use of cutting-edge technologies. Loriol (2002) notes that in areas with very high concentrations of medical provision, competition between hospitals (particularly between public and private organizations) has encouraged hospital managers to invest heavily in new equipment (for example, scanners and MRI) that is itself expensive to operate and leads to high levels of prescribing. All hospitals, irrespective of size, are engaged in a race to acquire the most comprehensive 'technical panoply' possible. Second, increasing importance is being attached to the question of the service relationship and service quality, which are becoming strategic tools in a competitive environment (Bonnici, 1998). Faced with the difficulties inherent in improving the technical aspects of their services, hospital managers are indeed emphasizing the quality of their provision by improving patient facilities and enhancing the appearance of sites and buildings. Another strategy is to compete on the range of services provided (Moisdon and Tonneau, 1996). In order to maintain or increase their 'market shares', hospitals are tending to increase the services they provide. Finally, competitive pressures are also causing hospitals to look for alternative solutions to standard hospitalization practices.

Conversely, however, (technological) innovation also influences the competitive environment. After all, while technology is a key factor in inter-hospital competition, it is also – and increasingly so – a key driver of inter-hospital cooperation. Pressure from local health authorities or sheer financial necessity is forcing hospitals to cooperate in the acquisition of expensive equipment. Many agreements on the shared use of such equipment (for example, scanners and MRI) have been concluded. Technology is also a key factor in the establishment of telemedicine networks and in many other ventures.

4.2.3 The Social and Societal Factor

The social and societal factor encompasses several dimensions: changes in demand, demographic developments and certain trends in healthcare provision and social welfare, such as the development of services for certain groups within the population, particularly the more vulnerable.

The demand for medical services has been changing significantly for several years, with the emergence and development of real 'medical consumerism' (Delaeter, 1991). Users (customers) of medical services, who are better informed and also more likely to be co-producers, have indeed become more demanding and disputatious.

The demographic aspect is an important factor in the evolution of hospitals in Europe and the USA, and their capacity to innovate. The main challenge is the ineluctable ageing of the population. The increasing share of the elderly in the population as a whole has significant consequences for healthcare provision and its various characteristics. First, existing provision has to be adapted to the level of needs. For example, in hospitals this adaptation generally involves the conversion of short-stay beds into medium- and long-stay beds. At the same time, provision has to be shifted out of hospitals, notably through the development of home care services or home-based health services, particularly 'high-tech home care'. Hence, in the last few years, the need to provide care and support for the elderly has led to experiments with many innovations, both within hospitals and elsewhere (Djellal and Gallouj, 2006).

One of the major forces driving the evolution of healthcare provision and social welfare is the requirement to develop approaches appropriate to the needs of particular groups. The most significant examples involve groups living in precarious situations. In addition to the ageing of the population, there are increasing levels of relative poverty for the poorest groups in many European societies and the USA. This is leading to a revival of the hospital as a provider of social welfare, a role once forgotten (Volovitch, 1998). The objective here is to put together innovative programmes that focus more specifically on the needs of vulnerable groups.

The evolution of healthcare and social welfare also has an epidemiological dimension, which may also exert significant influence on innovation. Because of their prevalence, some diseases require the establishment of highly specific procedures. However, these arrangements are seldom implemented. They concern new afflictions, such as AIDS. Delaeter (1991) notes that dealing with AIDS means that people have to rethink their approach to prophylaxis, their competences in infectology and their ethical codes.

4.2.4   Measurement and 'Transparency' of Output and Innovation

The management tools developed in order to give a more satisfactory account of local practitioner and hospital activity (and to provide a basis for a more justifiable and equitable distribution of resources) include the Programme de Médicalisation du Système d'Information (PMSI) in France. Launched in 1982, this is recognized as a major management innovation. The PMSI aims to measure hospital activity by replacing the traditional 'hotel' criteria (number of stays, number of days) with a typology of patients or diseases. Diagnosis Related Groups (DRGs) are used as a basis for calculating and comparing costs.

Like many management tools used in hospitals, the PMSI is a closed tool, the main focus of which is internal management and control. A number of difficulties arise when the traditional boundaries of a hospital become blurred, that is, when a hospital opens up to its external environment. It then becomes difficult to use the tool to track changes in the organization of the healthcare system, particularly changes in the boundary between hospitals and other care networks (Gadrey, 2002). Thus, the PMSI fails to take account of decompartmentalization and the opening up of hospitals to the external environment, which are fundamental aspects of innovation in hospitals.

The PMSI is relatively poor at identifying innovation, or more precisely makes it invisible. Gadrey (2002) shows that it fails to take account (except in a negative way) of hospitals' research and innovation activities. Such activities are not regarded as justifiable output for a hospital. Indeed, they are not even subjected to any specific evaluation. In certain hospitals, however, they may account for a relatively high share of total activity and use not insignificant volumes of resources and time. The fact that they are ignored by management instruments may well be damaging for hospitals in the long term.

Other studies (Gadrey, 2002; Suarez, 2002) have also noted that the PMSI ignores hospitals' relational and educational activities (whether involving patients or those close to them). These activities, which are excluded from the definition of hospital output, may make not insignificant contributions to recovery and prevention (particularly in some areas, such as psychiatry or geriatrics). They provide the basis for better patient care (and better care for patients' families) and for many innovations.

PMSI undoubtedly constitutes a major innovation, but one of its effects is to reduce the visibility of other innovations introduced in hospitals. It is necessary, therefore, to try to make innovation in hospitals even more visible, to raise its profile. This is the aim of the present study.

4.3 THE PRODUCTION FUNCTION APPROACH

Health economics was initially constructed around the notion of the hospital as a production function, in other words, like a private sector firm. After all, the notion of a production function was developed as a universal tool capable of accounting for any economic activity. Phelps (1992), for example, does not see the slightest difference between the production of cars and the production of healthcare. In both cases, the fundamental objective is to mobilize and combine production factors in order to create a product. In the case of a car, the production factors will include steel, plastic and labour, while in the case of health services, the production factors will be 'medical care', that is, a set of activities intended to restore or increase patients' health capital.

The production function can be written as follows: $H = g\,(m)$, where H denotes the product 'health' and m denotes 'medical care'. The marginal productivity of medical care is assumed to be positive. In other words, an increase in 'medical care' increases the restoration of health. In addition, returns to scale are assumed to be decreasing.

The medical care (m) that is described here, for simplicity's sake, as a homogeneous activity actually comprises a large number of variables. These include capital (for example, beds, diagnostic and therapeutic equipment, and operating theatres), supplies (for example, bed sheets and drugs) various types of workers (for example, nurses, doctors, secretaries and managers) and patients, since they are themselves participants in their own care (co-production). Similarly, the product (H) is not homogeneous since hospitals and doctors' surgeries are akin to multi-task workshops producing a range of different products, each of which is specially tailored to a specific patient. This production model does not differ fundamentally, therefore, from that of organizations such as hairdressing salons, motor vehicle and electronic equipment repair shops or grocery shops.

The notion of technique, it should be remembered, lies at the heart of the concept of production function, to the extent that technique is defined as a given combination of production factors (in this case, 'methods' of providing healthcare). Changes in techniques can be explained by changes in the relative prices of these production factors. They are reflected in a shift along the production function. Technological change is reflected in the shift in the production function. It expresses the notion that more health (H) is being produced with unchanged quantities of production factor inputs, that is, medical care (m). Alternatively, the same amount of health may be produced using less medical care inputs (m).

4.4   THE COMPETENCE APPROACH

In this set of studies the hospital is viewed as a set of technological and biopharmacological competences. The importance of innovation lies in extending and developing these technological and biopharmacological competences. The focus is thus placed on medical innovations, where the term is used to denote the introduction and/or development of tangible or intangible technological innovations, and medicinal innovations at the heart of a hospital's core business, that is, the provision of medical care. Within this generic category, three sub-groups can be identified:

1.   Biomedical or biopharmacological innovation (for example, new drugs, new chemical and pharmaceutical substances).
2.   Tangible medical innovation, that is, the introduction of technical systems, whether based on capital goods or various small items of equipment and whether used for diagnostic or therapeutic purposes.
3.   Intangible medical innovation, which encompasses treatment protocols and diagnostic or therapeutic strategies.

The main studies in this second group focus on: the nature of medical innovation; its dynamic; and its impacts.

4.4.1   The Nature of Medical Innovation

This is the subject with which the vast majority of studies by experts and practitioners, published regularly in the numerous specialist magazines, are concerned. These essentially descriptive articles constitute case study databases that social science researchers, who generally ignore this literature, could use to their advantage. For example, Schrayer (1995) identifies 18 categories or sectors, which can be divided into three groups: single-use equipment, capital goods, and implants.

Although they are much fewer in number, this group also includes some more theoretical enquiries into the nature of technologies. The classification developed by Thomas (1975), for example, identifies three categories of medical technologies. The first category is 'non-technologies' that are applied to little known and poorly understood diseases. These generally involve the provision of assistance and support for patients in situations in which remission is more or less inconceivable. This category would include the treatment of tuberculosis until the 1920s, infections until the 1950s and the treatment of AIDS until the introduction of combination therapy. The second category is 'half way technologies' that lead to a remission of the disease or enable patients' lives to be adapted to their illnesses, albeit at relatively high cost. These technologies help to slow down the development of diseases but have no real effect on the causes. They would include the treatment of tuberculosis in the 1930s by artificial pneumothorax and sending patients to sanatoriums. More recent examples include organ transplants, anti-cancer treatments (radiotherapy and chemotherapy), and dialysis and combination therapies for AIDS patients. The third category is 'high technologies' (or 'effective technologies') that are based on a real understanding of the pathological mechanisms of the diseases in question. These high technologies can be used to prevent and cure diseases at low marginal cost. Immunization programmes, antibiotics and vaccines fall into this category.

4.4.2 The Dynamics of Medical Innovation

The humanities and social science disciplines have been concerned with this second general theme. Economics occupies a central position. The main theoretical problems addressed are the diffusion of medical innovation, its life cycle and decreasing returns.

4.4.2.1 The diffusion of medical innovation

Numerous studies have revealed differentiated diffusion patterns, depending on the type of innovation in question. According to Majnoni d'Intignano and Ulmann (2001), innovations can be classified by the decreasing speed of diffusion: drugs and heavy equipment, complex procedures and innovations requiring a coordinated network of out-patient and in-patient facilities. Moreover, the diffusion of innovation depends on many other factors, such as the existence of specialist teams with specific training, the degree of acceptance of the innovation within the population at large and even within the medical profession itself, government standards and controls, and even the pricing system.

Although a wide range of themes is addressed in the literature on the diffusion of innovation, Paraponaris et al. (1997) take the view that this question can be considered from three different perspectives, which they denote by the terms normative, analytical/descriptive and prescriptive. Normative studies seek to define the optimal configurations for the use and diffusion (rates and scale of diffusion) of medical innovation, and its various elements. Analytical/descriptive studies are essentially concerned with examining the cognitive, socio-demographic and organizational factors that encourage or hinder the diffusion of medical innovations. Prescriptive studies, finally, seek to identify the financial and organizational constraints and incentives that encourage and promote more rational (use) of the resources allocated to the healthcare system.

4.4.2.2   The life cycle of medical innovation

Some studies have revealed that medical innovations have relatively short life cycles or, in other words, that they are renewed or replaced very rapidly. Weisbrod (1991) notes that of the 200 drugs and substances most widely used 20 years ago, only 50 or so are still widely used today. He also notes that most of the diagnostic techniques and treatment protocols and techniques currently in use did not exist less than 50 years ago. More recent studies by Frija et al. (2002) describe certain trends towards the replacement of invasive investigations with non-invasive procedures, of irradiating methods with non-irradiating methods, and of standard surgical procedures with therapeutic techniques based on interventional radiology.

By contrast, studies by De Kervasdoué and Lacronique (1981), Nègre et al. (1989) and Beresniak and Duru (1992) suggest that genuine substitutions are rare and that the life cycles of medical innovations can, in fact, be relatively long. In most cases, medical innovations are added to the panoply of existing diagnostic and therapeutic methods. For example, endoscopy has not supplanted radiological methods among gastroenterologists, despite its real effectiveness. In the sphere of medical imaging, the widespread use of scanners has not led to any significant reduction in the number of standard radiological examinations, while MRI has not significantly reduced the number of scans carried out (also see Chapter 5).

4.4.2.3   Decreasing returns to medical innovations

A number of studies have investigated the decreasing returns to medical innovations and the consequences thereof. Decreasing returns become evident as the innovation diffuses, whether as a result of its being repeated in the treatment of the same patient, or being applied to other patients or to other therapeutic indications (Durieux et al., 1986; Eddy, 1990; Moatti, 1991; Eisinger et al., 1995).

For any given pathology, the diffusion of medical innovations contributes to a deterioration of the cost-effectiveness ratio. According to Paraponaris et al. (1997), patient survival, or the quality of that survival (an indicator of the effectiveness of treatments), is increasingly less elastic to research and development (R&D) expenditure, to investment in innovative technological equipment or to the introduction of new therapeutic strategies. However, the deterioration in the cost-effectiveness ratio is all the more rapid when the technique in question is applied to new indications.

4.4.3 The Impacts of Medical Innovation

This question can be considered in relation to a number of potential targets such as quality of health, productivity, work organization, the nature of that work, health expenditure and externalities. Here we confine ourselves to examining the last three targets and, in particular, the question of the impacts of innovation on health expenditure and externalities, which seem to figure prominently in the literature. One additional, cross-cutting theme is the evaluation of medical technologies. The aim of evaluation is both to verify the performance of the technologies in their practical applications, and to assess their positive or negative consequences for individuals and the wider society (De Kervasdoué and Lacronique, 1981; Durieux et al., 1986; Béjean and Gadreau, 1996).

4.4.3.1 Medical innovation and health expenditure
Economists frequently tackle the question of medical innovation from the perspective of health costs. Medical innovation is often regarded as the main factor in explaining the rise in health expenditure (Altman and Blendon, 1977; Ginzberg, 1990; Newhouse, 1992; Fuchs, 1996). According to Newhouse (1992), medical innovation explains half of the increase in medical expenditure in the USA over half a century. In France, L'Horty et al. (1997) estimate that technical advances in medicine explain more than a quarter of the increase in health expenditure between 1970 and 1995. For his part, Weisbrod (1991), who draws on Thomas's typology (Thomas, 1975), takes the view that the sharp increase in health expenditure is linked to the fact that the collective treatment of many diseases has moved from stage 1 (non-technologies) to stage 2 (half-way technologies), with its associated high costs.

However, the direction of causality between medical innovation and health expenditure is far from obvious. Some authors wonder whether the causality might not in fact be reversed, with technological innovation being the result rather than the cause of increased health expenditure (De Kervasdoué and Lacronique, 1981). It should be noted, furthermore, that what is problematic is less the absolute level of health expenditure than the increasing ineffectiveness of this expenditure relative to the results achieved (Cutler, 1994; Majnoni d'Intignano and Ulmann, 2001).

4.4.3.2 Medical innovation, healthcare quality and well-being
A certain number of studies have focused on the relationship between medical innovation and healthcare quality and, more generally, on the

impacts of medical innovation on wellbeing, whether individual or collective. These studies assess quality on the basis of criteria such as technical effectiveness, safety and comfort, accessibility (physical and moral) and the cost savings achieved (De Kervasdoué and Lacronique, 1981). Any improvement in one or other of these variables is regarded as a contribution to healthcare quality and increased wellbeing, even if it has no effect on technical effectiveness (in the sense of reduced mortality, morbidity or infirmity).

There are also a number of studies on the general theme of evaluating the effects of technological progress and innovative procedures on the quality of patients' (extended) lives (Beresniak and Duru, 1992; Le Pen, 1997). Weinstein and Stason (1977) and Williams (1985) develop a synthetic indicator of the 'quantity and quality of survival' (QALY: 'quality adjusted life years'), which can be used as a basis for analysing a treatment in terms of both life expectancy and survival quality.

4.4.3.3 Medical innovation and the nature of work

Medical innovation fundamentally alters the nature of medical care. The relational aspect of providing healthcare tends to be replaced by a logistical process whereby the patient is transferred from one technical system to the other (Chandernagor et al., 1996). In consequence, technical acts increasingly replace relational acts and technical time is increasingly substituted for relational time. This also gives rise to changes in management and monitoring systems, since it is easier to measure technical time than relational time.

The new medical technologies are also contributing to the break-up of the traditional notion of a profession, and to the emergence of new professions. The medical professions are increasingly entering a period of integration, characterized by a blurring of the traditional boundaries between, for example, biology and clinical practice (development of predictive medicine), and between medicine and surgery (development of interventional techniques), as well as between research and clinical practice, and between health and social services (Anatole-Touzet and Souffir, 1996). The use of new technologies leads to the emergence of new competences. For example, the development of non-invasive techniques means that surgeons and their teams work with conscious patients, whereas they used to operate on patients under anaesthetic. The need to manage this new service relationship gives rise to changes in behaviour and competences for all operating theatre personnel.

4.5   THE INFORMATION APPROACH

Too often innovation in services is reduced to the introduction of new ICTs (Andersen et al. 2000; Boden and Miles, 2000; Gallouj, 2002). It is true that for several decades services have been the main users of this type of technology. Hospitals are not, of course, immune to the pervasive diffusion of ICTs. Consequently, a significant number of studies have taken as their starting point the notion of the hospital as an information system, and examined innovation in hospitals in terms of its relations with the informational paradigm. In surveying the literature that adopts this point of view, a distinction needs to be made between information technology applied to administration (informational and material flows) and information technology applied to medical care itself.

4.5.1 ICTs and the Management of Informational and Material Flows

Information technology swept through hospital administrative departments as early as the mid-1960s. It was only later that it was applied to logistical departments (management of material flows) and then medico-technical departments (Acker, 1995; Hémidy, 1996).

Studies such as Stanback (1987) and Sachot (1989) are concerned with the development of more or less sophisticated typologies of ICT applications or hospital management systems. Sachot (1989), for example, identifies four separate management systems: a patient management system (comprising an administrative and a medical component); a production input management system (that is, pharmacy and other supplies, as well as personnel); a system for managing production units; and a system for managing production itself (which extends from patient reception to discharge and billing).

There is nothing to separate this literature from that devoted to other types of service activities. The analyses primarily focus on the impacts of ICTs on various economic variables: quality, work organization and, in particular, productivity and employment. These last two variables are examined below.

4.5.2 ICTs Applied to Medical Care

We are dealing here with medical technologies. That is, with technologies applied to patient care, in whatever form that care may take, whether diagnosis, treatment or monitoring. These technologies have emerged much more recently than those deployed for administrative purposes (Berbain and Minvielle, 2001).

It is useful, in investigating the nature of these technological innovations, to make a distinction between two major groups of technologies. First, there are hybrid medical technologies that have an ICT component added to other technological elements (for example, robotics and transport).

Second, there are ICTs that facilitate the delivery of healthcare remotely (principally telemedicine).

Hybrid medical technologies (that is, those that combine ICTs with more traditional, material processing technologies) have been the subject of numerous studies (for example, Child et al., 1985; Blackburn et al., 1985) that are essentially analytical/descriptive in nature (description of the technology, analysis of its impact in organizational terms). The examples most frequently investigated include computer-assisted diagnosis, medical monitoring, automatic diagnostic equipment and video surgery. Imaging (for example, MRI, scanography and video endoscopy) is often regarded as the medical technology that has benefited most from progress in IT, automatics and video.

Telemedicine already has its particular spheres of application, such as obstetrics and, more generally, perinatality. But other areas are also affected. These include emergency services, out-patient clinics and treatment centres, prisons and retirement homes. In each of these areas there are many possible spheres of application, including remote consultations, video-communication, teleconferencing and telemonitoring. Over and above the sometimes very detailed description of the possible uses and the (sometimes unfulfilled) promises of the application of new ICTs to remote medicine, two major research concerns can be identified. First, investigations of telemedicine are often associated with more general enquiries into the development of care networks. The second major preoccupation is with hospital treatment provided in the home (Mehlman and Youngner, 1991; Arras, 1995). Studies in this second group focus in particular on the social and ethical implications of home care, the economic impact of high-tech home care, and the effects of new ICTs on patients and their families.

4.5.3 The Effects of New ICTs on Employment and Productivity

Studies that approach innovation from the perspective of ICTs, on the one hand, and from that of the hospital as a set of technological and biopharmacological capacities, on the other, share a number of concerns (diffusion, impacts on quality of healthcare and wellbeing, for example). However, one important differentiating characteristic is the focus in the first group on the effects of new ICTs on jobs and productivity. These last two questions are essentially, though not exclusively, associated with the administrative applications of new ICTs.

4.5.3.1   ICTs, employment and skills
A very large number of studies have investigated the effects of ICTs on employment, in both its quantitative and qualitative aspects. Important

examples include Stanback (1987), Silver (1992), Dent (1996) and Vendramin and Valenduc (2002). The main concerns of these studies include the volume of jobs, the nature of work and employment, the demarcation lines between tasks, the new professions, payment systems, monitoring of work and internal mobility (career opportunities). This is not, of course, an exhaustive list, nor can the individual themes be considered independently of each other.

Paradoxically, the finding on which there seems to be unanimity is that the introduction of ICTs seems to have had relatively little impact in terms of reducing the volume of hospital jobs. It appears that new technologies are supplementing rather than replacing existing functions and procedures. As far as the more qualitative aspects of employment are concerned, the findings also tend to show that the impact of ICTs has been positive rather than negative. In his studies of the American hospital system, Stanback (1987) found that the work done by administrative staff and nurses had widened in scope and that their responsibilities had increased. There were also new career opportunities, which reflected the increased need for professionals and specialists to operate and maintain the technical tools (for example, isotope technicians, IT specialists and electronics experts). Similarly, according to Vendramin and Valenduc (2002), new ICTs have not had much of a negative influence on the qualifications, competences and occupational status of workers in the hospital sector. Contrary to what has been observed in other service sectors, such as banking, insurance and distribution, the pressures on workers and working conditions following the introduction of new ICTs seem to be relatively weak. Little evidence has been found of stressful monitoring, increased labour turnover, increased involuntary part-time working or an increase in low levels of qualifications and skills.

Mention should also be made of some interesting studies on shifts in occupational boundaries resulting from the introduction of new ICTs. According to Silver (1992), for example, the increasing computerization of medical and administrative records is forcing nurses to act as secretaries when it comes to certain administrative tasks, while hospital IT services currently play very little part in their strictly medical duties. The number of bedside computers remains very small.

The introduction of new ICTs has led to certain changes in the structure and composition of occupational categories. A high proportion of the ICTs used in hospitals (although this is also true of all the new technical systems introduced in hospitals) now depend on specialists, who generally benefit from continuing training programmes provided by the manufacturers of the medical equipment themselves.

4.5.3.2   ICTs and the productivity question

As in other service sectors, the basic question running through the literature on this subject is that of Solow's paradox, which concerns the difficulties of generating productivity gains through the use of all-pervasive ICTs. Attempts to explain this paradox occupy an important place. Some interpretations are specific to hospitals. According to Fuchs (1990), for example, the increase in litigation for alleged professional negligence explains the low productivity gains. Indeed, health professionals have tended to increase the volume of records, reports and other documentation they produce in the course of treating patients as a precautionary measure against litigation. This increases the volume of work done by doctors and other health professionals but has absolutely no effect on output. Doctors are also conducting more examinations and devoting more time to each patient, without there being any corresponding change in pricing practices. Finally, they have a tendency to request increasing numbers of tests and analyses of various kinds for each patient.

Other explanations of Solow's paradox are more general and are applicable to all economic sectors. One is the phenomenon of hysteresis where, it is argued, a certain time must elapse before the use of ICTs has a real and measurable impact on productivity. If this is true, then the effect will also occur in health services (Stanback, 1987; De Kervasdoué, 1996). Another explanation is that methods used to measure productivity are flawed. In particular, they are ill-suited to services (Gadrey, 1996).

4.6   THE SYSTEMS APPROACH

This concept of the hospital is very different to the other three approaches for it marks a shift away from the technicist perspective towards one that places greater emphasis on service and the (internal and external) service relationship. The patient is not simply a patient in need of treatment, but also a consumer of a complex set of services, and efforts have to be made to satisfy this customer's needs, as well as those of their family.

Innovation in hospitals is not a black box, as in the production function approach. It is no longer simply the sum of the more or less highly developed and spectacular medical technologies, designed and used by a medical aristocracy, as in the approach that sees the hospital as a set of technical and biopharmacological capacities. Nor does it come down simply to a sophisticated and all-pervasive information system, as in the hospital-as-information-system approach. If innovation in hospitals is to be apprehended in its totality it is necessary to break into the black box of the organization. Penetrating the black box in this way puts the spotlight on the actors in innovation and on support functions (accommodation, catering, laundering and transport), which are also neglected.

In our experience, the specialist professional literature is less resistant to adopting an approach that is open to the multiple aspects of innovation in hospitals. A survey of this literature is facilitated by dividing it into two groups. The first comprises analytical studies that seek to develop broad, open typologies of innovation or focus on forms of innovation that are generally neglected. The few academic studies concerned with the same issues will be allocated to this group. The second comprises more descriptive studies that confine themselves to 'technical' presentations of case studies of innovation in hospitals. These case studies cover a very wide range of innovations.

4.6.1 The Typological and Analytical/Descriptive Studies

This first group includes the studies by Anatole-Touzet and Souffir (1996), who describe a veritable hospital 'innovation system' encompassing the following types of innovation. First, there are technological innovations in the strict sense of the term, for example, biotechnologies, IT and new medical equipment. Second, there are service innovations linked to changes in the way hospitals go about their work. That is, the introduction of new activities, such as out-patient services, medical and social services for the destitute, and the development of networks with doctors in private practice and/or voluntary organizations. Third, there are organizational innovations. These include the reorganization of administrative and logistical departments, the evaluation of healthcare quality, the development of treatment protocols and the organization of working time. Fourth, there are social and cultural innovations, such as the development of problem-based training schemes and programmes for improving working conditions.

This typology acknowledged the multiplicity of different forms of innovation that exist in hospitals, and belongs to what might be called the 'Schumpeterian tradition'. It suffers from a lack of any explicit definition of each of the categories, and from a certain degree of overlap between them. Thus, as the examples listed above show, the boundaries between service, organizational and social innovations are not clearly defined.

This group also includes the studies of Arbuz and Debrosse (1996), which concentrate more on 'non-technological' innovation. The authors criticize other studies for their excessive concentration on 'innovation in terms of medical equipment and practices', which leads to a serious underestimation of the important role played by the modernization of other activities, in particular the general running of hospitals and working conditions.

Academic studies that tackle the question of organizational innovation in hospitals can be characterized in different ways. First, there are relatively fewer of them than the others. Second, they tend to emphasize innovations in the organization of healthcare or of treatment units. Third, an increasing number of them are concerned with issues related to healthcare networks (for example, Larcher and Poloméni, 2001; Bonafini, 2002). Finally, a (relatively) large number of them tackle the question of organizational innovation as a secondary matter. In most cases, organizational innovation is losely associated with the introduction of medical technologies and new ICTs. De Kervasdoué (1996), for example, argues that the diffusion of technological innovations is reflected, first, in increased costs before giving rise to organizational innovations introduced with a view to fully exploiting the new potential for increased productivity. Organizational innovation, as a secondary effect, is made explicit in the studies by Lamarque (1984), who makes a distinction between key and peripheral innovations. Key innovations, which are strictly medical, are those involving technologies used for diagnostic or investigative purposes, for treatment or rehabilitation and for prevention. In other words, the triad of drugs, material resources (products and equipment) and techniques (procedures). Peripheral innovations are structural or organizational innovations introduced in order to bring about changes in the organization of healthcare provision.

4.6.2   Case Studies

Most of the available case studies belong to this second group. They include examples, case studies, monographs and accounts of experiments. One example in France is the journal *Gestions Hospitalières*. Every two years, since 1987, it has published the results of the 'awards for innovations in hospitals'. The various award winners that are listed constitute a very rich database of innovations in French hospitals. The case studies, taken together with other sources, provide an extremely wide list of innovations that cover a multiplicity of areas and specialities within hospitals.

If strictly technological innovations (medical, ICT-related and logistical) are excluded, the hundreds of innovations listed can be divided into the following five categories:[1]

1.   Organizational innovations. These include, first, all attempts to modernize the organization and functioning of non-medical hospital departments (for example, breaking down departmental boundaries and the establishment of new units in order to develop or take responsibility for new functions in spheres such as catering, accommodation, shops, maintenance and management). They also include all innovations in the

organization of healthcare provision. Examples include the establishment of new types of clinics within certain hospitals, 'the hospital at home' and day units.

2. Managerial innovations. This category comprises new management techniques and methods, such as new accounting and financial techniques and procedures, and new management practices. The latter includes the development of strategic approaches, client segmentation and the introduction of total quality management approaches. The Programme de Médicalisation du Système d'Information (PMSI), a management tool that seeks to measure hospital activity by means of a typology of patients or diseases, also falls into this category (Naiditch and de Pouvourville, 2000).

3. Relational or service innovations. This category includes all innovations affecting the nature of the interface between service providers and service users and their families, such as improvements in the quality of patient facilities, management of patient flows, reductions in waiting times and accommodation for patients' families.

4. Social innovations. Barreau (2002) defines social innovation as a process based on social bargaining and formal and informal compromises leading to changes in the rules governing coordination and incentives. These innovations take shape through the development of new attitudes to work organization, the exercise of power and decision-making processes. Examples include experiments with internal communications and voluntary working hours in excess of the standard (in France) 35-hour week or flexible time management.

5. Innovations in external relations. This type of innovation involves the establishment (in new and original forms) of particular relations with customers, suppliers, the public authorities and other businesses. Innovations in external relations can take a number of different, more or less complex forms (depending on the number of actors involved in the new relationship and the purpose of that relationship). The simplest innovations in external relations are those involving bilateral relations. Examples include agreements on the shared use of heavy equipment (whether medical or logistical equipment), agreements on the joint acquisition of such equipment, mergers between hospitals and the sale of services to other hospitals or to firms or organizations in other sectors. A range of different service activities may be involved here, such as catering, laundry services and logistics, as well as training, consultancy and renting out of premises for conferences or cultural activities. The more complex innovations in external relations involve healthcare networks. Increasingly diverse networks are being built up, whether formal or informal, integrated or otherwise and

dependent (or not) on the use of new ICTs. It might be said that the 'hospital as service provider' is also increasingly part of a network of healthcare and other services.

4.7 CONCLUSION

This chapter has highlighted the extent to which innovation in health services can be investigated from several very different theoretical perspectives. Health sector organizations, such as hospitals, can be viewed as separate atomistic entities. They can then be studied as production functions, as a set of technical and biopharmacological capacities or as an information system. Treating an organization as an independent entity has advantages and disadvantages. The alternative, which we have also discussed, is to treat health sector organizations as part of a larger system of service providers. In the literature the three atomistic perspectives predominate. The main focus of attention is, on the one hand, innovation processes involving an organization's 'operational centre' (its individual treatment units) and, on the other, the implementation of medical and/or IT innovations. As a consequence, the literature largely ignores certain aspects of innovation in organizations, such as hospitals, and consequently fails to investigate either the form or nature of that innovation or the departments (that is, the actors) involved in innovation.

This technological bias can be interpreted in various ways by drawing on economic and sociological arguments. First, economic theory, through the notion of the production function, favours a technological approach to innovation – one that tends to focus on process innovations. Second, medical and IT innovations are tangible and often spectacular. They can be described as pervasive when they are no longer concentrated in clearly identified areas, such as cutting-edge specialist hospitals (operating theatres, radiology departments and laboratories), but have spread widely, diffused across all health sector organizations (Chandernagor et al., 1996). These technologies constitute the 'shop window' of health sector organizations and testify to their degree of modernity and to their practitioners' level of competence. For example, a hospital's technical capacities not only enable it to attract good doctors but also patients and professional advisors. It is hardly surprising, therefore, that managers and medical staff should combine to highlight this aspect of innovation. Furthermore, medical organizations are dominated by the medical profession. This being so, the concentration on innovations involving this 'learned profession' can scarcely be regarded as illegitimate.

The strength of the system approach (and the weakness of atomistic approaches), lies in its highlighting the complexity of a set of interacting organizations that produce a wide range of outputs and services. Consequently, there may be many other sources of innovation available for exploitation, whether by researchers, actors in a particular organization or the public authorities. These new sources contain an abundance of technological innovations, as well as organizational innovations and service innovations. They bring into play actors other than medical personnel, including administrators and workers in services, such as catering, cleaning and so on.

Innovation is not the exclusive preserve of a particular function (or of the professionals attached to that function). Further, innovation is much deeper and broader than tangible technologies. The authors have developed a theoretical framework to capture the complexity of modern heath sector organizations (Djellal et al., 2004; Djellal and Gallouj, 2005) and in Chapter 7 of this book apply this framework to a set of case studies of hospital innovation. The aim is to capture the multiple forms of innovation that are encountered, and thereby gain a deeper understanding of both the nature and the extent of innovation in public sector health.

NOTE

1. The categories in question may overlap with each other. After all, the definitions adopted in the literature often vary depending on the studies and authors in question.

REFERENCES

Acker, F. (1995), 'L'informatisation des unités de soins et travail de formalisation de l'activité infirmière', *Sciences Sociales et Santé*, **13**(3), 69–91.
Altman, S.H. and R. Blendon (eds) (1977), *Medical Technology: The Culprit Behind Health Care Costs?* Washington, DC: Department of Health, Education and Welfare.
Anatole-Touzet, V. and W. Souffir (1996), 'Innovation technologique, organisation du travail et gestion des compétences', *Gestions Hospitalières*, **354**, 222–5.
Andersen, B., J. Howells, R. Hull, I. Miles and J. Roberts (2000), *Knowledge and Innovation in the New Service Economy*, Cheltenham, UK and Northampton, MA, USA: Edward Elgar.
Arbuz, G. and D. Debrosse (1996), *Réussir le Changement de l'hôpital*, Paris: InterEditions.
Arras, J.D. (ed.) (1995), *Bringing the Hospital Home*, Baltimore, MD: Johns Hopkins University Press.
Barreau, J. (2002), 'Les services publics français et l'innovation sociale', in F. Djellal and F. Gallouj (eds), *Nouvelle Économie des Services et Innovation*, Paris: L'Harmattan, pp. 165–85.
Béjean, S. and M. Gadreau (1996), 'Du calcul économique à l'évaluation organisationnelle des politiques de santé', *Revue Française d'Economie*, **XI**(1), 21–47.

Berbain, X. and E. Minvielle (2001), 'Informatique et gestion des unités de soins', *Sciences Sociales et Santé*, **19**(3), 77–106.

Beresniak, A. and G. Duru (1992), *Economie de la Santé*, Paris: Masson.

Blackburn, P., R. Coombs and K. Green (1985), *Technology, Economic Growth and the Labour Process*, New York: St Martin's Press.

Boden, M. and I. Miles (eds) (2000), *Services and the Knowledge-based Economy*, London and New York: Continuum.

Bonafini, P. (2002), 'Réseaux de soins: réforme ou révolution', *Politiques et Management Public*, **20**(2), 1–22.

Bonnici, B. (1998), 'L'hôpital enjeux politiques et réalités économiques, notes et études documentaires', no. 5079, 15 October, La Documentation Française.

Chandernagor, P., J.P. Claveranne and M. Krichen (1996), 'Le statut des équipements hospitaliers: stratégie(s) d'acteur(s) et ordre technicien', in A.P. Contandriopoulos and Y. Souteyrand (eds), *L'hôpital Stratège*, Montrouge, France: John Libbey Eurotext, pp. 257–67.

Child, J., R. Loveridge, J. Harvey and A. Spencer (1985), 'The quality of employment in services', in T. Forester (ed.), *The Information Technology Revolution*, Oxford: Basil Blackwell, pp. 419–38.

Cutler, D.A. (1994), 'Guide to healthcare reform', *Journal of Economic Perspectives*, **8**, 13–29.

De Kervasdoué, J. (1996), *La Santé Intouchable: Enquête sur une Crise et Ses Remèdes*, Paris: Editions Jean Claude Lattès.

De Kervasdoué, J. and J.-F. Lacronique (1981), 'L'état et la technique: l'apparition du rationnement', in J. De Kervasdoué, J. Kimberly and V. Rodwin (eds), *La Santé Rationnée: La Fin d'un Mirage*, Paris: Economica, pp. 89–116.

Delaeter, B. (1991), 'La conduite du changement à l'hôpital public: principes dégagés de la démarche stratégique menée au CHRU de Lille', *Cahiers Lillois d'Economie et de Sociologie*, **18**(2), 26–40.

Dent, M. (1996), *Professions, Information Technology and Management in Hospitals*, London: Avebury.

Djellal, F. and F. Gallouj (2005), 'Mapping innovation dynamics in hospitals', *Research Policy*, **34**, 817–35.

Djellal, F. and F. Gallouj (2006), 'Innovation in care services for the elderly', *Service Industries Journal*, **26**(3), 300–327.

Djellal, F., C. Gallouj, F. Gallouj and K. Gallouj (2004), *L'hôpital Innovateur*, Paris: Masson.

Durieux, P., C. Blum and D. Jolly (1986), 'Evaluation des technologies médicales à l'hôpital', *Journal d'Economie Médicale*, **2**, 103–12.

Eddy, D. (1990), 'Screening for cervical cancer', *Annals of Internal Medecine*, **113**, 214–26.

Eisinger, F., J.P. Giordanella, H. Allemand and J.M. Benech (1995), 'Dépistage du cancer du sein. Le coût du temps et de l'espace', *Revue Médicale de l'Assurance Maladie*, **2**, 128–33.

Frija, G., A. Kalaï, A. Hernigou, C. Grataloup and M.P. Revel (2002), 'Imagerie non isotopique', in G. Broun (ed.), *Le Plateau Technique Médical à l'hôpital*, Paris: Editions Eska, pp. 225–63.

Fuchs, V. (1990), 'The health sector's share of the gross national product', *Science*, **247**, 534–38.

Fuchs, V. (1996), 'Economics, values and health care reform', *American Economic Review*, **86**, 1–24.

Gadrey, J. (1996), *Services: La Productivité en Question*, Paris: Desclée de Brouwer.
Gadrey, J. (2002), 'Emploi, productivité et évaluation des performances dans les services', in J. Gadrey and P. Zarifian (eds), *L'Émergence d'un Modèle du Service: Enjeux et Réalités*, Paris: Editions Liaisons, pp. 57–89.
Gallouj, F. (2002), *Innovation in the Service Economy: The New Wealth of Nations*, Cheltenham, UK and Northampton, MA, USA: Edward Elgar.
Ginzberg, E. (1990), 'High tech medecine and rising health care costs', *Journal of the American Medical Association*, **263**(13), 1820–22.
Hémidy, L. (1996), 'L'informatisation des hôpitaux et ses enjeux', *Revue Française de Gestion*, June-July-August, 125–36.
L'Horty, Y., A. Quinet and F. Rupprecht (1997), 'Expliquer la croissance des dépenses de santé: le rôle du niveau de vie et du progrès technique', *Economie et Prévision*, **129–30**(3–4), 257–68.
Lamarque, D. (1984), 'L'innovation médicale et les dépenses de santé', *Gestions Hospitalières*, **240**, 8–25.
Larcher, P. and P. Poloméni (2001), *La Santé en Réseaux: Objectifs et Stratégie dans une Collaboration Ville-Hôpital*, Paris: Masson.
Le Pen, C. (1997), 'Théorie de l'utilité et mesure des états de santé: le débat QALYs-HYEs', *Economie et Prévision*, **129–30**(3–4), 37–54.
Loriol, M. (2002), *L'impossible Politique de la Santé Publique en France*, Paris: Eres.
Majnoni d'Intignano, B. and P. Ulmann (2001), *Economie de la Santé*, Paris: PUF.
Mehlman, M.J. and S.J. Youngner (eds) (1991), *Delivering High Technology Home Care*, New York: Springer.
Moatti, J.P. (1991), 'Ethique médicale, économie de la santé: les choix implicites', *Annales des Mines*, **22**, 74–80.
Moisdon, J.-C. and D. Tonneau (1996), 'Concurrence et complémentarité: stratégies de l'hôpital et de sa tutelle', in A.P. Contandriopoulos and Y. Souteyrand (eds), *L'hôpital stratège*, Paris: John Libby Eurotext, pp. 21–45.
Naiditch, M. and G. de Pouvourville (2000), 'Le programme de médicalisation du système d'information (hospitalier): une expérimentation sociale limitée pour une innovation majeure du management hospitalier', *Revue Française des Affaires Sociales*, **1**, 59–95.
Nègre, M., B. Cayrol and H. Sebah (1989), 'Substitution ou complémentarité des techniques médicales: la pratique endoscopique et radiologique des gastro-entérologues', *Journal d'Economie Médicale*, **6**, 19–30.
Newhouse, J.P. (1992), 'Medical care costs: how much welfare loss?', *Journal of Economic Perspectives*, **6**(3), 3–23.
Paraponaris, A., J.-P. Moatti, P. Mossé and P. Huard (1997), 'Economie de l'innovation médicale: bilan et perspectives', in J.-C. Sailly and T. Lebrun (eds), *Dix Ans D'avancées en Économie de la Santé*, Montrouge, France: Editions John Libbey Eurotext, p. 225–33.
Phelps, C. (1992), *Health Economics*, New York: Harper-Collins.
Sachot, E. (1989), 'La productique entre à l'hôpital', *Politique Industrielle*, Winter, 135–41.
Schrayer, S. (1995), *Les Technologies Médicales: Une Industrie de la Santé*, Paris: Editions Pradel.
Silver, H. (1992), 'Vers une gestion flexible des services professionnels? Le cas des hôpitaux et des services juridiques aux Etats-Unis', in J. Gadrey and N. Gadrey (eds), *La Gestion des Ressources Humaines dans les Services et le Commerce*, Paris: L'Harmattan, pp. 165–80.

Stanback, T. (1987), *Computerization and the Transformation of Employment: Government, Hospitals and Universities*. Boulder, CO: Westview.

Suarez, B. (2002), 'La télémédecine: quelle légitimité d'une innovation radicale pour les professionnels de santé', *Revue de l'IRES*, **39**(2), 157–86.

Thomas, L. (1975), *The Lives of a Cell*, New York: Bantam Books.

Vendramin, P. and G. Valenduc (2002), *Technologies et Flexibilité: Les Défis du Travail à L'ère Numérique*, Paris: Editions Liaisons.

Volovitch, P. (1998), 'L'hôpital public en plein chantier', *Alternatives Economiques*, **155**, 59–62.

Weinstein, M. and W. Stason (1977), 'Foundations of cost-effectiveness analysis for health and medical practices', *New England Journal of Medecine*, **296**, 716–21.

Weisbrod, B. (1991), 'The health care quadrilemma: an essay on technological change, insurance, quality of care, and cost containment', *Journal of Economic Literature*, **29**, 523–52.

Williams, A. (1985), 'Economics of coronary artery bypass grafting', *British Medical Journal*, **291**, 326–9.

PART II

Case studies

5. The adoption and diffusion of technological and organizational innovations in a Spanish hospital

Manuel García-Goñi

5.1 INTRODUCTION

The innovation process has been studied using a variety of different approaches in the past. What is more, there is a strong debate on whether fundamental differences exist between innovation in (private sector) services and manufacturing. The focus of this chapter is the process of innovation observed within a public organization in the health sector, specifically, the publicly owned La Princesa Hospital in Madrid. The chapter analyses the process of adoption and diffusion within the context of a public health system, paying particular attention to the origin of the innovation, the agents involved in diffusion and the different stages of the diffusion process. The analysis considers the adoption and diffusion of two recent innovations at La Princesa Hospital. One is digital radiology, a technologically intense innovation. The other is ambulatory surgery, an organizationally intense innovation. These case studies are used to critically evaluate key theories and hypotheses about innovation. In particular, the question of whether the innovation process in public services is different to that found in private sector services and manufacturing is addressed.

Two types of innovation processes are prevalent in health service provision: technological innovations and organizational innovations. This chapter presents a detailed case study for each of these types of innovation and identifies the similarities and differences of their diffusion. The two case studies examine the adoption and diffusion of digital radiology, a technologically-intense innovation, and the adoption and diffusion of ambulatory surgery, which is an organizationally intense innovation. These case studies were selected because they provide a clear insight into policy learning and technical and administrative innovations in the public sector.

We find that both cases are consistent with innovation processes described in the health economics and services innovation literature. Notably, they support the relationship between the diffusion of knowledge and the stage of the life cycle in Barras's reverse product cycle (see Section 5.2), and highlight the impact of different actors (as beneficiaries of an innovation) on the identification of solutions to bottlenecks in service provision. Importantly, the findings are consistent across the two case studies. Therefore, even if technological and organizational innovations are at different stages of diffusion, they can be analysed using a common theoretical model of innovation.

Digital radiology (DR) is a direct substitute for analogue radiology (AR). Its adoption has led to various changes in the activities of agents involved in providing the service. These range from changes in the physical process of image development (a technical change), to the transportation of images to the physician, the storage of images and the examination of the X-ray. DR reduces the time needed to provide the same service, improves communication among specialists and image storage. The relative importance of this innovative process stems from the fact that radiology is one of the most intensively used services in a hospital. In La Princesa Hospital, 150 000 patients were analysed each year, accounting for more than 20 per cent of all services provided by the hospital. Radiology is not one of the most expensive in terms of unit costs (see Table 5.1 for details on the size of the expenditures at the hospital for different materials). However, its management has an enormous effect in the other services provided by the hospital. This is because most diagnoses require patients to be sent to the radiology department. In this chapter we measure the economic gains (or losses) of the new technology, comparing the time series of the services accomplished by the radiology department before and after the gradual adoption of DR. We also examine the quality of the service provided. As an indicator of quality we consider the demand for radiology services by different areas of the hospital over time. If the relative weight of radiology services increases for a number of areas of the hospital, this indicates an increase in the quality of the service provided.

Ambulatory surgery (AS) is a response to post-operative drawbacks of traditional surgical (TS) intervention. It is believed that AS originated in the Glasgow Royal Hospital for Sick Children in 1909 (Nicoll, 1909). AS (sometimes known as out-patient surgery) is an organizational innovation. Technically, there are two different types of AS. The first is where patients are able to leave the hospital on the same day as surgery is performed, but stay in hospital the night before. The second is where patients enter and leave hospital on the same day surgery is performed. Here we include both types of procedure under the general heading of ambulatory surgery. While AS is an organizational innovation – it radically alters the way in which service activities are structured – it is related (complementary) to technical innovations. For example, the post-surgery trauma of laser treatment for

Table 5.1 Consumption of different types of materials in hospital (euros), 1996–2002*

Type of material	1996	1997	1998	1999	2000	2001	2002
Office material	160 706	166 594	174 261	202 412	215 042	216 926	196 263
Informatics	202 795	164 503	149 604	181 067	163 828	192 150	220 756
Health instruments and tools	148 721	169 663	145 082	147 410	67 900	167 070	143 089
Other instruments and tools	81 310	189 634	52 106	38 657	136 832	56 819	61 301
Clothes	208 495	178 381	199 980	176 297	243 996	230 032	177 037
Food	551 961	580 466	174 261	570 713	405 896	263 606	–
Implants	2 524 612	3 224 942	3 410 727	3 101 760	3 865 594	4 015 541	4 241 620
Laboratory material	574 767	556 928	477 469	481 831	531 269	595 400	585 069
Reactive analysis	2 602 077	2 725 023	2 734 460	2 839 834	3 060 727	3 312 940	3 432 102
Radiology	398 466	460 036	414 160	439 573	430 008	438 620	482 834
Radioactive material	112 338	112 675	125 960	70 670	50 752	15 883	14 912
Sterilization	71 917	9 094	19 265	20 912	25 256	17 189	17 245
Dialysis	398 830	382 545	404 251	349 282	399 796	326 764	221 630
Other health material	3 979 456	4 145 088	3 955 684	4 220 342	4 694 823	4 908 230	4 838 748
Other non-health material and reparations	345 677	442 934	283 253	327 405	357 604	436 909	426 206
Other materials	209 274	211 213	236 137	231 612	240 914	244 858	254 643
Personnel expenditures	42 274 562	42 813 734	44 601 870	46 634 038	49 752 010	53 308 301	57 207 212

Source: Author's data using information at La Princesa Hospital

Note: * Variation of the costs of different types of materials from year to year stems from changes in the policy of providing specific services from other health centres or the hospital or from the hospital to other health services.

cataract surgery (ophthalmology) is far less than the manual surgery that used to be performed at the hospital. Combining laser treatment with AS can significantly reduce the length of stay, from three days to just a few hours. Hence, an important aspect of this case study is an appreciation of how this organizational innovation is related to, and facilitated by, complementary technological innovations.

The key benefits of AS are: a significant saving in pre- and post-surgery costs by freeing up of hospital beds; increased efficiency enabling waiting lists to be reduced; and reduced disruption of patients' lives. The innovation thus offers a substantial financial saving because hospital care is far more expensive that out-patient care. At the same time, patients have a higher level of comfort. They are able to return home much sooner, reducing the impact of surgery on their work and family.

The main change taking place in the introduction of AS occurs at the organizational level. Different procedures and protocols are adopted by medical staff (doctors, nurses and other medical workers) and also by patients. AS allows a higher rate of services per unit of time (Table 5.2) and a richer utilization of resources. We shall define the gains of the AS system, through the perception of quality by patients, taking into account the evolution of ambulatory practices and the entrance and exit of the waiting lists for those practices.

It is important to note that DR and AS both involve technological and organizational change for the hospital. We shall discuss the differences in the implementation processes, and how well they have solved (or not solved) particular bottlenecks in the hospital. In Section 5.2, after briefly describing the innovations, we discuss the theories of services innovation that will be critically evaluated, the relationship between innovation and expenditure, and how this relationship is treated differently by public sector and private sector institutions. Section 5.3 provides a detailed account of the institutional context and a technical analysis of the innovations explored here. Section 5.4 analyses the extent to which the case studies do or do not support existing theories of service innovation. Finally, Section 5.5 concludes with some policy implications learned from this study.

5.2 EXISTING THEORIES AND DATA ON SERVICES INNOVATION IN THE HEALTH SECTOR

There is a strong debate in the services literature on whether fundamental differences exist between innovation in (private sector) services and manufacturing. This literature stresses the specific characteristics of services: their intangible nature, their [services] being impossible to store, and the

Table 5.2   *Frequency of ambulatory and non-ambulatory surgery performed per year, 1998–2003**

	1998		1999		2000		2001		2002		2003		Total	
	Freq.	%	Freq.	%	Freq.	%	Freq.	%	Freq.	%	Freq.	%	Freq.	%
Ambulatory	2963	28.31	3637	33.10	2870	27.69	3052	28.93	3981	33.75	4081	33.37	20 584	0.31
Non-ambulatory	7503	71.69	7352	66.90	7494	72.31	7499	71.07	7815	66.25	8147	66.63	45 810	0.69

Note: The final column represents the total number of ambulatory and non-ambulatory surgeries performed during 1998–2003.

overlap between the production and consumption of services.[1] Innovation processes can be classified into two different types: those that correspond to technological advances and those that do not correspond directly to technological advances.

Barras (1986) presents a model of services innovation that focuses on the relationship between the improvement of the processes and their diffusion along the product life cycle. He found that the key stages in the diffusion of service products are the reverse of those found in manufacturing products, leading him to develop the 'reverse product cycle' thesis for services. In stage 1 the innovation is introduced. However, the drive for competitive innovation in stage 2 of the service industries studied by Barras was in process innovations (cost reduction). This was primarily achieved through the introduction and exploitation of new capital goods – new vintages of IT capital that replaced older vintages of IT capital. In stage 3 the drive was product differentiation, leading to a focus on product innovation. The pattern of innovation in stages 2 and 3 is the opposite of that found in studies of manufacturing innovation. There are two different factors that affect the speed of diffusion. The first is a lag between the availability of new (IT) capital goods and their adoption. The second is a lag between the installation of the new capital goods and the realization of the potential benefits associated with them.

The diffusion process of innovation has been explored from other points of view, but these do not necessarily contradict the reverse product cycle hypothesis. While the Barras thesis is based on case studies outside the health sector, Cutler and Huckman (2002) and Cutler and McClellan (2001a) identify two types of technological diffusion in the health sector that are compatible with the thesis. First, there is the substitution of old medical treatments by new treatments. This is the substitution of old technology goods by new technology goods, discussed in stage 2 of the reverse product cycle, although this may occur in health regardless of whether the unit cost of the new technology is higher or lower than the old technology. The second is treatment expansion. Here, competing firms seek new health improvements and, if the treatment is effective, it is used by more consumers. This is equivalent to product improvement in stage 3 of the reverse product cycle.

The structure of an industry is thought to be a key determinant of the diffusion process. Still, there is an ongoing debate about whether innovation rates are higher in private sector markets with many small firms and little market power, or when market concentration is higher, with fewer larger size firms and greater financial resources for R&D (Schumpeter, 1942). This may be too simple a characterization. Large firms in one sector, for example, a capital goods sector, may be the initial producers of an innovation, while implementation and adoption of the innovation have impacts in sectors with different levels of market concentration (stage 2 of the reverse life cycle). In addition, in stage 3 it may well be new entrants or existing small firms that pursue product differentiation using the new innovation. This idea has been refined by Barras (1990), and there is some evidence that industries containing small firms may adopt some innovations, such as IT, more easily (Stock et al., 2002). However, this is challenged by Windrum and de Berranger (2003).

There are other factors that influence diffusion. These include supply side factors (such as the capacity for financing), demand side factors and institutional constraints. These may provide incentives for efficiency gains and, therefore, influence the propensity to innovate. In the health sector, a very important determinant is the spillover from the positive strategic complementarities between R&D expenditures of different (public and private) institutions in the same sector (González, 2003). This spillover effect operates after stage 1 of the reverse product cycle. It is important to note that the quicker the diffusion process through the spillover effect, the greater the level of equity in the provision of health care by different regions or hospitals.

Gallouj and Weinstein (1997) present a theory that seeks to explain both technological and non-technological innovation processes. It begins with the specificities of service goods but seeks to construct a framework in which both innovation in services and manufacturing can be studied. Their framework uses Lancaster's approach, defining a product as a set of service characteristics that are offered to the end-user. Gallouj and Weinstein generalize this, defining products as two sets of characteristics: technological characteristics and service characteristics. Through this manipulation it is possible to characterize innovation processes of goods and services of all types. The final product is characterized by a matrix consisting of the internal and external properties of the product (tangible and intangible), resulting from the combination of two different matrices; one consisting of the technical characteristics and the other consisting of competences, including the ability to use the technical characteristics. The innovation processes might stem from improvements on either technical characteristics or competences. As a result, there can be different combinations of product characteristics through the substitution or addition of service characteristics. This framework is relevant to the health economics literature on how a new product or treatment is configured in different stages of the product cycle. In Djellal and Gallouj (2005), and in Chapter 7, the framework is applied to innovation in hospitals. Different types of innovation are classified according to whether the source of the innovation is competences, material operations, informational operations, methodological operations, or contractual or relational service operations.

As mentioned above, innovation can increase the efficiency of production. In growth accounting, productivity growth has three components: the marginal productivity of labour, the capital stock and a residual factor. Given that changes in the marginal productivity of labour and the capital stock are easily observed, through time series of wages (by different types of workers) and investment, the focus falls on the residual term. Harberger (1998) breaks down the residual into three parts: technical change, real cost reduction and total factor productivity. The latter includes the spillover effect and variations derived from human capital. Consequently, Harberger weights organizational change heavily. This can be related to Barras's reverse product cycle, however. Real cost reduction arises from the standardization of new processes in the second stage of the cycle, and total factor productivity includes the spillover effect that occurs when utilization of the new process is expanded in the third stage. This contrasts with Harberger, who only studies one aspect of the residual term, that is, real cost reduction.

It is implicitly assumed in the innovation literature that innovations invariably lead to an increase in productivity. However, this is something that needs to be empirically tested. In the health sector there will be an increase in productivity if the benefits of medical advances exceed the costs. Examining several innovations in different medical treatments, Cutler and McClellan (1996; 2001a) find an increase in productivity for most new treatments, such as for heart attacks, cataracts and depression. However, productivity growth is not clear in some treatments, such as for breast cancer. In general, Cutler and McClellan (2001b) find that innovations lead to increased productivity in healthcare. In addition, Lichtenberg (2003) finds a significant positive effect of new drug launches on average lifespan.

On the other side of the cost-benefit account is the impact of innovations on total costs. Even if there is a fall in the marginal cost of the health service provided (through the substitution effect of a new process), there is often an increase in total costs due to increased demand for more effective treatments (Baker et al., 2003). Hence, technical innovations in health are thought by some to be an important driver behind increasing health expenditures (Weisbrod, 1991; Newhouse, 1992; Fuchs, 1996). The key issue here is the extent to which the application is expanded following the introduction of a new, more effective treatment (Gelijns and Rosenberg, 1994).

The institutional aspect is a key determinant of diffusion in health. Thus, in Spain private sector health institutions are quicker to adopt high technology medical equipment than public sector institutions (González, 2003). One possible reason is the lack of incentives for increasing efficiency in not-for-profit public institutions with retrospective reimbursement.

There is also a tendency for very high degrees of vertical integration in public sector hospitals in Spain, such as the one that we investigate in this chapter (Puig-Junoy and Pérez-Sust, 2002). This, it is suggested, results in a lower adoption rate for organizational innovations. Finally, public and private sector institutions have very different aims and objectives. Public institutions invariably deal with local/regional problems, sometimes unaware of outside problems. The decision-making process tends to be strongly influenced by political and socio-economic issues. Public sector health institutions are further concerned with social welfare, that is, all innovative processes should address the real needs of patients (Oteo and Repullo, 2003). By contrast, private sector institutions must be efficient in order to survive and need to generate profits that satisfy their stakeholders (Ghaffar et al., 2004).

Technological Change in Health Care (2001) suggests that the structure of the health market, that is, the relative proportion of private and public sector institutions that make up the sector, affects the diffusion of health innovations. The report finds that supply side incentives are particularly important. The diffusion of innovations is slower in countries, such as Canada or Sweden, in which the health system is publicly owned and organized centrally than in countries, such as the USA, where hospitals have a high degree of autonomy and there is a significant private sector component. Danzon et al. (2003) analyse the impact of price regulation on the launch delay of new drugs. They find that countries with lower expected prices or smaller market sizes (with lower market power for private firms) experience longer delays in access to new drugs.

5.3   THE INTRODUCTION AND DIFFUSION OF INNOVATIONS IN LA PRINCESA HOSPITAL

This section examines the innovation process observed in La Princesa Hospital in Madrid, Spain. The aim is to identify common aspects in the diffusion of two different innovations, while placing these within the local context. In this way, the specificities of a technological innovation and an organizational innovation can be analysed using data generated at the hospital.

5.3.1   The Context: Origin, Viability and Goals

The innovation process is initiated following the identification of a need within the infrastructure of La Princesa Hospital. This may be due to the lack of an existing service or to a need to offer an improved service. It tends to be medical practitioners – particularly, doctors and nurses who are in permanent contact with patients – who are the first to recognize this need. As well as being in close contact with patients, doctors and nurses have expertise in medical procedures and techniques, and so are aware of the potential medical benefits of new or improved services. Only a small proportion of the innovations stem from patients' suggestions. What is more, suggestions tend to come from a minority group of patients: those who are highly educated and read about the existence of new procedures or the discovery of new medical conditions in the foreign or specialized press. When suggestions from patients are not applicable (for example, the application of laser technology to services where it is not feasible), it is the task of the physician to convince the patient of the advantages and disadvantages of treatments that are applicable and available. Sometimes an innovation is driven by political factors, for example, a political pledge by the national government. This may lead to an increase in the funding of innovations in a particular area. However, it may be the case that, rather than there being an increase in the overall budget, funding is redirected from other areas and from other innovations. It is at this point that conflicts can arise between the views of politicians and the views of medical professionals on the prioritizing of different innovations.

When medical practitioners identify the need for an innovative alternative to a given procedure, they present a proposal to the relevant section of management within the hospital. The first, and main, constraint on innovation is the hospital budget, which is controlled by the management. Sometimes managers cannot provide the financial resources needed to develop the innovation and it stops or is restricted. If a budget can be found, there remains a set of difficulties that still need to be overcome. To start with, most organizational innovations meet resistance to change. This is particularly so when changes involve modifications to the working conditions of hospital employees. Employees, especially low-skilled employees, in Spanish public institutions (including hospitals) tend to be paid a fixed wage that is incremented with each year of service. Hence, there is a problem of incentives and rewards for innovation by these employees (see Chapter 1). Indeed, at first sight, they may consider innovations to be a source of problems. New medical techniques require time and effort to learn, and innovations do not usually work first time. Resistance to change can include hostile or sceptical attitudes, and difficulty maintaining the enthusiasm of programme staff (Borins, 2001). Other difficulties arise from the administrative organization of medical tasks, that is, a set of activities or procedures must be conducted in a certain way. A lack of administrative flexibility in a hospital restricts the speed with which an innovation can be adapted and diffused. The fact that it is a public health institution is a factor in itself. An innovation must first be seen to work properly before it is widely adopted. This is very different to consumer goods and services. There the diffusion process is reasonably robust to the occasional recall of faulty goods and services. The production line is halted, the problem fixed and production is restarted. This is simply not an option for new public health services.

In contrast to the resistance to change observed amongst low-skilled employees, doctors and highly skilled medical personnel tend to be the active champions of new procedures. As supported by Maslow's hierarchy of needs theory (Maslow, 1954), high-skilled workers usually have a higher motivation than low-skilled workers. Highly skilled medical personnel are the local 'innovation entrepreneurs' in Spain, holding a positive attitude towards innovations, and are usually connected to research networks in their fields, as shown by the increasing number of biomedical or clinical medicine international publications (González, 2003). Our findings suggest that innovation positively impacts the job satisfaction of these employees for the same reason that it negatively impacts the job satisfaction of low-skilled personnel. Successful innovations directly improve their working life, and are an important means of advancing their career prospects.

Of course, the main beneficiaries of innovations in the long run are patients. But innovations make the practitioner's task easier. Doctors and other health workers are usually the first to identify the need for innovation, and are the people best placed to understand the limits of current practices and machinery, and the way in which improvements can be made. They have a privileged position within the innovation process, are innovators in their own right and directly benefit from successful innovations.

5.3.2 The Diffusion of Digital Radiology in the Hospital

At the core of digital radiology is the digitalization of an X-ray. The first experiments in electronically transmitting radiological images occurred in the 1950s, although the first use of DR was in the early 1990s in Austria. La Princesa Hospital was not one of the first adopters of DR technology in the world. Rather, it adopted in the second stage of the technology's diffusion. DR technology was first introduced in La Princesa Hospital in 1999, and has gradually replaced AR technology since that time. In the last few years its use has increased dramatically. Now, six out of the seven radiology rooms work with the new DR system.

Using DR the information contained in the X-ray is transmitted to the hospital's main computer, and is available to any physician or specialist connected to the hospital intranet. Images can be printed on paper using laser printing technology. This is a substitute for the photochemical (acetate plate) technology of analogue radiology. Differences in the costs of raw material mean that laser printed images are far cheaper than acetate plates. In addition, eradicating printing chemicals means that DR is much more environmentally friendly.

It is still possible to print a DR recorded image on an acetate plate, if this is necessary, although the image quality of acetates is lower than laser printed images. Still, printing DR images on acetate plates enables savings of 75 per cent to be made on raw material costs. This is because differences exist in the way images are printed on the acetate plate. With AR a darkroom and chemicals are needed to develop an X-ray. Processing an image (that is, developing, fixing, washing and drying) usually takes about two minutes per X-ray. Unfortunately, sometimes the process does not work. In this event, the entire process needs to be repeated – this involves taking another X-ray of the patient and exposing the patient to twice the amount of radiation. According to the Director of Radiology at La Princesa Hospital, around 5 per cent of all X-rays had to be repeated when AR technology was used.

Aside from the cost savings and reduced environmental impact for each image taken, far more important advantages – as far as the specialist and patient are concerned – are the improvements that DR makes to the speed and quality of diagnosis. A patient's X-ray can immediately be observed from the specialist's computer, significantly cutting down waiting time. What is more, the X-ray itself is readily manipulated by the specialist (enlarged/reduced, light contrasts altered and so on). This is said to increase the quality of the diagnosis.

In order to examine the cost-effectiveness of DR in La Princesa Hospital, it is important to conduct a detailed analysis of the differences between AR and DR technologies. To this end, we next present the specific areas in which savings were made through the substitution of AR by DR. These fall under two generic categories: savings in raw materials and space, and service quality improvements and non-economic effects.

5.3.2.1 Savings in raw materials and space

As noted, AR technology requires a darkroom for processing images onto acetates. This is not required by DR. Removing the need for a darkroom saves on expensive hospital space and chemicals, and reduces the chemical contamination of the environment. This contamination is not quantified and is left out of the formal cost–benefit analysis.

Different chemicals are used in the three stages of developing an image onto an acetate plate. First, a combination of chemicals are used to develop an image, then a fixing agent stabilizes the image (that is, stops the processing chemicals and makes the image stable in daylight), and finally a washing agent removes the remaining residues of developer and fixing agent. This processing takes around two minutes per plate. After this the acetate must be dried. DR technology dispenses with this processing technology.

Acetate plates can be generated using AR or DR. However, a key difference is that plates must be generated if one uses AR, while with DR one has the alternative option of using a computer to observe images held on the hospital intranet (with the aid of specific software). Using AR, plates differ in size according to the part of the body that is X-rayed. Using DR, all the plates can be made of equal size. Standardizing the size of the plates as in the DR technology decreases the cost of this printing stage.

A cost that is exclusive to DR technology is the computer system. DR presupposes the existence and maintenance of a central system containing a server capable of storing all recorded images, and making these images accessible to all the computers logged onto the hospital intranet.

While the space taken up by a digital image is smaller than an acetate, and DR avoids the need for a darkroom, space is required to site the computer server needed for DR. As noted, this is not required by AR technology. Therefore, there are important opportunity costs associated with the (expensive) hospital space that each system requires.

DR equipment is more expensive than AR equipment. But it is important to note that capital equipment used in AR can be readapted to work with DR technology. There is an associated conversion cost, and a difference in the waiting time for each patient's X-ray. The adaptation is called 'computer radiology' (CR) and needs a special chassis to be placed in the AR equipment in order to capture X-ray images in a digital manner.

With regards to ongoing maintenance costs, these are highest for AR. CR still has some significant maintenance costs and DR has almost zero maintenance costs. La Princesa Hospital has radiology rooms in which all three types can be found.

5.3.2.2   Service quality improvements and non-economic effects
A first quality indicator to be considered is the time taken to provide the service per patient. Here we consider the total number of patients receiving radiology services per unit of time. It is found that the time taken to perform the service, including the transportation of the image, has decreased. There are several explanations for this. First, it is observed that hospital workers have not resisted change but, rather, have adapted very quickly to the new DR technology. Second, as discussed previously, AR dispenses with acetate plates, and the time it takes to develop and dry acetate. Further, it is estimated that around 5 per cent of AR X-rays were defective and had to be repeated. In addition to increased raw material costs, this significantly increased the time taken before an X-ray reached the specialist.

The second quality indicator is professionals' satisfaction with the diagnosis given to patients using the different technologies. At the very least, the quality of diagnoses using DR is at least as good as that using AR technology. Interviews with specialists indicated that the increased flexibility of image manipulation with DR increases the quality of diagnoses that they believe they are making. Further, the increased availability of images, held on the hospital intranet, can contribute to improved communication among specialists. From our face-to-face interviews we learned that this opportunity is not entirely exploited by specialists.

A further potential consequence of increased confidence in diagnosis, due to improvements in service quality, is a rise in the demand for radiology services by doctors and specialists in other services departments within the hospital. Hence, increased internal demand following the diffusion of DR is a key indicator of (perceived) improvements in service quality by fellow practitioners.

Finally, it is important to note that, while the differences may not be large, there is evidence that the time patients are exposed to radiation is lower under DR than under AR, and is therefore a benefit to patient health (Canto, 2000). Further, we note that patients were exposed to double the amount of radiation in the estimated 5 per cent of cases where AR X-rays were defective.

5.3.3   The Diffusion of Ambulatory Surgery in the Hospital

Ambulatory Surgery (AS) was first introduced in La Princesa Hospital in 1994. So, again, it was not one of the very earliest adopters of this innovation worldwide, but was among the second cohort (the early majority) of adopters. AS was first adopted by the hospital's Ophthalmology Department. Over time it has diffused to other departments within the hospital. Still, as Table 5.3 shows, the Ophthalmology Department remains the highest user of AS, accounting for almost 40 per cent of all AS procedures in La Princesa Hospital. Thoracic, general digestive, cardiovascular, neurosurgery and maxillofacial surgeries make up around 30 per cent of AS procedures conducted in La Princesa Hospital. The high rate of AS accounted for by the Ophthalmology Department may in part be explained by the fact that it is the first, and most established, user of AS in the hospital. In part it is due to the high and increasing number of older patients who are requesting cataract operations. Since the Ophthalmology Department is by far the largest user of AS procedures at La Princesa Hospital, we will focus on the cost and benefits of introducing AS in this department.

One of the difficulties identified in our case study was resistance to change on the part of patients, particularly elderly patients, when AS was

Table 5.3   Services performed using ambulatory surgery (AS), 1997–2004

Active service	Number of AS	Percentage of AS	Total surgeries	Relative weight of AS
Cardiology	2	0.01	10	20.00
Dermatology	592	3.04	1 145	51.70
Digestive	22	0.11	77	28.57
Gynaecology	10	0.05	74	13.51
Haematology	7	0.04	239	2.93
Internal medicine	2	0.01	4	50.00
Nephrology	38	0.20	60	63.33
Ophthalmology	8 065	41.44	11 105	72.62
Otorhinolaryngology	835	4.29	3 667	22.77
Surgery	6 017	30.92	26 815	22.44
Traumatology	3 870	19.89	16 026	24.15
Total	19 460	100.00		

Source: Author's data

first introduced. They did not completely trust AS procedures and preferred to stay overnight in the hospital. They were afraid of being at home if post-surgery complications arose. This fear was particularly strong for elderly patients who live alone at home. This information and perception problem needed to be rapidly solved by doctors, that is, by explaining to patients that they are not discharged from the hospital unless a doctor is satisfied that the surgery has been successful, and that out-patient care is provided in home visits. Today patients have a positive perception about reduced hospital stays.

5.3.3.1 Monetary savings
The key financial saving of AS is due to the freeing up of (expensive) hospital beds. However, the total number of beds in La Princesa Hospital has not fallen since the introduction of AS in 1994. Indeed, the total number of beds increased slightly between 1998 and 2002 (Table 5.4). The net impact of AS has been a reallocation of beds from one set of hospital patients to another set of patients. Indeed, as observed in Table 5.4, the average hospital stay has actually increased from 10.29 days in 1998 to 10.89 days in 2002. This is because beds are now allocated to patients receiving treatments that require post-surgery hospital stays, and for which the average stay is longer than for treatments now allocated to AS. Given this, there is not an absolute saving on the number of hospital beds in La Princesa Hospital, and it is difficult to establish a clear set of financial savings associated with the adoption and diffusion of AS.

Table 5.4   Structure of the hospital and description of stays, 1998–2002

	1998	1999	2000	2001	2002
Working beds	501	501	501	504	504
Programmed surgical rooms working	10.36	10.36	10.36	11.00	11.00
In-patient entrance	16 112	15 307	15 657	15 821	15 631
Average stay	10.29	10.85	10.99	10.50	10.89

Source: Author's data.

It is clear that the benefit of AS in the reallocation of different sets of patients with hospital beds and the financial cost of applying AS with new technology (for example, the laser technology applied in the Ophthalmology Department in the cataracts procedure) is higher than the traditional methodology. First, higher costs are due to the initial investment of machinery. Second, there is a difference between the protocols of the surgical procedures. Under the traditional method, some materials were reutilized after sterilization for different patients. By contrast, the new cataract procedure using laser technology does not allow for reutilization.

5.3.3.2   Quality change

There is an opportunity cost for a patient undergoing surgery. Before the cataract procedure was generally practised under the AS system, the average hospital stay was three days. Now, the time spent at the hospital for the same procedure after the adoption of the innovation is only several hours.

Surgical waiting lists have evolved over time due to the adoption of AS. Table 5.5a shows the number of patients that enter waiting lists for surgery, by service and by year. *Ceteris paribus*, procedures with lengthening waiting lists are due to an increased flow of patients demanding that service. In the case of ophthalmology, the waiting list increases each year from 1997 to 2003 (from 1749 to 3936 patients). It is necessary to combine this information with the net flow of patients represented in Table 5.5b (the number of patients who enter the waiting list minus the number of patients that are treated and taken off the waiting list). The net flow of patients on waiting lists is decreasing over time, as is the waiting time for individual services at the Ophthalmology Department (Table 5.5c).

Table 5.5a   Number of new patients entering waiting lists by service, 1997–2003

Active service	1997	1998	1999	2000	2001	2002	2003	Total
Cardiology	358	210	6	1	4	1	2	582
Dermatology	0	28	62	255	363	169	199	1076
Endocrinology	1	0	0	0	0	0	0	1
Gynaecology	76	65	2	1	1	3	1	149
Haematology	3	0	0	0	0	1	0	4
Internal medicine	0	0	0	0	0	1	0	1
Nephrology	0	0	0	0	0	0	3	3
Ophthalmology	1749	2362	2193	3030	3675	3795	3936	20740
Otorhinolaryngology	514	492	505	675	628	668	687	4169
Surgery	2955	3331	3897	4225	4568	5401	5403	29780
Traumatology	2239	1945	1895	1857	1914	1853	1887	13590
Urology	1210	1200	1238	1235	1410	1227	1531	9051
Total patients	9105	9633	9798	11279	12563	13119	13649	79146

Table 5.5b   Net flow of patients on waiting list by service, 1997–2003

Active service	1997	1998	1999	2000	2001	2002	2003	Total
Cardiology	9	−9	0	0	0	0	0	0
Dermatology	0	5	−1	51	−35	−7	31	44
Endocrinology	0	0	0	0	0	0	0	0
Gynaecology	7	−7	0	0	0	1	−1	0
Haematology	0	0	0	0	0	0	0	0
Internal medicine	0	0	0	0	0	0	0	0
Nephrology	0	0	0	0	0	0	0	0
Ophthalmology	822	−88	−170	198	272	−36	190	1188
Otorhinolaryngology	70	52	10	117	−55	2	−10	186
Surgery	805	116	84	145	−71	639	−352	1366
Traumatology	601	−248	117	206	−13	−197	120	586
Urology	246	−125	116	−80	47	−48	120	276
Total patients	2560	−304	156	637	145	354	98	3646

Falling waiting lists have important implications for patient welfare. For example, the sooner a patient with cataracts is treated, the sooner they recover their vision and enjoy a higher quality of life.

The adoption of AS has led to a change in the composition of waiting lists, and beds have been reallocated from patients receiving one set of procedures to more patients receiving other treatments. This is observed in

Table 5.5c   Waiting time spent (in months) by service, 1997–2003

Active service waiting time	1997	1998	1999	2000	2001	2002	2003
Cardiology	0.32	0.48	0.00	0.00	0.00	0.00	0.00
Dermatology	0.00	0.29	0.65	2.60	1.72	1.26	1.77
Endocrinology	0.00	0.00	0.00	0.00	0.00	0.00	0.00
Gynaecology	0.89	0.92	3.00	1.00	0.00	2.00	0.00
Haematology	0.00	0.00	0.00	0.00	0.00	2.00	0.00
Internal medicine	0.00	0.00	0.00	0.00	0.00	1.00	0.00
Nephrology	0.00	0.00	0.00	0.00	0.00	0.00	0.67
Ophthalmology	5.15	4.66	3.82	3.32	3.37	3.67	3.46
Otorhinolaryngology	1.99	1.89	2.74	4.59	4.49	3.72	3.86
Surgery	3.06	3.06	3.20	3.53	2.89	3.45	3.27
Traumatology	3.17	2.40	2.57	4.21	4.50	3.73	3.82
Urology	2.38	1.87	2.03	1.88	1.53	1.38	1.84

Source: Author's data.

Tables 5.5a, 5.5b and 5.5c. The AS system has led to a fall in waiting time in the Ophthalmology Department, despite an enormous increase in the demand for its services (as seen by the larger number of patients entering the waiting list each year). This has been achieved by significantly increasing the number of procedures carried out each year.

An important contribution to increasing efficiency has been made by the introduction of the shifts within the hospital (see Table 5.6). After 2000 there is a significant increase in the use of surgical theatres in the evening. The change led to a fall in waiting times for most departments but, interestingly, initially led to an increase in waiting time for ophthalmology procedures. However, in 2003 and 2004 there is a significant increase in the proportion of ophthalmology procedures conducted in the evening shift. Consequently, the introduction of the AS system prompted changes in other organizational procedures and led to new innovations.

5.4   REFLECTIONS ON EXISTING LITERATURE

La Princesa Hospital was not one of the very first adopters of AS or DR worldwide. Rather, it made up what Rogers (1983) calls the cohort of early majority adopters. The Director of Radiology of La Princesa Hospital was the key person who championed the idea of DR and acted as a public sector entrepreneur, convincing peers, organizing and obtaining the funding

Table 5.6   Operations performed in different shifts in surgical theatres, 1998–2004

| | 1998 | | 1999 | | 2000 | | 2001 | | 2002 | | 2003 | | 2004[a] | |
	Freq.	%	Freq.	%	Freq.	%	Freq.	%	Freq.	%	Freq.	%	Freq.	%
Morning	8 736	83.48	9 365	85.23	8 626	83.23	8 389	79.51	9 118	77.30	9 392	76.81	8 831	65.07
Night	174	1.66	254	2.31	283	2.73	287	2.72	349	2.96	370	3.03	404	2.98
Evening	1 555	14.86	1 369	12.46	1 455	14.04	1 875	17.77	2 329	19.74	2 466	20.17	4 337	31.96

Notes: [a] 2004 contains only data until November.

Source: Author's data.

necessary to ensure that DR was adopted and then further developed within the hospital. The Director of Radiology was aware of the existence of DR, and had studied the possibility of introducing this technique at La Princesa Hospital. He organized a cost–benefit analysis and a proposal was submitted to the head of the hospital. This is the standard procedure at La Princesa Hospital for considering all new treatments. The other key facilitators of DR were the hospital management. The attitude of management was very positive and the project was quickly approved, with DR being introduced in 1999. Since that time, DR has gradually replaced AR.

The adoption of AS was not driven by a single leader/entrepreneur but by a team of specialists who actively promoted AS. Most of the team were based in the Ophthalmology Department of the hospital. Members of the team were aware, through contacts with medical practitioners in other hospitals and by reports in specialist international journals, of the benefits that AS had brought in other hospitals. Because AS facilitates the introduction of laser treatment, specialists in the Ophthalmology Department were the key advocates who promoted its introduction at La Princesa Hospital. As with all new innovations, they needed to engage and persuade the hospital management in order to secure its introduction. Again the positive attitude of the hospital management was a key facilitating factor of this innovation.

According to the literature (Weisbrod, 1991; González, 2003), a key factor influencing the speed of diffusion is the set of incentives that exist for promoting efficiency. Incentives for efficiency appear when agents benefit from savings. However, low-skilled employees at La Princesa Hospital are paid a fixed wage. There is no monetary incentive linked to improving the quality of services delivered or to improving patient satisfaction. New innovations, which alter organizational work routines, may be perceived by low-skilled employees as negative unless there is a positive non-financial reward. For instance, improvements in service quality are accompanied by a set of working practices that either simplify the procedure or make it easier to perform.

With regards to resistance to change it was feared, in both the case of DR and AS, that low-skilled personnel at La Princesa Hospital might initially resist their introduction. Yet in neither case did this materialize. As discussed earlier, there was no group that resisted DR. With AS there was initial resistance, not from hospital staff but from patients, particularly elderly patients, who had fears about post-surgical complications occurring at home. In the beginning it was difficult to convince them that it is medically safe to leave the hospital on the same day that surgery is performed. Today the concept of out-patient surgery is no longer new and patients' attitudes are very positive towards AS.

A finding that strongly emerges in both case studies is the importance of the support of medical staff, particularly medical specialists and nurses, in determining the success (or otherwise) of innovations. AS is strongly supported by this group because it enables surgical procedures to be carried out more effectively, and has a significant impact in reducing waiting lists. This group strongly supports DR because it reduces the time taken between a patient's X-ray and a patient's consultation, specialists are able to manipulate the DR image themselves (size, contrast and so on), which is believed to be an important contribution to improving the accuracy of diagnosis, and there is instant and multiple access to images held on the hospital intranet.

The case studies have interesting implications for the theories of services innovation discussed in Section 5.2. Let us start with the reverse product cycle thesis. According to the thesis, the emphasis is placed on efficiency improvements for an existing service in stage 1 of the cycle. A new technology is adopted if its unit costs are lower than the unit costs using the old technology. It is in stage 2 of the cycle that one sees the development of new, improved treatments and the substitution of old treatments by these new treatments, that is, of AR by DR. A consequence of this substitution is an increase in demand for new, better treatment and an expansion of provision on the supply side.

Evidence of this is provided in Table 5.7. There was a small increase in the number of procedures performed, following the introduction of DR. Around three times as many procedures are now performed, which is a dramatic increase. Most of this improvement is explained by the removal of the bottleneck in the provision of X-rays. However, there is a reduction in the number of consultations between 2000 and 2001. According to the hospital personnel that were interviewed, a small but significant proportion of the increase is due to doctors ordering both AR and DR X-rays. Interviewees suggested that this was part of the learning process, doctors ordering both and comparing them until they were convinced of the merits of DR.

Table 5.7   Unit costs of radiology services (euros)

	1997	1998	1999	2000	2001	2002
Radiology	460 036.17	414 159.74	439 573.28	430 008.38	438 619.82	482 834.46
Consultations	53 729	54 019	102 692	200 557	160 320	154 631
Cost per consultation	8.56	7.67	4.28	2.14	2.74	3.12

Source: Author's data.

We only have access to a gross classification of annual expenditures in the hospital and, therefore, we cannot identify the individual cost of each X-ray room. Further, it is too early to evaluate possible gains in hospital space. Consequently, the indicator that is used is the unit costs of the Radiology Deparment, which is obtained as the total expenditure by department divided by the number of services performed (Table 5.7). Per unit service costs fall 50 per cent between 1997 and 2002. This is in line with the predictions of stage 1 of the life cycle. However, it rises slightly in the last two years.

Using two indicators we are able to identify improvements in the quality of services due to DR. The first is the amount of time required to provide the service (the number of services per unit of time). The second is the satisfaction of professionals in other service areas of the hospital (the utilization rate of radiology in other service areas). Table 5.8 shows that utilization has increased significantly in two service areas, oncology and

Table 5.8   Change in relative share of radiology services (%), 1999–2003

Radiology service	1999	2000	2001	2002	2003	Difference 1999–2003
Allergy	4.94	3.35	1.49	0.93	0.67	-4.27
Cardiology	7.94	10.35	8.28	7.52	8.15	0.20
Dermatology	2.79	1.60	1.67	2.04	1.99	-0.80
Digestive	17.13	15.33	11.55	11.31	13.50	-3.64
Endocrine	7.25	6.22	6.02	5.64	5.48	-1.78
Gynaecology	17.12	19.74	23.16	132.34	115.69	98.57
Haematology	10.61	11.03	7.48	8.34	9.52	-1.10
Internal medicine	45.94	56.02	25.85	24.73	25.76	-20.19
Nephrology	29.13	38.30	26.51	20.42	21.41	-7.72
Neurology	28.93	18.58	18.50	21.16	24.24	-4.70
Ophthalmology	3.28	2.79	1.50	1.22	0.85	-2.42
Oncology	111.65	114.11	107.40	114.65	139.12	27.47
Otorhinolaryngology	10.82	7.76	6.48	7.53	7.38	-3.43
Pneumology	25.40	19.02	16.29	16.79	18.83	-6.57
Psychiatry	3.44	4.33	2.30	1.64	1.04	-2.39
Radiology	4.64	3.11	3.79	3.57	3.46	-1.18
Rehabilitation	4.70	6.96	8.58	3.60	1.47	-3.22
Rheumatology	21.60	21.75	18.92	17.92	17.95	-3.65
Surgery	35.99	33.23	20.89	21.24	21.75	-14.24
Traumatology	61.30	43.08	29.00	31.85	30.56	-30.74
Urology	41.50	39.71	40.40	44.13	41.08	-0.42

Source: Author's data.

gynaecology, given the improvement in the quality of diagnosis using digital images. What is more, this increase occurred following the adoption of DR. A possible explanation is that consultants in these service areas saw radiology as a bottleneck. Once the new technology was adopted, the perceived bottleneck was removed and the demand for DR increased in services that had not previously used radiology inputs. Again, this is in line with the reverse product cycle. It predicts new applications of improved quality services, leading to an increase in demand for services.

AS also follows the stages predicted by the reverse life cycle. The initial focus in applying AS was on efficiency gains. In stage 2 there was a standardization of the procedure (observed in Tables 5.5a, b and c), enabling more patients to be treated while simultaneously reducing the average waiting time for procedures. The focus then shifted to improvements in the quality of services provided. There was an expansion of AS to surgical operations conducted by departments other than Ophthalmology. This expansion of treatment has led to economies of scale. This impact is discussed by Harberger (1998) but is not considered in Barras's reverse cycle model.

There are other long-term implications of more effective treatments that are not considered by Barras, but which are considered in the health economics literature, for example, Cutler and McClellan (2001a) and Cutler and Richardson (1999) on the gain in the quality of life perceived by patients. Through new, improved surgical procedures it is possible to treat patients at an earlier stage of illness. For example, one can treat cataract patients who have a higher initial quality of vision. This has important economic and policy implications. Applying procedures to healthier patients leads to a fall in improvement per patient over time and, hence, a fall in the quality adjusted life years (QALYs). This is a key indicator of healthcare. Policy makers may take into account the rise in total social welfare due to treatments being extended to more patients, but this depends on the objective function of the policy maker.

The health economics literature (for example, Weisbrod, 1991; Newhouse, 1992; Fuchs, 1996) predicts that successful innovations lead to an increase in total costs. This occurs because the increased demand for services outweighs the substitution effect (that is, marginal costs fall but total costs rise). For DR there is evidence of treatment expansion in two areas of the hospital, although not for all areas. The prediction is supported, since the large increase in the number of consultancies outweighs the decrease in the unit costs, leading to an increase in the total cost of radiology (see Table 5.7). The prediction is supported by the adoption of AS in the hospital. While AS has lowered the marginal costs of performing each cataract operation, there has been a significant increase in demand for this procedure and, hence, an increase in the total number of operations performed by the hospital. Further, the fixed stock of hospital beds has been reassigned to procedures which have longer recovery times than was the case for cataract operations under the old system.

DR corresponds to a combination of two types of trajectory described by the Djellal and Gallouj (2005) model. It has some of the properties of both the logistical and the material transformation trajectory. It involves the mechanization of imaging, changing from analogue to digital technology. It also involves logistical and information processing, lowering communication costs and improving networking through the use of new IT systems. The other trajectories discussed by Djellal and Gallouj – the methodological trajectory of knowledge-intensive services or treatment protocols, pure service trajectory and relational trajectory – are not significant in DR. Therefore, the diffusion of DR leads to changes in the two vectors: the vectors of competences and technical factors. Changes in both vectors are necessary, since without technical change we cannot talk about digital radiology, and without change in competences and human capital (improvements in communication through the use of new IT, such as the internet and intranet), the new technology would not diffuse.

AS also represents a combination of the innovation trajectories discussed by Djellal and Gallouj. In part, it is a logistical and material transformation trajectory because it was derived from the adoption of laser technology and, therefore, there is a tangible medical innovation related to the adoption of AS. However, the organizational nature of AS is knowledge intensive, with changes in protocols and treatments. This makes it an innovation with a methodological trajectory. Additionally, AS follows a relational trajectory because it introduces new ways of bringing together customers (patients) and a health service provider (the hospital). It is not a 'pure' service trajectory because it contains a technologically tangible improvement. Equally, it is not a 'pure' logistical and information processing trajectory because IT does not play a significant role, as it does in the adoption of DR.

If we examine the vector of final service characteristics, we not only observe a change in characteristics but also the emergence of new sets of connected technical characteristics and service characteristics. For example, there is the development of a standard size of plates with DR technology, and there is the development of appropriate software that facilitates physicians' examination of images on computers. According to the classification of Gallouj and Weinstein (1997), DR is a recombinative innovation because the interaction of the use of new techniques and competences/knowledge leads to the development of new service characteristics.

With AS, changes occur in the vector of technical factors through the application of laser technology. Changes also occur in the vector of competences. These include all the changes that occur in the organization's protocols as AS protocols displace the original organizational protocols. The vector of service characteristics also changes, with a higher utilization rate and increased patient satisfaction. There is a substitution of old services by new service characteristics. Finally, it is important to note that the changes are tied together; new service characteristics are the result of complementary changes that occur in technical factors (laser surgery) and in competences (AS protocols). According to Gallouj and Weinstein (1997), AS is a radical innovation because the vector of service characteristics is enormously improved once the technical characteristics have also improved. Even if there are elements in common with the service and technical characteristics before the innovation (the patient is cured of cataracts), it is a radical innovation because it changes the 'internal structure' of the service provision.

A key driver of innovation within an organization is the identification of bottlenecks (see Saviotti, 1984; Hughes, 1987; Chapter 1). Once one bottleneck is removed, the focus shifts to the next bottleneck that makes its presence felt. The quality of radiology services, using the old AR technology, was perceived to be a bottleneck by medical practitioners elsewhere in the hospital. Following the introduction of DR the demand for radiology services increased. Hospital beds are a key bottleneck in the flow of surgical operations. AS combined with new treatments removed this constraint for certain types of surgical procedure. A new bottleneck has now been identified: the efficient use of surgical theatres. New shifts have been recently introduced, with certain operations conducted in daytime shifts and other operations conducted in evening shifts.

5.5   CONCLUSIONS

This chapter has discussed two innovation processes at La Princesa Hospital in Madrid, Spain. One is primarily a technological innovation (the adoption of digital radiology), the other is primarily an organizational innovation (the adoption of ambulatory surgery). These were selected because they provide a clear insight into policy learning, and technical and administrative innovations in the public sector and are important in the context of the hospital.

Both innovations overcome bottlenecks in service provision, leading to improvements in service quality. These improvements benefit patients by raising the quality of individual care and by increasing the number of patients that can be treated. In this way, the original bottlenecks that propelled the innovation process are removed. In removing one bottleneck, a new bottleneck makes its presence felt and the search for new innovation starts again. The adoption of DR solved the bottleneck in the provision of X-rays, and the adoption of AS solved (at least partly) the bottleneck of the number of beds. With better use of hospital beds, a new bottleneck has been identified – the number of surgical theatres. Other innovations are being now being experimented with, such as the use of shifts in surgical procedures.

Using these case studies this chapter addressed a number of hypotheses regarding innovation that are put forward in the services innovation literature and the health economics literature. The reverse product cycle theory is, in general, supported by these public health innovations. As suggested, the focus of innovation is on efficiency improvements during the first stage of adoption, and the emphasis shifts to improved quality and the substitution of old services by new, improved services in stage two. This leads to an increase in demand. During the third and final stage, there is an expansion of the new treatments which promotes further innovations.

The studies have, however, identified an important difference between the public health services and the private sector services on which reverse product cycle theory is based. In the private sector, efficiency gains are driven by the desire to reduce unit costs, as this confers a competitive advantage to firms. As we have seen, unit costs are not necessarily the key driver for efficiency improvements in public sector institutions.

With regard to barriers and enablers of diffusion, the literature highlights the importance of incentives for efficiency and the motivation of workers as key factors affecting the speed of diffusion. In the case of DR, there was a single public sector entrepreneur who organized and drove the process. In the case of AS, the process was driven by a team of doctors. In both cases, the actors are high skilled, able to identify the bottleneck, know the needs of the hospital and understand the potential benefits of the innovation for patients. These practitioners have incentives to innovate; they directly benefit from successful innovations. Still, patients are the final and true beneficiaries of the innovations through the improvement of service quality, reductions in waiting times and the ability to treat larger numbers of patients.

Finally, this chapter tested a key hypothesis regarding the impact of innovation on unit and total costs in public health. First, it was proposed that the time required to deliver a unit of service will fall over time, leading to a fall in unit cost. This was found in the DR case but not in the AS case. Second, it was proposed that productivity improvements lead to an expansion in the total number of treatments performed and an increase in total cost. In these two cases total costs have indeed risen as predicted.

To summarize, the general patterns of innovation predicted by the reverse life cycle theory hold for the case studies, as do the predictions regarding unit and total costs. Having said this, there are important differences. Notably, unit costs were not the sole driver for process innovation, but one of a number of drivers. Another key driver in public health service innovation is the reduction of waiting time per patient, which improves their quality of life. The final beneficiary must be society through improvements to the health of patients. The studies also highlight the importance of key professionals, 'public sector entrepreneurs', in the innovation and diffusion process. This is a key lesson for policy makers.

Finally, this chapter has highlighted key lessons for policy learning and for future research. It is important for policy makers to evaluate the possible benefits and costs of the innovation processes. This is important because, given limits on resources, only a limited set of innovations can be adopted by public institutions. The case studies have highlighted the need to anticipate the new bottlenecks that can arise once the innovation has removed the current bottleneck(s). Proper evaluation of the services derived from an innovation needs to include these costs. The case studies prompt further research into the various incentive structures that promote innovation by workers and managers in public sector institutions. They also highlight the importance of the interaction between economic, social and political spheres in shaping public sector innovation. This has been neglected in the past.

NOTE

1. See Coombs and Miles (2000), Drejer (2004) and Windrum (2006) for a detailed discussion of whether innovation in services is fundamentally different to innovation in manufacturing.

REFERENCES

Baker, L., H. Birnbaum, J. Geppert, D. Mishol and E. Moyneur (2003), 'The relationship between technology availability and health care spending', *Health Affairs*, July–December, supplement web exclusives W3-537-51.

Barras, R. (1986), 'Towards a theory of innovation in services', *Research Policy*, **15**, 161–73.

Barras, R. (1990), 'Interactive innovation in financial and business services: the vanguard of the service revolution', *Research Policy*, **19**, 215–37.

Borins, S. (2001), *The Challenge of Innovating in Government*, Innovations in Management Series, The PricewaterhouseCoopers endowment for the Business of Government, Arlington, VA: PricewaterhouseCoopers Endowment.

Canto, R. (2000), *Telemedicina: Informe de Evaluación y Aplicaciones en Andalucía*, Seville, Spain: Agencia de Evaluación de Tecnologías Sanitarias de Andalucía.

Coombs, R. and I. Miles (2000), 'Innovation, measurement and services: the new problematique', in J.S. Metcalfe and I. Miles (eds), *Innovation Systems in the Service Economy*, Boston, MA: Kluwer, pp. 85–103.

Cutler, D.M. and R.S. Huckman (2002), 'Technological development and medical productivity: the diffusion of angioplasty in New York State', National Bureau of Economic Research working paper W9311.

Cutler, D.M. and M. McClellan (1996), 'The determinants of technological change in heart attack treatment', National Bureau of Economic Research working paper 5751.

Cutler, D.M. and M. McClellan (2001a), 'Is technological change in medicine worth it?', *Health Affairs*, **20**(5), 11–29.

Cutler, D.M. and M. McClellan (2001b), 'Productivity change in health care', *American Economic Review*, **91**(2), 281–6.

Cutler, D.M. and E. Richardson (1999), 'Your money and your life: the value of health and what affects it', in A. Garber (ed.), *Frontiers in Health Policy Research*, *vol 2*, Cambridge, MA: MIT Press, pp. 99–132.

Danzon, P., Y.R. Wang and L. Wang (2003), 'The impact of price regulation on the launch delay of new drugs – evidence from twenty five major markets in the 1990s', National Bureau of Economic Research working paper 9874.

Djellal, F. and F. Gallouj (2005), 'Mapping innovation dynamics in hospitals', *Research Policy*, **34**, 817–35.

Drejer, I. (2004), 'Identifying innovation in surveys of services: a Schumpeterian perspective', *Research Policy*, **33**(3), 551–62.

Fuchs, V. (1996), 'Economics, values, and health care reform', *American Economic Review*, **86**(1), 1–24.

Gallouj, F. and O. Weinstein (1997), 'Innovation in services', *Research Policy*, **26**, 537–56.

Geljins, A. and N. Rosenberg (1994), 'The dynamics of technological change in medicine', *Health Affairs*, Summer, 28–46.

Ghaffar, A., A. de Francisco and S. Matlin (2004), *The Combined Approach Matrix: A Priority-Setting Tool For Health Research*, Geneva: Global Forum for Health Research.

González, B. (2003), 'Adopción y difusión de tecnologías en sanidad', in: V. Ortun (ed.) *Gestión Clínica y Sanitaria. De la Práctica Diaria a la Academia, ida y Vuelta*, Barcelona: Masson pp. 143–60.

Harberger, A.C. (1998), 'A vision of the growth process', *American Economic Review*, **88**(1), 1–32.

Hughes, T.P. (1987), 'The evolution of large technological systems', in W.E. Bijker, T.P. Hughes and T.J. Pinch (eds), *The Social Construction of Technology Systems*, Cambridge, MA: MIT Press, pp. 51–82.

Lichtenberg, F. (2003), 'The impact of new drug launches on longevity: evidence from longitudinal, disease-level data from 52 countries, 1982–2001', National Bureau of Economic Research working paper 9754.

Maslow, A.H. (1954), *Motivation and Personality*, New York: Harper & Row.

Newhouse, J.P. (1992), 'Medical care costs: how much welfare loss?', *Journal of Economic Perspectives*, **6**(3), 3–21.

Nicoll, J.H. (1909), 'The surgery of infancy', *British Medical Journal*, **2**, 753–4.

Oteo, L.A. and J.R. Repullo (2003), 'La innovación en los servicios sanitarios; consideraciones desde la perspectiva del Sistema Nacional de Salud español', *Revista de Administración Sanitaria*, **1**(2), 307–32.

Puig-Junoy, J. and P. Pérez-Sust (2002), 'Integración vertical y contratación externa en los servicios. Integración vertical y contratación externa en los servicios', *Gaceta Sanitaria*, **16**(2), 145–55.

Rogers, E.M. (1983), *Diffusion of Innovations*, New York: Free Press.

Saviotti, P.P. (1984), 'Technical change', in M. Gibbons and P. Gummett (eds), *Science, Technology, and Society Today*, Manchester: Manchester University Press, pp. 117–30.

Schumpeter, J. (1942), *Capitalism, Socialism, and Democracy*, New York: Harper.

Stock, G., N. Greis and W. Fischer (2002), 'Firm size and dynamic technological innovation', *Technovation*, **22**, 537–49.

Technological Change in Health Care (TECH) (2001), 'Technological change around the world. Evidence from heart attack care', *Health Affairs*, **20**(3), 25–42.

Weisbrod, B. (1991), 'The health care quadrilemma: an essay on technological change, insurance, quality of care, and cost containment', *Journal of Economic Literature*, **29**(2), 523–52.

Windrum, P. (2006), 'Innovation in services', in Horst Hanusch and Andreas Pyka (eds), *The Elgar Companion to Neo-Schumpeterian Economics*, Cheltenham, UK and Northampton, MA, USA: Edward Elgar.

Windrum, P. and P. de Berranger (2003), 'The adoption of intranets and extranets by SMEs', MERIT research memoranda 2003-023, University of Maastricht.

6. Health innovation processes at the public–private interface

Andrea Mina and Ronnie Ramlogan

6.1 INTRODUCTION

Interaction between private and public organizations is a fundamental source of innovation, and a crucial framing condition for reaping the benefits of new technologies through their diffusion in regulated domains. Focusing on the health sector, this chapter investigates the emergence of one of the most important medical innovations of the last few decades – coronary angioplasty – and uncovers the dynamics of its emergence at the interface between hospitals, firms and regulatory agencies. Coronary angioplasty has become the main surgical treatment for heart disease, the primary cause of death in advanced economies. We undertake a multi-method study (interviews, inspection of secondary sources and a network analysis of bibliometric data) of the origin, development patterns, opportunities and constraints of the new procedure. The chapter investigates the entrepreneurial efforts of the pioneers and the seminal interaction between the science base, technological know-how and clinical practice in order to gain a deeper understanding of the relationship between the characteristics of complex new treatments and the rationales, modes and diffusion patterns in the context of public service provision.

Our core focus is the mechanisms through which medical knowledge emerges, grows and transforms itself at the interface between biomedical research, the manufacturing of drugs and devices, and the delivery of clinical services. Innovation in the health sector is a process that is distributed across time, space and epistemic and organizational domains. It involves the development of correlated understandings about the nature of medical problems, and the search for solutions to these problems through clinical practice. On the one hand, it entails a shift from the exploratory undertakings of inquisitive individuals to the more systemic interactions of dispersed groups of practitioners competing and cooperating to solve scientific and technical puzzles in a variety of institutional settings, using various communication channels, and responding to different incentive structures. On the other hand, it crucially relies upon extensive applied research, ranging from highly experimental to routine-type activities that generate chains of radical and incremental innovations.

The reliance of medical knowledge upon clinical practice implies strong interdependencies between innovation and the diffusion of medical technologies. The reason is that the benefits and risks of innovative procedures are only fully realized over the long term and, through extensive mechanisms of feedback, gathered in a systematic way from the dispersed adoption decisions of clinicians. Only through the widespread application of a technology can a full understanding of its implications be gained. Given this, organizational change in the modes of delivery of clinical services can never be independent from the processes of innovation in drugs and devices. Changes in one can induce far-reaching consequences on the other. In fact, while it is important to recognize that the characteristics of innovative technologies are important determinants of their diffusion patterns, it is equally important to emphasize that it is through the process of diffusion that technologies evolve, as new insights are generated for further innovation. In other words, the framework that enables and constrains adoption decisions is fundamental, not only as a set of conditions that determines who benefits from new treatments and to what extent, but also as a platform for further technological advance. Hence, the evolution of medical technologies jointly depends on the activity of innovative suppliers and on that of those organizations – medical research centres and hospitals above all – where the associated new clinical services are delivered.[1]

In turn, the delivery of clinical services results from the coordination of a number of different markets (that is, for general supplies, drugs and devices, specialized labour and insurance) and on the interaction of a diverse set of organizations, within and across the public and private realms (that is, regulatory agencies, universities, firms, hospitals, patient associations, charities and other funding bodies). Furthermore, the boundaries between public and private, and the openness to change, are contingent on the institutional set-up, values and historical tradition of national (and occasionally regional) health sectors. This makes it extremely difficult to uniformly transfer clinical and organizational practice from country to country and across institutions. As a result, innovation in healthcare systems is a lengthy and costly process whose outcomes are uneven, often contestable and far from predictable.

6.2 MEDICAL INNOVATION AS A LONG-TERM LEARNING PROCESS

The literature on innovation management and health policy present several analyses of medical devices markets, and provide numerous opportunities for deepening our understanding of the micro-dynamics of invention, innovation and the diffusion of medical technologies. Many important insights have been gained and a number of characteristics of the medical device sector have been profiled. To begin with, innovation processes are typically non-linear with progress relying on mechanisms of feedback between research and development, and practice (Gelijns and Rosenberg, 1994). The main reason why feedback from clinical practice is so important is the radical uncertainty associated with new treatment options. Whether these enable the achievement of new goals or provide more efficient tools to solve known problems, the reaction of the body (as in all complex systems) cannot be predicted in a reliable way (Gelijns et al., 1998). As a consequence, advancement in the treatment of diseases has much in common with the trial-and-error learning typical of engineering-based innovation processes, where incremental improvements and eventual drawbacks are discovered through the actual use of new techniques (Vincenti, 1991; Constant, 1980).

Feedback from practice also means that the involvement of users (von Hippel, 1976, 1988) has been identified as a fairly robust regularity of innovation in medical devices. Expert users are not just a source of information. They know the need and at the same time articulate plausible ways to satisfy it. In this sense, they are genuine sources of invention, and are capable of generating new innovations when they possess the entrepreneurial motivation and skills necessary to turn new ideas into business. The literature is rich in anecdotal, as well as more systematic, examples of this.[2]

Both the reliance of manufacturers on users and the latter's activities in academic and commercial domains, suggest that innovation in medical devices originates rather systematically at the interface of different institutional settings (Blume, 1992) and involve, above all, university departments, academic medical centres, general hospitals, firms and regulators. It is across their boundaries that scientific and technological learning occurs and technology transfers take place. The main avenues for technology transfer are extensively discussed in Campbell et al. (2004), who (net of communication flows between innovators and regulators) identify three main paths:

1. General dissemination of knowledge
2. University–industry relationships
3. Commercialization activities.

The first encompasses education and training for practitioners, the organization of dedicated conferences and meetings, and publication activities. The second includes university profits from honoraria, consulting fees, research support by trading research expertise and intellectual property. The third accounts for the activities of university technology transfer offices and university patenting.[3]

With respect to all three types of technology transfer process, research hospitals and, more generally, research foundations/institutes, where clinical services are also delivered, are especially important institutions. On the one hand, they tend to be teaching institutions and are an integral part of academic institutions. In this sense they are the prime mechanisms for the inter-generational diffusion of knowledge, whose tacit components are often predominant in the field of medicine. On the other hand, research hospitals provide the organizational links between basic science, mostly produced in universities, with experimental phases of research where firms are involved as partners in the development of prototypes (be they drugs or devices) or as the suppliers of products that must be tested in clinical trials in order to receive market approval. In this case, firms often act as sponsors for trials. The trials are expected to provide unbiased evidence of the safety and comparative advantage of the innovations on which the decision of the regulators to approve their introduction in the marketplace will depend.

Another important, but often neglected, aspect of the innovative process is the role of diffusion not only in its own right, as the process through which new treatments reach an increasing number of patients, but also as the context in which innovations are modified, adapted, improved and better understood. Gelijns et al. (1998) argue that 'innovation is a learning process that takes place over time, and a fundamental aspect of learning is the reduction of uncertainty' (p. 694). Uncertainty, they argue, results from the complexity of the human system, which poses severe limits on the possibility of predicting the effects of new procedures. The typically narrow target of clinical trials, and the heterogeneity of patients recruited to test new drugs and new devices in the early phases of development, add to the difficulty of finding unexpected benefits associated with new treatments in the short run. As a consequence, the experience gathered in clinical practice, and the resulting post-innovation improvements of experimental techniques, can hardly be overstated.[4]

Post-innovation improvements provide strong indications that the process of accumulation of medical knowledge occurs along trajectories of change that emerge over time in the search for better and better solutions to clinical problems (Metcalfe et al., 2005). Innovations are rarely if ever uniquely circumscribed events and outcomes. They are better seen as trajectories of improvement sequences in which devices or procedures are progressively refined and extended in their scope of application. Moreover, the devices are only the signatures of knowledge and practice, as one innovation problem is solved so others range into view and form new foci for innovative effort within the broad objective to improve the efficacy of the overarching procedure. All innovation is an exploration of the unknown; it is a discovery process that is neither random nor completely canalized. Rather it proceeds through exploring a design space in a largely path–dependent fashion within bounds set by the perception of the problem (Metcalfe et al., 2005). Progress means finding new problems and the solutions to these problems may lie in different domains of knowledge and communities of practice.

Communities of practice (Brown and Duguid, 1991) are important loci for the development of new knowledge, and it is often at this level that new problems emanate and are identified. It is through the performance of clinical practice that particular 'glitches' and potential solutions become apparent. These cannot be independent of the organizational and institutional bases of relevant networks of individuals. As a consequence, scientific and technological knowledge co-evolve with the social networks in which the process is embedded. Not only is knowledge distributed within communities, it is also distributed across communities linked through a variety of formal and informal mechanisms of exchange. The advancement of medical knowledge relies on continuous feedback between science and technology, and the nature and intensity of interaction across communities at different points in time are of great importance to the emergence, growth and transformation of medical micro-innovation systems.

6.3 A CASE STUDY OF INTERVENTIONAL CARDIOLOGY

Interventional cardiology is a sub-speciality of the broad field of cardiology that deals with mechanical (mainly surgical) solutions to a vast array of heart diseases. Among these, coronary artery disease (CAD) constitutes the principal cause of death in developed countries (WHO, 1999; OECD, 2003). It results from a process called atherosclerosis, through which deposits (plaque) form on the inner layer of the coronary arteries and obstruct the flow of blood to the heart. While no symptoms are felt by the patient in the first stage, chest pains of varying degree and shortness of breath begin to emerge as the disease progresses. If untreated the likely outcome is a heart attack.

The now dominant surgical procedure for CAD is 'percutaneous transluminal coronary angioplasty' (PTCA). This emerged in the late 1970s as a substitute for the principal surgical alternative at that time, coronary artery bypass surgery, and complemented a growing range of pharmacological tools. PTCA is today considered one of the most important medical innovations of the last decades.[5] Not only has PTCA proven, with the benefit of experience, to be an effective and efficacious mode of treatment, it has transformed the division of labour in cardiology. So much so that medical boards around the world now recognize interventional cardiology as a separate speciality within the broader field of cardiology. The growth of this speciality reflects the concomitant evolution of a medical industrial complex that supplies devices, materials and drugs, and forms an integral part of the associated medical innovation system. This rapid commercialization reflects a more fundamental point: the growth of the market, and the associated extension and transformation of the modes of delivery of new clinical services.

6.3.1 Old and New Solutions

As recently as the 1960s, treatment options for angina (chest pain) or acute myocardial infarction (heart attack) consisted of few medications (mainly nitroglycerin), rest and hope. In the 1960s and 1970s beta blockers and calcium channel blockers were added to the cardiologist's arsenal for dealing with angina. However, while these provide effective relief from angina by reducing the frequency and force of the heartbeat, they do not cure the underlying problem. Surgical treatments also improved from the 1960s, with the development of coronary artery bypass surgery. This is a major invasive and complicated surgical procedure, taking between three and six hours to perform. It requires general anaesthesia, the use of a heart-lung machine to substitute for heart and lung functioning during surgery, and a lengthy period of post-surgical recuperation. Most patients tend to be discharged after five to six days, and return to work in five to six weeks. The idea is to improve the blood flow to the heart muscle by bypassing blockages using blood vessels harvested from the leg (saphenous vein) or chest wall (internal mammary artery).

At the time of its introduction, bypass surgery was regarded as truly revolutionary. The idea of stopping a heart, restoring its blood supply and then restarting it bordered on the miraculous. The technique spread rapidly, although figures about the volume of procedures undertaken in the early period are patchy. In 1973 around 25 000 operations were performed in the USA. This had increased to 70 000 by 1977 (OTA, 1978). Elsewhere, the absolute numbers of procedures were small in comparison. In the UK, for example, 2297 operations were carried out in 1977, increasing to 4057 by 1980 (British Heart Foundation, 2004).

The diffusion of the procedure was not without controversy, however, primarily due to the evidence base on which bypass surgery was being promoted. A debate raged throughout the 1970s about the quality of evidence that was being assembled on the efficacy of bypass surgery relative to medical therapy. So much so that the US Office for Technology Assessment (OTA, 1978) was decidedly lukewarm about the procedure, arguing that, in terms of survival, the VA randomized trial (and a number of others) showed that surgery did not appear to bring any appreciable longevity benefit when compared with medically treated patients. The OTA did concede the point that bypass surgery gave 'excellent symptomatic relief from angina pectoris' (OTA, 1978, p. 43), although it was careful to caution about placebo effects associated with surgery.[6]

Coronary angioplasty was developed against this background of uncertainty about the efficacy of coronary bypass surgery. It secured the name of its pioneer, the German radiologist Andreas Gruentzig, in the annals of medical history. Gruentzig's key insight was to use a balloon-tipped catheter to dilate the constricted coronary artery, and was based on the already known techniques of cardiac catheterization and percutaneous transluminal angioplasty. Cardiac catheterization is a diagnostic procedure in which a catheter (a thin flexible tube) is inserted into the right or left side of the heart. This procedure could be used to produce angiograms (X-ray images) of the coronary arteries and the left ventricle, the heart's main pumping chamber, and/or used to measure pressures in the pulmonary artery and to monitor heart function. Percutaneous transluminal angioplasty (PTA) was a technique developed in the 1960s by the American Charles Dotter. In this technique a catheter is used to reopen occluded peripheral arteries (initially the iliac artery in the lower abdomen) by pushing it through the plaque.[7]

Gruentzig was exposed to the Dotter method by one of Dotter's followers (Eberhardt Zeitler) in the mid-1960s at the Ratchow Clinic in Darnstadt (Germany), where he was a Research Fellow in Epidemiology studying coronary artery disease. He then decided to become a cardiologist and moved to the University of Zurich in 1974. Here he began to think about whether the Dotter method could be applied to the heart, recognizing that 'any application of the dilatation procedure to other areas of the body would require technical changes' (King, 1996, p. 1624). Encouraged by his colleague, and Joint Head of Cardiology, Wilhelm Ruttishauser, Gruentzig proceeded to develop himself a prototype balloon catheter, the foundation for PTCA. Two crucial developments followed. First, in 1972 he introduced a PVC balloon, a tough, less compliant material than latex, with which he had experimented earlier. In 1975 he developed a single and then a double lumen catheter. One catheter is used to inflate the balloon and the other catheter is used to inject contrast media and monitor intravascular pressure. In 1976 Gruentzig presented the results of animal experimentation to a less than enthusiastic audience at the American Heart Association meeting. Regardless, he succeeded in doing the first PTCA on a patient in Zurich in 1977.

Despite the initial conservative reaction to his work, Gruentzig's pioneering insights and early successes opened up tremendous opportunities for further improvements in the new technique. A growing number of practitioners started experimenting with PTCA, and a growing range of devices started to be developed. The next phase of the diffusion process involved the taking up and further development of PTCA by a community, which itself is newly formed. In this respect, the nature of the innovation process of PTCA mirrors that of other significant medical innovations: it is an uncertain co-evolutionary process of knowledge and technique.[8] In the next section we take up this subsequent phase of the innovation/ diffusion process.

6.3.2 Trajectories of Change

In this section we apply techniques of longitudinal network analysis that can generate parsimonious maps of citation networks, and illustrate branches of developments that the medical community selects over time as being important (through quoting relevant contributions). More specifically, we use a variation of the Main Path Algorithm, described in Batagelj (2002), which identifies the citation paths that are most frequently encountered among all the possible 'chains' of citations from the most recent records to the oldest.[9] The results enable us to identify, at each time period and across time periods, scientific and technological developments that branch out in the search space, and their patterns of convergence or divergence over time.

The complex history of medical techniques is extremely well documented in the records of medical journals, where practitioners regularly publish the results of their research, and in the patent records covering the property rights granted for innovative drugs and devices. These can be used to provide systematic evidence of the long-term evolution of clinical knowledge and associated technical equipment. For this purpose we created two databases. The first is a bibliographic database of papers published between 1979 and 2003. It was extracted from the Institute for Scientific Information (ISI) online resources, and contains basic details and bibliographic citations for 11 240 papers published in the field of interventional cardiology. The second dataset includes patent documents extracted from the United States Patent Office, and contains information on 5136 patents granted in the USA to angioplasty-related inventions between 1976 and

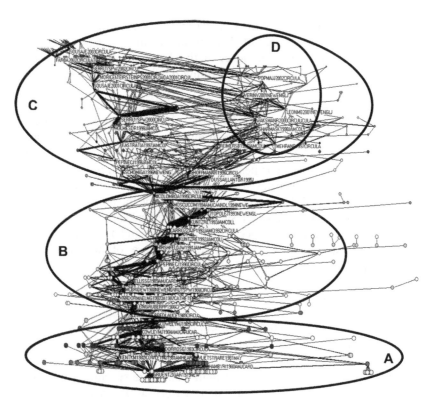

Figure 6.1   Time evolution of scientific knowledge

2003. Both datasets were extracted by keyword searches derived from major university textbooks of interventional cardiology with constant feedback from medical practitioners.[10]

Using the Main Path Algorithm on the datasets we can generate the time evolution research in interventional cardiology over the past three decades (Figure 6.1).[11]

Inspection of the map reveals that nodes broadly contained in cluster A are strongly connected to the original breakthroughs of Gruentzig, and clearly illustrate a phase of intense exploration of the search space opened up by the first appearance of coronary angioplasty.[12] Analysis of a number of these papers reveals that these were concerned with the efficacy of PTCA, and the conditions under which the procedure could work. Among them, special mention must be made of the study by Cowley et al. (1985), which was produced under the sponsorship of the National Heart Lung and Blood Institute, and provided early evidence on the effective use of balloon angioplasty procedures in medical centres across the USA and in other countries.

Between 1986 and 1995, cluster B papers reported various developments of the technique, and began to focus on the problem of restenosis (for example, Pepine et al., 1990). This occurs when plaque eliminated by the mechanical action of the balloon catheter reforms after surgery, dramatically reducing the efficacy of the treatment and raising its real cost.[13] During the latter part of the 1980s, one solution to this problem gathered momentum. It was the application of a stent – a scaffolding structure, applied either with balloon angioplasty or on its own (a self-expanding stent). This solved two problems. First, it acted as a support structure to prevent the collapse of the inner vessel, which sometimes occurred, and thus limiting the need for emergency surgery. Second, it reduced the impact of restenosis by mechanically maintaining the artery patency and thus the need for multiple angioplasty procedures.

It is in relation to this specific device that we can explain the visible convergence of the epistemic network between clusters B and C, marking a step change in the progress of clinical research. Until the mid-1990s, results from clinical trials where stents were used failed to meet the expectations that had been raised. This was due to the great variability in the outcomes of surgery. The watershed in the evolution of the network, identified in the study by Colombo et al. (1995), coincided with the emergence of persuasive evidence of the advantages of stenting compared to 'simple' balloon angioplasty, and to the finding that the success rate of the procedure heavily depended on the placement of the stent graft.

After this, new scope for exploration opened up to new contributions – papers in cluster C. The aim was not only to improve upon the use of stents, but also to deal with the problem of plaque reforming inside the stent – the so-called problem of in-stent restenosis. This triggered the emergence of parallel trajectories of research. Finally, among the various solutions explored in the period of cluster D were stents coated with drugs (drug-eluting stents) that locally deliver to the point of the lesion, pharmacological therapies that precede or follow stenting and radiation therapies.

Will we find similarities between the evolutionary patterns of scientific understanding and those of technical knowledge, as documented in patents? Figure 6.2 shows the network evolution of PTCA-related devices.

Gruentzig's contribution is again identifiable (Patent No. 4195637) among the most important ones. His prototype catheter was developed, of all places, in his kitchen! He later entered into a relationship with Schneider, a Swiss medical needle manufacturing company based in Zurich, for manufacturing a marketable device and applied for a patent

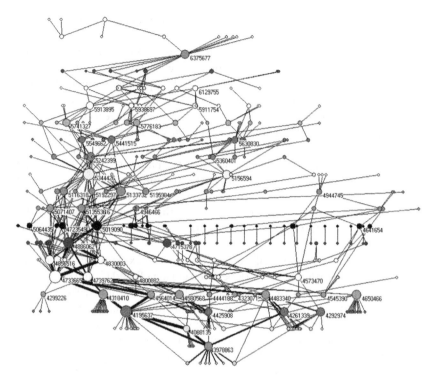

Figure 6.2   Time evolution of technological knowledge

with the US Patent and Trademark Office in 1977. This was granted in 1980 and paved the way for the diffusion of coronary angioplasty in the USA.

Citations reveal that Gruentzig's patent built upon other catheters, both specific and generic (bottom layer of the graph and node 3798863), and it was developed along with a number of other designs that proved less successful. The map also shows the importance of a number of incremental and complementary improvements to Gruentzig's double-lumen catheter. Above all, it highlights the contribution of Simpson (Patent No. 4323071), who developed the steerable guide wire in the USA in 1982. This device enabled operators to access the most distal lesions by allowing greater direction control of the catheter through the coronary system. It increased the angiographic success rate from 83 to 93 per cent, a clinical success (angioplasty) rate from 79 to 91 per cent, and a lowering of the emergency bypass surgery rate from 7.2 to 2.8 per cent by 1984 (King, 1998).

In the same cohort of patents we find Gianturco's (Patent No. 4580568). This is a fundamental precursor of the first stent to receive market approval, the so-called Palmaz stent (Patent No. 4733665). This Palmaz stent appears to be the source of several streams of research, branching rather neatly from the left lower section of the graph that relates to improvement in stent devices. Prototypes of the Palmaz design were used for two early randomized trials whose results were included in an evidence-based consensus document published by the American College of Cardiology (ACC) in 1996.[14] By the time this document appeared, stents were being used in more than 50 per cent of PTCA procedures. The pace of scientific and technical knowledge about stent improved rapidly, so much so that, by the time the ACC published a second consensus document two years later, neither of the two stents approved by the Food and Drug Administration (FDA) for use in the treatment of discrete *de novo* lesions (to prevent restenosis and acute or impending artery closure) were in use, having been replaced by improved versions (Suwaidi et al., 2000). Stents were widely used by 1997, and the by end of the decade they accounted for 80 per cent of all angioplasty procedures (Schaaf, 2001).

To summarize, the focus of technical research moved over time from generic catheters to coronary catheters, followed by an expansion of stent delivery systems that typically included a specially designed catheter apparatus. Then, a phase of relative maturity seems to be reached in the latter period. An increasing number of stent designs were patented independently of catheter systems, reflecting a greater degree of specialization in the second half of the 1990s.

Insofar as the advancement of codified knowledge is concerned, in our systematic analysis of over 11 000 scientific publications and more than 5000 patents, we find substantial similarity between the development of a scientific understanding of the disease and the technological tools used to diagnose and treat the conditions. This is a clear indication of the strong complementarities (though not linear dependency) between basic and applied medical research. Furthermore, as science and technology co-evolved, so did the set of interdependent problems that emerged along the search for satisfying cures to the disease. As one problem was solved, others presented themselves. Partly in reaction to newly found solutions, opportunities for further market entry emerged (the case of stents is emblematic). The resulting picture of medical progress in this clinical area takes the form of a series of coherent trajectories of change that converged and diverged along specific sequences of problems. These can only be appreciated *ex post* as the result of a process of path-dependent emergence through multi-level mechanisms of selection. Over time, knowledge that is judged to be ineffective is weeded out through clinical use by communities of relevant practitioners. These communities of practitioners typically operate across the boundaries of science, technology and clinical practice, especially in the early phases of the development of new treatments.[15]

6.4   ENTREPRENEURSHIP AND THE SEEDS OF THE PTCA MICRO-INNOVATION SYSTEM

Inspection of citations patterns, both for papers and patents, clearly reveals the importance of Andreas Gruentzig in the development of the new technique. While it is important to recognize his pivotal role, it is also important to emphasize that not only his innovative efforts built on previous knowledge but also relied on the cooperation of a number of partners in research and clinical practice which constituted a distinctively entrepreneurial community. His ability in the classroom and his fairly conservative style contributed greatly to the acceptance of the technique he championed and the diffusion of related equipment. Furthermore, his teaching was as important as the originality of his ideas and the extent of his technical competence. It would be a mistake to overlook it and to only consider his scientific production and his limited – but extremely influential – contribution to the advancement of technical know-how.

Gruentzig presented his first results to the American Heart Association conference in 1977. This generated enough interest for him to receive numerous requests from other cardiologists wanting to learn the technique. A close-knit – and practice-based – micro community developed around Gruentzig that constituted the backbone for the diffusion of the technique.[16] It included, among others, Richard Myler who, together with Simon Sterzer, was the first to perform angioplasty in the USA in 1978 (King, 1998). Over time Gruentzig's connections with the USA intensified to the point that in 1980 he moved from Zurich to Emory University, where there were fewer constraints on the laboratory time that he was allowed by his employer. At Emory not only could he work on an increasing number of cases but was also provided good teaching facilities, which he was very keen to have. He was convinced that a critical mass of expert practitioners needed to be trained as well as possible to avoid the formation of imperfect skills that would have jeopardized the long-term success of the new technique.

It is in this community that we find the seeds of science, as well as the seeds of the industrial complex that was to grow over the following three decades. Gruentzig was not only scientifically minded but was involved in the invention and development of devices. He was very cautious about the production and commercialization of his catheters.[17] In the early days in Zurich he exerted tight control on the sale of the first angioplasty catheters, produced under his instructions by Schneider, a small Swiss company later to be acquired by Pfizer in 1984 and sold on to Boston Scientific in 1998. It has been reported that he required practitioners who bought catheters to receive training or counselling from him on how best to use the device.[18] This significantly contributed to a reduction in the rate of failure of the procedure due to improper use in a phase of the diffusion process that was most delicate for the future success of angioplasty.

When the procedure started to be experimented with on a larger scale, the need also emerged to evaluate the performance of the technique in a systematic way. John Abele, who went on to found one of today's market leaders (Boston Scientific) and who started collaborating with Gruentzig in the development of double-lumen catheters, recalls that there were informal discussions between Gruentzig, Myler and himself about creating a registry to document what was being learned in clinical practice wherever the technique was used. They then developed a very simple but comprehensive form where results of every procedure could be recorded. The registry that resulted from the collection and organization of the forms lasted for no longer than 18 months but was not to disappear. In 1979 the National Heart, Lung and Blood Institute (NHLBI) – the relevant branch of the National Institutes of Health – invited a small working group to discuss how evaluation of PTCA could be managed. It was agreed that a workshop should be held to review the preliminary evidence and that a voluntary registry should be set up. The PTCA registry was established in March 1979 (Mullins et al., 1984) and was really a formalization of the earlier database started by Gruentzig and others.

Thus, in this process of division of social labour, the monitoring function of the system passed to the NHLBI while the regulation of medical devices shifted to the FDA in the same years. Both these complementary modes of regulation proved crucial to the extension of understanding and practice, and to the growth of the market on which investment by commercial firms depended. Market institutions do not usually, if ever, operate independently of wider regulatory norms and these norms – formal and informal – like the market itself are created and co-evolve with it.

Prior to the 1980s, as we have mentioned, Gruentzig and Myler personally exerted informal control on the availability, quality and safety of catheters. In a way, they acted as the first regulators of angioplasty devices before the FDA started implementing the reform of Medical Devices Law passed in 1976, and became the ultimate arbiter for regulation of medical technologies. The FDA then became the institution that exerted in the public interest the functions of evaluation and selection of the variety of drugs and devices stemming from the wealth of R&D activities that followed the sparse experimentation of the early years. Needless to say, its role grew in importance along with the increasing commercial interests associated with angioplasty, which grew fast especially in the USA where the centre of gravity of the community shifted both scientifically and technologically. Also, as the technique developed, a number of complementary and competing solutions were found in the community gathered around Gruentzig. From there, these new solutions found their way to the market very often through the activities of a number of physician-entrepreneurs such as John Simpson, inventor of the steerable guidewire, who founded no less than ten product innovation-based start-ups and then sold them in rapidly expanding knowledge markets to larger device manufactures (Guidant, Abbott Laboratories and Boston Scientific among others).

The stylized facts that emerge from an analysis of the origin of the PTCA micro-innovation system provide a picture where the creative vision of a few lead developers and users became shared by an increasing number of practitioners and spilled over, on the one hand, on the formation of growing profit expectations and, on the other hand, on the need for coordination mechanisms that included a wide range of collaborative agreements between public and private organizations, different funding schemes, including the provision of venture capital, and standard regulatory processes. Gruentzig was a creative and skilled surgeon but was also endowed with a sense of cautious discipline and an active interest in community building. He was actively involved in creating the initial informal connections between clinical research, manufacturing and service delivery and in establishing the first means of coordination and technology transfer across institutional boundaries.

The growth of knowledge of the disease benefited and in turn extended the diffusion of clinical practice, without which the true value of the innovators' creativity would be lost to the final beneficiaries. In order to bring the benefits of new treatments to patients, complementary innovations in the allocation strategies and modes of service delivery are needed. In the case of angioplasty, for example, the reaction of local health sectors was pivotal to the success of the new technique in relation to alternative treatments. This was contingent to the specific ethos, financial structure and strategic orientation of different national health providers (OECD, 2003), which adapted to different degrees and at different rates to the new treatment within the constraints embedded in the established healthcare systems.

6.5   DISCUSSION AND CONCLUSION

This chapter has examined the history of coronary angioplasty, from academic debate to technological research, to clinical practice. Medical research is of enormous significance to society, and constitutes a rich area for studying innovation, especially as new and urgent issues are emerging with respect to economic sustainability, social acceptance and access, and the ethical conduct of the medical sector. A fundamental element of interest is the interdependence between services and manufacturing. Medical progress crucially depends on the interaction between the clinical delivery of healthcare services and a global research and manufacturing system that develops and delivers new drugs and new devices to enhance the delivery of local clinical services. Thus, service innovation is premised on complementary innovations in manufacturing, and those manufacturing innovations are shaped by clinical innovations and related co-developments in the delivery of services. We argue that it is a mistake to treat them as separate processes.

A second finding of this chapter is that feedbacks from clinical practice are essential to the advancement of medical science and technology, as in few other sectors of the economy. The conduit of medical progress resides in the tight connection between the provision and use of new treatments, where feedback from intermediate adopters (clinicians) and final beneficiaries (patients) is essential in shaping the innovation process. As a consequence, the development of entrepreneurial activity is premised on the scale and scope of clinical practice – an element that has traditionally characterized the US health innovation system, and that is both related to the availability of high budgets for biomedical research, a high propensity to risk, and a very favourable attitude of patients to innovation (Kim et al., 2001).

The health sector is a clear example of a system in which public and private organizations closely cooperate and compete to meet socially recognized needs, and where different interdependent markets co-exist under a variety of institutional arrangements. Close interaction between firms, public service providers and regulators is likely to facilitate the emergence and development of scientific, technical and social innovation. Creativity, which thrives in the presence of variety and openness to change, is only sustainable through rigorous and transparent evaluation processes and selection mechanisms of new applications. On this basis, enhancing the conditions for self-organized interaction between individuals and across organizations, as typified in the early phase of the development of coronary angioplasty, has genuine potential to help the formation of new micro communities of innovators and lead users of new technologies.

Looking ahead, the complexity of health innovation and diffusion systems is such that straightforward answers to general resource allocation problems are often missing because they necessarily depend on the values, traditions and strategic orientation of local institutions. With specific reference to the clinical area of heart disease, extensive comparative analyses of the performance of different national health systems (McClelland and Kessler, 1999) reveal that the identification of optimal solutions can hardly go beyond general agreement that supply-side incentives are a strong determinant of the diffusion of new costly treatments. What seems to be clear, however, is that technology is the most important determinant of the rising costs of healthcare, both in the aggregate (Newhouse, 1992) and in the specific clinical area of heart disease (Cutler and McClelland, 2001). As a consequence, in the face of tighter financial constraints being implemented in several countries to prevent escalating health costs, it has become necessary to find better tools for evaluating the benefits and costs of health technologies. These should also include quality-adjusted measures for the systemic impact of organizational change in the delivery and teaching of new procedures. Furthermore, the need has emerged to improve the transparency of modern private–public partnerships in biomedical research, and to monitor the effect of current variations in health expenditure on long-term innovation rates and productivity growth. These, we believe, are important challenges that lie ahead for future research.

ACKNOWLEDGMENTS

This chapter is an extension of the joint work of the authors with Prof. Stan Metcalfe and Dr Gindo Tampubolon of the University of Manchester, who have provided invaluable conceptual and technical insights. It has been carried out in CRIC under the Innovative Health Technology Programme coordinated by Prof. Andrew Webster (University of York) and funded by the UK Economic and Social Research Council (ESRC) and Medical Research Council (MRC).

NOTES

1. Also, hospital administrators, payers, insurers and regulators are increasingly influencing the rate and direction of medical innovation by explicitly identifying priority needs, and redefining modes of financing that incentivize the emergence and diffusion of cost-reducing technological solutions in the face of escalating health expenditures (Newhouse, 1992).
2. Among others, Hauptman and Roberts (1987) provided evidence from a dataset of biomedical firms located in the US state of Massachusetts, de Vet and Scott (1992) from Californian suppliers of medical devices, Shaw (1986) from a sample of UK firms and Biemans (1991) from a subset of Dutch medical device companies.
3. As widely discussed in the literature, although there is still disagreement on the long-term risks versus benefits of these decisions, investments by universities in applied research aimed at patenting increased dramatically after the implementation of the Bayh–Dole

Act in the USA, and Bayh–Dole types of policy intervention in other countries. With respect to this issue, see Gelijns and Rosenberg (1999) and Zinner (2001) on the specific field of medical innovation.

4. As Gelijns and Rosenberg (1994) recall, innovations may not come from biomedical research in the first place, but from other fields (for example, ultrasound, laser and magnetic resonance), and the development of medical devices is especially dependent on a number of technological competences that are not core to medical sciences (for example, optical engineering) but which, nevertheless, cannot be understood if not in association with the surgical practice in which they are utilized, and the broader contest of their approval, marketing and distribution.

5. A recent survey by Fuchs and Sox (2001) of general internists actively involved in patient care, ranked PTCA as third (only behind MRI and CT scanning, and ACE inhibitors) of the 30 most important medical innovations over the last 25 years.

6. One of the interesting features of the spread of bypass surgery is how quickly it was taken up for cohorts of patients for whom the medical evidence was not indicated (Anderson and Lomas, 1988). A study carried out in Ontario, Canada, expressed concern about the apparent change in clinical policies towards the use of bypass procedures in the elderly, without solid evidence on efficacy or cost-effectiveness in support of such a change. While the increased procedure rates observed might be based on the assumption that the effectiveness demonstrated in the non-elderly could be generalized to the elderly, this assumption may or may not be supportable. The over 65 age groups were not represented in any of the three major randomized trials that had been reported by the early 1980s. Yet in Ontario and the USA in 1983 they respectively accounted for 23 per cent and 37 per cent of bypass surgeries.

7. Werner Forssmann is credited with being the first to introduce a (urological) catheter into the right atrium (his own!) in 1929. Branded as 'crazy' by his contemporaries, his immediate reward for this achievement was dismissal from his German hospital (he went on to win the Nobel Prize in 1956). By the 1950s, however, following the work of Cournand, Seldinger and others, diagnostic catheterization had become established as the main technique for investigating cardiac function. The American Charles Dotter faced the same degree of scepticism when he developed the technique of transluminal angioplasty, based on the therapeutic potential of catheters, after he inadvertently reopened an occluded right iliac artery by pushing through it with the angiography catheter (Rosch et al., 2003). His insight proved so successful that European radiologists later institutionalized the term 'dottering' (of patients) to refer to improving the patency of arteries by the introduction of a series of coaxial catheters.

8. See, for example, Gelijns and Rosenberg (1994); Gelijns et al. (1998); and Gelijns et al. (2001).

9. For more details on the application of the algorithm, see Ramlogan et al. (forthcoming).

10. Significant efforts have been made not only to validate the search strategy and results, but to balance the need to be economical in the number of searches, so as to impose as little structure as possible upon the data, and the need to maximize the probability of capturing relevant patents.

11. To visualize the data we use the freely available software Pajek developed by mathematicians from the University of Ljubljana for mapping large networks (Batagelj and Mrvar, 2003).

12. Due to space constraints, the detailed bibliographies of the maps have not been included. They are available from the authors upon request.

13. Restenosis tends to occur during the first three to six months after the procedure. It is not atherosclerotic in nature but results from the outgrowth of endothelial cells that normally line blood vessels. It has been likened to 'over exuberant' tissue healing and regeneration similar to scar formation after the trauma of angioplasty.

14. It was through the production of the Palmaz stent that J&J entered the profitable interventional cardiology market.

15. This does not imply that the outcomes are necessarily optimal or could not have been different.

16.	See also interview with John Abele (Cohen, 1996), Part III, accessed September, 2006 at www.ptca.org/nv/interviewframe.html.
17.	Interview with Heliane Canepa (Cohen, 1996), then President of Schneider Worldwide and former collaborator of Gruentzig, accessed September, 2006 at www.ptca.org/nv/ interviewframe.html.
18.	Interview with John Abele (Cohen, 1996), accessed September, 2006 at www.ptca.org/nv/ interviewframe.html.

REFERENCES

Anderson, G.M. and J. Lomas (1988), 'Monitoring the diffusion of a technology: coronary bypass surgery in Ontario', *American Journal of Public Health*, **78**, 251–4.
Batagelj, V. (2002), 'Efficient algorithms for citation network analysis', Department of Theoretical Computer Science, University of Ljubljana working paper.
Biemans, W.G. (1991), 'User and third-party involvement in developing medical equipment innovation', *Technovation*, **11**, 163–82.
Blume, S. (1992), *Insight and Industry: On the Dynamics of Technological Change in Medicine*, Boston, MA: MIT Press.
British Heart Foundation (2004), 'Coronary heart disease statistics: factsheet', British Heart Foundation Health Promotion Research Group.
Brown, J.S. and P. Duguid (1991), 'Organisational learning and communities of practice: towards a unified view of making, learning and innovation', *Organisational Science*, **2**, 40–57.
Campbell, E.G., J.B. Powers, D. Blumenthal and B. Biles (2004), 'Inside the triple helix: technology transfer and commercialization in the life sciences', *Health Affairs*, **23**, 64–76.
Cohen, B. (1996), interview with John Abele, part III, and interview with Heliane Canepa, accessed September 2006 at www.ptca.org/nv/interviewframe.html.
Colombo, A., P. Hall, S. Nakamura, Y. Almagor, L. Maiello, G. Martini, A. Gaglione, S.L. Goldberg and J.M. Tobis (1995), 'Intracoronary stenting without anticoagulation accomplished with intravascular ultrasound guidance', *Circulation*, **91**(6), 1676–88.
Constant, E. (1980), *The Origins of the Turbo Jet Revolution*, Baltimore, MD: Johns Hopkins University Press.
Cowley, M.J., S.M. Mullin, S.F. Kelsey, K.M. Kent, A.R. Gruentzig, K.M. Detre and E.R. Passamani (1985), 'Sex-differences in early and long-term results of coronary angioplasty in the NHLBI PTCA registry', *Circulation*, **71**(1), 90–97.
Cutler, D.M. and M. McClellan (2001), 'Is technological change in medicine worth it?', *Health Affairs*, **20**, 11–29.
Fuchs, V.R. and H.C. Sox Jr (2001), 'Physicians' views of the relative importance of thirty medical innovations', *Health Affairs*, **20**, 30–42.
Gelijns, A. and N. Rosenberg (1994), 'The dynamics of technological change in medicine', *Health Affairs*, Summer, 28–46.
Gelijns, A. and N. Rosenberg (1999), 'Diagnostic devices: an analysis of comparative advantages', in D. Mowery and R. Nelson (eds), *Sources of Industrial Leadership*, Cambridge: Cambridge University Press, pp. 312–59.

Gelijns, A.C., N. Rosenberg and A.J. Moskowitz (1998), 'Capturing the unexpected benefits of medical research', *New England Journal of Medicine*, **339**, 693–8.

Gelijns, A.C., J.G. Zivin and R.R. Nelson (2001), 'Uncertainty and technological change in medicine', *Journal of Health Politics, Policy and Law*, **26**(5), 913–24.

Hauptman, O. and E.B. Roberts (1987), 'FDA regulation of product risk and its impact upon young biomedical firms', *Journal of Product Innovation Management*, **4**, 138–48.

Hippel von, E. (1976), 'The dominant role of users in the scientific instrumentation innovation process', *Research Policy*, **5**, 212–39.

Hippel von, E. (1988), *The Sources of Innovation*, Oxford and New York: Oxford University Press.

Kim, M., R.J. Blendon and J.M. Benson (2001), 'How interested are Americans in new medical technologies? A multicountry comparison', *Health Affairs*, **20**, 194–201.

King, S.B. III. (1996), 'Angioplasty from bench to bedside to bench', *Circulation*, **93**, 1621–9.

King, S.B. III. (1998), 'The development of interventional cardiology', *Journal of the American College of Cardiology*, **31**, Supplement B, 64B–88B.

McClelland, M. and D. Kessler (1999), 'A global analysis of technological change in health care: the case of heart attacks', *Health Affairs*, **18**, 250–5.

Metcalfe, J.S., A. James and A. Mina (2005), 'Emergent innovation systems and the delivery of clinical services: the case of intra-ocular lenses', *Research Policy*, **34**(9), 1283–304.

Mullins, S.M., E.R. Passamani and M.D. Mock (1984), 'Historical background of the National Heart, Lung and Blood Institute Registry for percutaneous trans-luminal coronary angioplasty', *American Journal of Cardiology*, **15**, 3–6C.

Newhouse, J.P. (1992), 'Medical care costs: how much welfare loss?', *Journal of Economic Perspectives*, Summer, 3–21.

Organization for Economic Co-operation and Development (OECD) (2003), 'Study of cross sectional differences in the treatment, costs and outcomes of ischaemic heart disease', OECD health working papers no. 3, Paris.

Office for Technology Assessment (OTA) (1978), *Assessing the Efficiency of Safety of Medical Technologies*, Washington, DC: US Government Printing Office.

Pepine, C.J., J.W. Hirshfeld, R.G. Macdonald, M.A. Henderson, T.A. Bass, S. Goldberg, M.P. Savage, G. Vetrovec, M.J. Cowley, A.S.L. Taussig, H.B. Whitworth, J.R. Margolis, J.A. Hill, A.A. Bove and R.A. Jugo (1990), 'Controlled trial of corticosteriods to prevent restenosis after coronary angio-plasty', *Circulation*, **81**(6) 1753–61.

Ramlogan, R., A. Mina, G. Tampubolon and J.S. Metcalfe (forthcoming), 'Networks of knowledge: the distributed nature of medical innovation', *Scientometrics*.

Rosch, J., F.S. Keller and J.A. Kaufman (2003), 'The birth, early years and future of interventional radiology', *Journal of Vascular and Interventional Radiology*, **14**, 841–53.

Schaaf, T.A. (2001), 'Young at heart', accessed at www.devicelink.com/mx/archive/99/09/schaaf.html.

Shaw, B. (1986), 'Appropriation and transfer of innovation benefit in the UK medical equipment industry', *Technovation*, **4**, 45–65.

Suwaidi, J.A., P.B. Berger and D.R. Holmes Jr. (2000), 'Coronary artery stents', *Journal of the American Medical Association*, **284**, 1828–36.

de Vet, M.J. and A.J. Scott (1992), 'The southern Californian medical device industry: innovation, new firm formation, and location', *Research Policy*, **21**, 145–61.

Vincenti, W. (1991), *What Engineers Know and How They Know It*, Cambridge: Cambridge University Press.

World Health Organization (WHO) (1999), *The World Health Report 1999*, Geneva: World Health Organization.

Zinner, D.E. (2001), 'Medical R&D at the turn of the millennium', *Health Affairs*, **20**, 202–9.

7. Innovation dynamics in hospitals: applied case studies in French hospitals

Faridah Djellal and Faïz Gallouj

7.1 INTRODUCTION

The aim of this chapter is the development of a general integrative analytical framework that enables one to understand innovation in hospitals in all its diversity, that is, to understand the diversity of possible innovation loci. The chapter is an emprical application of the discussion contained in Chapter 4 of this book and previous conceptual research conducted by the authors in Djellal and Gallouj (2005). The chapter draws on research carried out for the French Ministries of Social Affairs, Work and Solidarity and Health, the Family and the Handicapped. It is based, first, on extended interviews conducted in several hospitals and their health authorities and, second, on a secondary analysis of empirical material found in the specialist literature.

This chapter is divided into four sections. Section 7.2 briefly outlines the analytical framework, put forward in Djellal and Gallouj (2005), for analysing hospital output and hospital innovation. The framework views the hospital as a 'package', or architectural service, which combines a wide range of constituent services. This general morphology of the hospital provides a basis for the construction of a typology of the organizing principles driving innovation in hospitals. In Section 7.3 the typology is illustrated using a number of concrete examples and case studies on French hospitals. Section 7.4 concludes by showing that our framework is heuristic which not only makes it possible to widen the field of hospital innovation, but also the field of its possible actors. The field, which is too often reduced to medical professionals (primarily doctors), is enlarged both vertically (towards medical actors other than doctors) and horizontally (towards the actors of any elementary service, whatever it is, which make up the hospital product). This widening of the field corresponds to a certain democratization of innovation activity, both at the individual and organizational levels.

Peripheral (individual) actors, as well as other hospitals, play (or can play) a part in the innovation processes within hospitals. Section 7.4 also shows how the framework can be used both as a prospective tool and as an audit tool.

Innovation in hospitals is not a new topic. Knowledge and innovation in the area of health are inextricable elements of universal human history. This heritage undoubtedly explains a certain general tendency, in both the humanities and social sciences, to underestimate innovation in hospitals. After all, it is medical innovation (in the sense of technical care systems and biopharmacology) that usually lies at the heart of investigations in this area. This bias concerning the nature of innovation goes hand in hand with a biased approach to the actors involved in innovation – the medical profession occupies centre stage in the hospital innovation system. However, as discussed in Chapter 4, hospitals are complex service organizations that provide an extensive and open-ended range of services which support and influence the quality of care. To this end, one needs to develop and apply a broader conceptualization of innovation; one that is applicable to the study of hospitals. This is issue is taken up in the next section.

7.2 AN ANALYTICAL FRAMEWORK FOR ANALYSING HOSPITAL OUTPUT AND HOSPITAL INNOVATION

Here we briefly outline the analytical framework put forward in Djellal and Gallouj (2005). Using this framework, we suggest, one can grasp all the key facets of hospital output and innovation. In other words, the framework integrates the four existing approaches to hospital innovation discussed in Chapter 4, that is, the production function approach, the capabilities approach, the information approach and the systems approach.

7.2.1 A Functional Breakdown of Hospital Output

An arithmetic definition of hospital output as the association of different constituent services cannot capture all the key facets of hospital output and innovation. Rather, one must break into the 'black box' of each constituent service. Drawing on the findings of the economics of (private sector) services (Hill, 1977, 1999; Gadrey, 1996, 2000) and the economics of (private sector) services innovation (Gallouj and Weinstein, 1997; Gallouj, 2002), we envisage hospital output as a complex activity that is captured by linking four variables (see Table 7.1). These are the constituent services (S_i), the principal medium of service delivery (M, I, K, R), the basic service characteristics or use values (Y) and the service providers' competences (C).

Table 7.1 A functional breakdown of hospital output or service

Constituent services	Competences mobilized	Service medium, corresponding operations or functions and associated technologies				('External') use, final or service characteristics or functions
S_i	*C*	*M*	*I*	*K*	*R*	*Y*
	Competences in (the use of) technologies or competences directly mobilized	'Material' operations (plus corresponding sciences and technologies)	'Informational' operations (plus corresponding sciences and technologies)	'Methodological' operations (plus corresponding sciences and technologies)	Contractual or relational service operations (plus corresponding sciences and technologies)	Service functions and characteristics (plus corresponding disciplines)
S_1: Medical treatment/ nursing care		XXXXXXXX	XXXXXXXX			
S_2: Accommodation						
Maintenance						
Reception						
Transport						
Management, administration						
Catering						
Creche						
Laundry						
Leisure						
Retail activities						
Funeral services						
Cleaning, waste processing						

Note: The shaded area represents the main concerns of the literature devoted to innovation in hospitals.

The 'basic constituent service' of a hospital is the medical treatment itself. However, hospital services cannot be reduced to an individual treatment or care. Hospitals are complex organizations that provide a wide range of other services. The constituent services that make up a hospital's output can be categorized into three main groups:

1. Services of the hotel/catering type
2. Administrative and managerial services
3. Medical and paramedical services.

In reality, there are other constituent services that fall outside these three categories. These can include, for example, the various retail activities (shops) located within a hospital, recreational activities, beauty treatments and child-minding services.

Each constituent service (S_i) combines four groups of operations (and of corresponding technologies) in differing proportions, depending on the medium through which the service in question is provided (tangible object, codified information, knowledge and the clients themselves). These operations are:

1. Logistical and material transformation operations (M) which involve the processing of tangible objects.
2. Logistical and information processing operations (I) which involve the processing of codified information.
3. Methodological operations involving the intellectual processing of knowledge (K) using codified methods and intangible technologies.
4. Relational service operations (R) in which the principal medium is the customer.

The service characteristics are located downstream in our breakdown of output. Difficulties in identifying and labelling these can vary depending on the type of constituent service in question. They describe the utilities derived from the deployment, during the various types of operations that make up the service provision, of the internal technical components and/or competences.

The service providers' competences are located upstream in our breakdown of output. These relate to individuals or to small groups (the team or teams involved in delivery of the service). Competences are derived from various sources. They include initial education and training, continuing training, experience and, more generally, the various interactions that are sources of learning. They may be competences in the technologies deployed and the various types of operations carried out or they may be competences that are directly mobilized, without any technical mediation, in order to produce utilities Y (the 'pure service' situation).

Table 7.1 therefore provides a representation of hospital output in all its functional and technological diversity. Hospital output can be represented as the aggregate of various types of constituent services S_i but each S_i can itself be a combination, to varying degrees, of basic operations carried out on objects, information, knowledge or individuals. This framework refers to hospitals in their totality, that is, at the organizational level. However, intra- and inter-organizational perspectives are also possible and likely to enrich our analysis of innovation. This means that each constituent service (for example, medical services, accommodation services or catering services) can be broken down into a further set of constituent services s_{ij}, which could constitute independent units of analysis. The inter-organizational level, for its part, takes account of a hospital's integration into the external environment.

7.2.2 A Framework for Analysing Innovation in Hospitals

The general framework outlined above is an attempt to break into the 'black box' of hospital activity. It captures not only a hospital's end product but also all its intermediate products, and the products developed in collaboration with external actors. It provides us with a general framework for analysing innovation in hospitals.

Innovation can take place in any square of Table 7.1. Innovation may also involve adding or eliminating squares of the table. Over and above the diversity of innovation that is captured, the framework can also be used to highlight a limited number of 'organizing principles' that drive innovation in hospitals. These organizing principles can be described as extensive, regressive, intensive and combinatory.

7.2.2.1 The extensive and regressive organizing principles

We analyse together the extensive and regressive principles as far as they are similar in nature. Both act on the rows of Table 7.1.

At the organizational, intra-organizational or inter-organizational levels of analysis, the extensive organizing principle leads to rows being added to the table. In other words, constituent services (S_i or s_{ij}) are added to the core service. To some extent, this extensive model of innovation comes within the framework of certain types of differentiation strategies, and in particular of so-called improvement strategies, which involve considerable enhancement of a service provision through the addition of new characteristics that are valued by customers or users. Extending the range of specialities and services on offer, and competing on the range of services provided, seem to be important elements in hospitals' strategies.

Conversely, the regressive organizing principle involves the elimination of constituent services. That is, the elimination of rows from the table.

7.2.2.2   The intensive organizing principle

For a given constituent service S_i (for example, medical treatment, accommodation services and cleaning), the intensive mode of innovation involves changing at least one component of a hospital's output. This may occur by adding new competences and/or (tangible or intangible) technologies (which may be accompanied by the elimination of old competences and/or technologies) or by increasing (or sometimes reducing) the significance of existing competences and/or technologies. Hence, the intensive principle manifests itself in (positive or negative) action on the columns of Table 7.1. This intensive mode of innovation can follow five different trajectories: a logistical and material transformation trajectory; a logistical and information processing trajectory; a methodological and cognitive trajectory; a pure 'service' trajectory; and a relational trajectory.

The logistical and material transformation trajectory   This trajectory operates on the part of the service that relates to logistics and material transformations. This is a traditional (or 'natural' in the words of Nelson and Winter (1982)) trajectory based on increasing mechanization and the exploitation of economies of scale. It accounts for developments relating to the transportation and transformation of material substances, whether human or physical. It encompasses the development of biomedical/ bio-pharmacological innovations and 'tangible' medical innovations (such as imaging), as well as technologies for processing material substances within hospitals (for example, transportation systems for individuals or equipment, cooking and refrigeration systems, cleaning systems and various kinds of dispensing machines).

The logistical and information processing trajectory   This trajectory operates on the logistical/information components of a service. Its principal features are reductions in communication costs, the establishment of networks, the production of new information and new ways of using information. It corresponds to the dynamics highlighted by the information approach to hospital innovation (see above and Chapter 4).

The methodological and cognitive trajectory   This trajectory operates on the production and evolution of formalized methods of processing knowledge (that is, codified routines). It is mainly encountered, though not exclusively, in intellectual services. For example, it also plays a role in some operational services, such as cleaning or transport (see Djellal, 2000, 2002; Sundbo, 1996, 1998).

The pure 'service' trajectory   The service trajectory is an ideal type of trajectory that describes service innovations which evolve independently of any technological medium, that is, through the direct mobilization of competency C to provide the service functions or characteristics Y. They may be embodied in a particular organization and, therefore, they are to some extent organizational innovations (in which technical systems are not important).

The relational trajectory   The relational trajectory is a path taken by innovations in the direct service component. This accounts for the introduction of contact service functions and characteristics or new forms of client/provider relationship and their evolution over time. A particular characteristic of this trajectory is that, in some situations, it can be co-produced by the client and the service provider. It is difficult, therefore, to separate the relational trajectory from the pure service trajectory and from the material, informational or methodological trajectories.

7.2.2.3 The combinatory principle
Combinatory or architectural innovation is the most commonly encountered principle. It encompasses all innovation mechanisms associated with the various principles outlined above (extensive, regressive and intensive). In other words, the combinatory model of innovation is based on the association and dissociation of constituent services, and of the corresponding technologies and competences. It can also be at work at the organizational, intra-organizational and inter-organizational levels.

In Table 7.1 this combinatory principle affects several rows and/or columns, which it combines and/or separates in order to produce an innovation. In this sense the innovation process is rather like a puzzle in which various squares in the grid are combined in order to obtain a new service.

7.3   EMPIRICAL APPLICATION OF THE FRAMEWORK

Having outlined the theoretical framework, this section applies its organizing principles to a set of innovation case studies. These case studies are drawn from a mixture of existing case studies (primarily conducted in France) and expert interviews conducted by the authors in French hospitals. We examine each of the organizing principles and trajectories in turn.

7.3.1   The Extensive Organizing Principle

The constituent services that are added may be drawn from any of the major groups of hospital services previously identified; that is, medical and paramedical services; accommodation, catering or retailing services; and managerial or administrative services. As previously noted, innovation within hospitals (and the research conducted by social scientists) tends to focus on medical and paramedical services at the expense of others. However, the other groups' potential for expressing extensive innovation is very considerable. It should not be ignored, just as we should not ignore the opportunities for innovation offered by other categories of services (leisure activities, recreation and so on).

The literature provides a large number of examples of innovations related to this extensive organizing principle. Some of these are very well known: bookshops, gift shops, mini-supermarkets, florists, toy shops, sweet shops, photographers, pharmacies, recreational activities for children, fitness centres and childcare service. Others are more unconventional: banks, shoe repairers, dry cleaners, travel agencies, legal advice units (Swindley and Thompson,1992); the provision of classes in various fields, such as bicycle repairs, dancing and coping with divorce (Sasaki, 2003); and the provision of taxi services for people who have been drinking. In the field of non-medical services other examples are the introduction of new administative departments, such as management control, communications and quality assurance departments, as well as the provision of new accommodation modes: hotels or family houses in hospitals for patients receiving out-patient treatment and/or their families, luxury hospital suites, and restaurants for in-patients and their families.

7.3.2   The 'Regressive' Organizing Principle

In contrast to regional and/or teaching hospitals, local hospitals are characterized by limited technical capacities and services, which can be analysed as the elimination of many of the constituent services provided by regional and teaching hospitals. Thus, in a sense, the regressive organizing principle is at the basis of the distinction between these two types of hospitals.

The regressive principle might also reasonably be considered to manifest itself in two other situations. It is undoubtedly at work in the outsourcing strategies that have been implemented particularly in logistical functions within hospitals (Cubbin et al., 1987). It is also at the heart of the establishment of hospitals specializing in very strictly defined diseases (for example, hand surgery or foot lesions suffered by diabetics). The development in the USA of the MinuteClinic concept is one example among others. This is a mini doctor's surgery which treats a limited number of common complaints, such as ear, bladder and sinus infections, strep throat and so on, with a waiting time commitment (less than 15 minutes) and without the need to make an appointment. Teboul (1999) also provides an example of a private clinic that only treats patients with inguinal hernias. It does not accept, for example, obese people suffering from hernias or patients declaring a history of heart disease. By offering highly standardized surgical treatments, labour productivity is very high.

7.3.3 The Intensive Organizing Principle

As discussed in Section 7.2.2.2, the intensive organizing principle can follow five different trajectories: a logistical and material transformation trajectory; a logistical and information processing trajectory; a methodological and cognitive trajectory; a pure 'service' trajectory; and, finally, a relational trajectory.

7.3.3.1 The logistical and material transformation trajectory

Examples of innovations related to this trajectory are also numerous. They can be divided into two groups according to the medical or non-medical dimension of the process. Examples of technologies associated with the (non-medical) 'processing' of physical or human matter are motorized bed-moving equipment, new cooking equipment, new food transport systems and multi-functional vehicles adapted for the specific needs of hospital logistics. In the field of laundering services, examples include the introduction of automatic feeders, automatic stackers and tunnel finishers (Sachot, 1989). Other examples are the introduction of microfibre technology in cleaning equipment and processes, automatic cleaning robots and so on. The (medical) logistical and material transformation trajectory can be illustrated by the following examples: the introduction of new or improved drug treatments or medicines and the use of new technical tools (ultrasonic dissectors, high-tech hip protectors for elderly patients, and disposable and single-use items, such as syringes).

Further examples of innovations falling within the scope of the logistical and material transformation trajectory are provided by Planchon (1996) and Bertrand et al. (1994). Planchon (1996) examines the introduction of a multi-purpose vehicle at the Centre Hospitalier du Blanc. The idea of designing a multi-purpose vehicle, suited to the needs of the Centre Hospitalier du Blanc, originated within a working group that was established around the hospital director. Apart from the director, the working group consisted of the senior supervisor in charge of safety and hygiene, the technical services manager and a nursing aide in charge of personnel.

The hospital needs to deal with the problem of logistical inefficiency caused by carts used for a number of different purposes (for example, carrying meals, linen, household waste and goods for shops) on three different sites and in extremely varied conditions. The items transported may be packaged very differently (for example, in bags or containers), they may have to be loaded and unloaded at ground level or at variable heights, and so on. In order to solve these difficulties, and realize productivity gains, the working group put forward the idea of developing removable and interchangeable containers, of variable height, that could be placed on a transporting vehicle. The working group proposed five different types of container: one container for the kitchens, one 'clean' container (linen, shop goods), one 'dirty' container (linen, dustbins), a trailer for bulky objects, and a container with three compartments and side access (a meal compartment, a 'clean' compartment and a 'dirty' compartment) designed to meet the logistical requirements of residential homes for the elderly. This proposal was passed on to an external coach builder who developed it.

Bertrand et al. (1994) examine the establishment of a discharge preparation unit at the Lannion-Trestel general hospital. The functional rehabilitation centre at this hospital established a discharge preparation unit for disabled people with reduced mobility. The unit's purpose is to assess disabilities and encourage rehabilitation and the development of a certain degree of autonomy in daily life (at home and for car journeys). The discharge preparation unit is based around three technological systems:

1. A therapeutic apartment consisting of five rooms (kitchen, bedroom, bathroom, toilet and laundry room), which places disabled people in real-life situations so that their disabilities can be assessed and architectural problems evaluated.
2. An apartment simulator, which enables the layout of the apartment to be adapted to each individual's particular disability. In this simulator, the partitions, as well as the various items of equipment (washbasin, shower, bath and so on), can be moved and adjusted.
3. A specially equipped car (fitted out in collaboration with a manufacturer and a driving school). The various pieces of equipment in this car are also scalable and adjustable.

7.3.3.2 The logistical and information processing trajectory

Management constituent services are obviously a relevant locus for the development of the informational trajectory in that their main activity is dealing with information. Examples of innovations falling within the scope of this trajectory are automatic payment stations for hospital revenue collection,[1] electronic interactive systems for work schedules, ultra-sophisticated processing and dispatching centres for emergency calls. However, management constituent services are not the only locus for the informational trajectory. It is also at work in the management of material flows (digital kitchen, stock management, software for health waste elimination tracing and so on) and it is increasingly pervasive in medical services (telemedicine, barcode use, portable skin-screening camera for cancer detection).

The teleworking experiment at the Pierre-le-Damany hospital in Lannion (Ponchon et al., 1998; Ponchon, 1999) is a good example of an innovation with an information processing trajectory. In 1998 the Pierre-le-Damany hospital found itself facing space problems as a result of an ongoing refurbishment and conversion programme. The management of the Admissions and Patient Management Department decided to experiment with teleworking. The experiment was part of a complete reorganization of the hospital's administrative functions. The starting point for the experiment was a recognition that various administrative tasks (such as management of service users' records, input of payment orders and input of variable pay elements) can be carried out without the need for workers to be physically present at the hospital.

The experiment lasted six months. It involved one volunteer from the hospital's administrative department. The volunteer was linked to the hospital's local area network through a computer installed in his home. In this way, the whole of the existing office system was transferred to the employee's home. However, in order to avoid isolation, he was required to work in the office for one day a week and to attend department meetings. The experiment was relatively inexpensive and saved a considerable amount of office space. When it came to an end other possibilities for creating new (administrative) jobs for teleworkers or converting existing jobs were examined.

7.3.3.3   The methodological and cognitive trajectory

The term 'methodological trajectories' denotes the development and improvement of a wide range of intangible technologies (which are sometimes described as invisible technologies) at work in hospital services. Once again, a starting point for analysis is to divide them into two groups, the first one consisting of those deployed in medical treatments and the second group consisting of those deployed for other (that is, non-medical) purposes (services, management and so on).

The first group of intangible technologies, those deployed in medical treatments, contains two particularly fertile sub-groups. They are, first, treatment protocols, therapeutic strategies (care maps, critical paths, practice guidelines) (Coffey et al., 1991; Hoffman, 1993; Lumsdon and

Hagland, 1993) and hygiene protocols (including those drawn up to combat nosocomial diseases). They are, second, measurement or diagnostic methods. In the field of healthcare for the elderly, for example, measurement and diagnostic methods are a fertile field of research and innovation that is directed at a multitude of different targets: assessment of the degree of dementia, dependency, memory, pain; the design of indicators of well-being, quality of life and so on. Thus, there are a multitude of international assessment scales (Borrel, 1996; Dubuisson and Gardeur, 2000): the ADL (Activities of Daily Living) scale, the Mini-Mental State Examination, the Clinical Dementia Rating, the Geriatric Index of Comorbidity (these scales emphasize the medical dimension, that is, the identification of mental or physical pathologies), the Barthel scale (which relates to daily activities such as washing, dressing and so on), the Lawton and Brody scale (which relates to the ability to perform instrumental activities such as telephoning, shopping, taking medication and so on) and the Feifer scale (used to assess cognitive capacities). Innovation trajectories in this sphere are driven by the following factors: the object or target of measurement, the initial level of application (local, national, international) and the degree of novelty in the method. An innovation may involve the introduction of new assessment systems directed at new targets (or even a combination of several new and/or old targets). Equally, it may involve the adaptation of existing tools to new contexts, for example, by simplifying them or making them more generally applicable.

Methodological trajectories are also evident in non-medical services. The literature provides a wide range of examples of innovation falling within the scope of these trajectories: management of meals, sophisticated toxic waste cleaning protocols, quality procedures for stretcher bearers (Bernardy-Arbuz and Bannier, 1999), methodologies against the forging of medical prescriptions (Gestions Hospitalières, 1994), trend charts for quality and risk management (Bonhomme et al., 1994).

Other examples are a creativity process at Poitiers teaching university, the AGGIR model and the Resource Use Groups. Huteau (1996) discusses the development of a creativity process at Poitiers teaching university. Since the mid-1990s, Poitiers teaching hospital had been seeking to create conditions that would encourage the emergence and development of a creativity process in the hospital. This move was initiated by the nursing department and nursing teams. It concerned all occupational categories: nurses, disinfection staff, ancillary staff, nursing auxiliaries, nursery nurses and auxiliary nursery nurses, dieticians, physiotherapists and supervisors. The purpose of this initiative was to improve the quality of care, and to create a new corporate culture and a new image for the hospital. More precisely, the objectives were:

- To turn individual and collective initiatives to good account.
- To give greater recognition to nurses' achievements, which frequently go unrecognized.
- To motivate nursing teams and encourage them to develop novel solutions within their units.
- To show how creativity contributes to improvements in patient services.
- To develop team spirit and teams' internal dynamic.

The various projects, which took place over a period of about 15 months (12 months to plan the project and a maximum of three months to prepare and carry out the work), ended with a final presentation during 'creativity days' organized in the hospital.

Another key example is the Autonomie Gérontologique Groupes Iso-Ressources[2] (AGGIR) model with Resource Use Groups. The AGGIR model is used to evaluate the degree of personal autonomy loss among elderly people and to define homogeneous groups of dependent people. It comprises ten discriminatory variables that assess the loss of physical and psychological autonomy (for example, coherence, orientation and dressing) and seven illustrative variables that assess loss of domestic and social autonomy (such as management, food preparation, household tasks). Six dependency or Resource Use Groups (RUG) are identified on this basis, ranging from RUG 1 where elderly people are confined to bed or an arm-chair and whose intellectual functions are seriously impaired to RUG 6 where individuals still have their autonomy in performing the basic acts of everyday life.

7.3.3.4 The pure service trajectory

This can manifest itself at any level of an organization. However, it seems to be particularly important in front-office activities involving direct contact with customers or users (for example, reception services and admissions). There are many examples in the literature, such as reception services targeted at specific groups, such as disadvantaged patients and foreigners. Diebolt et al. (1995) examine the Foreign Patients Unit at Broussais hospital in Paris. At the beginning of the 1990s foreign patients accounted for more than 16 per cent of admissions to the Broussais hospital. At the same time the hospital was dealing with a sharp increase in the number of stays that were not paid for. These accounted for more than 7.5 per cent of the total sums to be recovered for the group. It was against this background that the hospital decided, in 1991, to set up the Foreign Patients Unit. Its task was to deal with the problems associated with the admission of foreign patients. The unit's purpose, therefore, was to regulate requests for admission on behalf of foreign patients, and to attempt to reconcile clinical imperatives with administrative and financial constraints. This was necessary in order to stay within the limits of underwritten and/or recoverable costs and to reduce the losses borne by the hospital in respect of patients without healthcare cover.

The originality of this unit principally lies in its multi-disciplinary composition. It comprises, on a voluntary basis, four representatives of the medical staff (two physicians, a surgeon and an anaesthetist), three employees from the admissions/cost recovery department and two social workers. The establishment of the unit was accompanied by an internal information campaign aimed at nursing managers and department heads. The unit operates on the basis of a system of standbys for emergency duties and weekly meetings for the staff concerned. The task of the staff on standby (available 24/7) is to regulate patient hospitalization flows. The staff who undertake this task include an administrator and a representative of the medical staff, who can be contacted at any time. The weekly meetings are attended by all the staff involved in the unit and provide a forum for permanent review of foreign patient admissions. A formal system for monitoring patient files has also been established by the unit's administrative staff.

The unit has helped to effect a radical change in the medical care of foreign patients. In particular, it has reduced the length of hospital stays (for equivalent quality of care). It has also contributed to a sharp reduction in unpaid bills (by more than a half), despite the fact that attendance at the unit is increasing. There seem to be good prospects for further developing the experiment. The aim of the project's proponents is to develop and intensify contacts outside the hospital, particularly with reception facilities and social security funds abroad. Furthermore, the success of the initiative offers encouragement to those seeking to extend it to other groups of patients.

Lebas (1995), Lebas and Chauvin (1998) and Loriol (2002) examine consultations for those socially excluded. 'Clinics for the socially excluded' or 'vulnerable persons units' are relatively small departments, which were set up in hospitals from the beginning of the 1990s onwards. Their objectives are logistical (relieving pressure on accident and emergency departments) and medico-social (providing services for insolvent patients with the support of social workers). The units are often run by teams of nurses rather than a doctor. The first initiative of this kind was launched in 1992 at the Saint-Antoine hospital in Paris, under the name of the 'Baudelaire scheme'. Some 3500 people per year are now assisted under the scheme. Each person attending the clinic is given a medical and a social assessment. The primary purpose of the social assessment is to open up access to social security benefits. The cost of the unit, at 350 francs per month per patient

in 1996, is minimal compared with the savings made by avoiding inappropriate hospital stays (the hospitalization rate for these patients is only 1
per cent).

A number of schemes of this kind have been set up since 1994. However,
their expansion is constrained by a conflict between two opposing perceptions. On the one hand, they are seen as an attempt to provide care and
support for those socially excluded in accordance with an enlightened
social and civic value system. On the other hand, they are regarded as
schemes governed more by market or commercial values (reducing the pressure on accident and emergency departments, cutting costs and isolating
vulnerable populations from other patient groups in order to maintain a
certain image) that are providing 'healthcare on the cheap' (by economiz-
ing on human and technical resources).

7.3.3.5   The relational trajectory
It is often difficult to consider relational trajectories independently because
they may merge with various other trajectories. For example, the following
innovations also have a strong relational component and also belong to a
relational trajectory: a reception unit for foreigners, a mobile psychiatric
emergency service, the establishment of experimental administrative units
in nursing departments in order to provide comprehensive patient reception services (see Ponchon, 1999), and internal and external systems for
transporting equipment and people (self-propelling vehicles, wheelchairs,
robots and so on).

More generally, it can be said that most of the experiments targeted
towards customer/patient loyalty fall within the scope of both methodological and relational trajectories. For example, strategies devoted to
waiting times reduction seek greater customer satisfaction (relational trajectory), but are not possible without the implementation of specific
methods and work organization (methodological trajectories).

An example of an innovation falling within the scope of the relational
and informational trajectories is provides by Argacha (1991). Pau hospital
in the south of France has set up interactive information stations. They are
aimed at several different types of users (both internal and external), but
primarily at patients and their families. On the basis of a detailed study
of the hospital's reception functions, two broad groups of users were
identified. The first group is 'scheduled users'. These are patients who have
appointments in a department and who already have some initial information. This group's needs are essentially twofold: confirmation of the initial
information and directions to the department where they are expected. The
second group is 'unscheduled users'. These are mainly families and visitors
who need basic information to orient themselves (for example, room

number and visiting hours) as well as more detailed information on admissions, the stay in hospital and the management of appointments.

Implementation of this project was based on detailed job analyses (studies of reception and patient support functions, and management of day-to-day operations) and on existing, albeit fragmented, communications networks. The project's success rested on cooperation between several internal and external actors, notably the hospital's reception team, switchboard, admissions department, nursing management, IT department and communications department, as well as an IT company that had already been involved in a number of projects with the hospital.

The advantages of this innovation are threefold. First, for the hospital as a whole, the information stations are an important vehicle in the dissemination of the hospital's image. The information stations have played their part in opening up the communications network and provide reliable, updated information on the main aspects of the hospital. Second, for hospital staff, the information stations facilitate the identification and personalization of various areas of activity in the hospital and the sharing of common values, such as increased opportunities to compare opinions, and the development of common reference points. Finally, for patients, the information stations provide immediate access to accurate information about the hospital, the location of the various departments (orientation/directions) and the main medical personnel people will deal with. They also provide information for patients on the functioning of the hospital (for example, admission conditions and out-patient clinics) and the services provided, as well as general information on the hospital's public service mission and the part it plays in civic life.

7.3.4   The Combinatory Organizing Principle

The combinatory principle is the most commonly found innovation principle. It is at work at different analytical levels. It is at work in the frequent hybridization of material and informational trajectories in hospitals. Trajectories can intertwine and become inseparable. Indeed, microelectronics and IT have gradually pervaded all physical or human material operations (medical instrumentation, equipment or patient transport systems). Examples of hybrid medical technologies are quite numerous and often spectacular: computer-aided diagnostics, medical supervision, automated diagnostic equipment, video surgery, imaging (magnetic resonance imaging, scanography, video endoscopy and nuclear medicine, particularly scintigraphy). The pervasive and generic dimension of the informational trajectories (that is, their ability to merge not only with the material trajectory but also with all the other trajectories) is illustrated by the evolution

towards the so-called digital hospitals, that is, hospitals where fully integrated systems are available from the kitchen to the administration to the
patients' bedsides.

The introduction of orthopaedic robotics and surgery at the Eaubonne-
Montmorency hospital and of an autonomous robot at Montpellier
teaching hospital are examples of the combinatory principle (at the intra-
organizational level). The Eaubonne-Montmorency hospital was the first
French hospital to fit a total hip prosthesis with assistance from a robot called
CASPAR. The hospital carried out a medical/medico-technical assessment
of the robot in collaboration with the Agence Nationale d'Accréditation et
d'Evaluation en Santé (ANAES) at the beginning of 2000. CASPAR is a
flexible and upgradeable multi-functional robot that is equipped with six
joints, giving it a high degree of mobility. CASPAR can be used with different
instruments, such as drills, oscillating saws and reamers. Its purpose is to
assist the surgeon in both planning and performing operations. Computer-
assisted pre-operative planning, using 3-D images, takes place outside the
operating theatre. The surgeon prepares for the operation by using planning
software to programme the fitting procedure – this also constitutes a radical
innovation compared with standard pre-operative planning. As a result of
this procedure the reaming is both more accurate (to within one-tenth of a
millimetre) and safer. The data are then transmitted to the robot.

For both the patient and the surgeon, CASPAR has many advantages
with regards to safety, reliability and traceability (the entire operation can
be retraced because it is recorded in the program), as well as reproducibil-
ity and manoeuvrability. It considerably increases the chance of success,
and contributes to a considerable improvement in quality of the outcome.
CASPAR was designed as a universal system for bone and joint surgery.
The robot is currently used in hip replacement surgery and in knee liga-
mentoplasty but many new applications are envisaged, such as total or
partial knee prostheses, corrective knee osteotomy, the fitting of pedicle
screws in spinal surgery and even shoulder prostheses.

Storper and Labrouve (1996) discuss the introduction of an autonomous
robot at the Montpellier teaching hospital. An automatic mobile robot,
known as HelpMate, was first trialled in 1995. HelpMate is an Amercian
technology, distributed in Europe by Otis, and had previously been used in
a number of US and Canadian hospitals. The trials at the Montpellier
teaching hospital used HelpMate in the transport department to deliver
tissue and blood samples. However, many other uses can be envisaged. In
particular, there is the transportation of meal trays, different types of
instruments, medical files, test results, and letters and parcels.

HelpMate is the result of the combination (hybridization) of different types of technologies: computing, robotics, transport, infrared and

ultrasound. The robot has a powerful on-board computer which can be programmed to store the routes that are to be negotiated, whether horizontally (through the hospital corridors) or vertically (using the goods lifts). All that has to be done is to enter the coordinates of the destination on a numerical keypad. HelpMate moves about totally independently and is able to take the lift, open automatic doors and go round obstacles using its infrared and ultrasonic detectors. Furthermore, it is fitted with a voice synthesizer that can deliver more than ten different messages.

The combinatory principle can also be envisaged at another level – the creation of a new type or concept of hospital. This can be analysed as the building of a new institution by the combination of constituent services (S_i), of technologies (M, I, K) and competences C. When the concept is particularly new, innovation and change cover a large area of our analytical table, if not the entire area. This is the case, for example, in the Jeanne de Flandre hospital in Lille. The hospital combines a wide range of innovations in the services it provides, such as the organization, the architectural and ergonomic features, the technologies used and so on.

The combinatory principle is also at work, at an inter-organizational level, in most network structure experiments. These include community health networks and coordinated care networks. Networks bring together and combine different constituent services and their corresponding actors. Network experiments are not a homogeneous group. They differ according to the number and nature of actors involved, their objectives and the technologies mobilized.

Community health networks that bring together doctors in private practice and those working in hospitals and other actors are very diverse. They have been established in a very wide range of different medical and sociomedical areas (gerontology, perinatology, HIV, diabetes, hepatitis C and in social exclusion) and sometimes at the intersection of different areas (for example, the provision of care for pregnant drug addicts and their children).

Networks may take other forms and be more or less sophisticated. The simplest forms are probably networks established between several hospitals in order to jointly purchase and/or share the use of expensive equipment, such as scanners and MRI machines. But more complex networks are also possible. For example, hospital mergers, cooperation between public and private structures and the takeover of one hospital by another. Another form of networking is also frequently encountered; the creation within hospitals (or close to them) of units intended to create links with generalists. Examples include walk-in treatment centres for minor emergencies that are operated and managed by (outside) doctors and nurses, and geriatric units run by (outside) general practitioners and social workers.

Other experiments fall within the scope of the combinatory principle. Home-based treatment is one of these. It uses technologies, methodologies and competences in order to combine hospital and home, whether this is to introduce the hospital to the home or vice versa (Arras, 1995; Bentur, 2001). Another interesting example is provided by the ways in which patients' associations involve hospitals in inter-organizational activities and determine research in particular fields (Rabeharisoa and Callon, 1998).

A number of case studies have been conducted which highlight innovations that fall within the scope of the combinatory principle (at the inter-organizational level). To start with, there is the Barcet et al. (2002) case study of a network involving a local authority, a public hospital and patients' homes in the Lyon area. The network brought together a wide range of actors from very different backgrounds in the non-commercial public and commercial private sectors. They included healthcare providers and professionals (public and private hospitals, doctors, nurses and medical laboratories), as well as social and political actors (local authorities and various associations) and industrialists (a number of producers of medical equipment and products).

The aim was to provide home care for patients receiving hospital treatment for serious illnesses or else with a high level of dependency because of concurrent multiple diseases (polypathology). The experiment had three aims. First, to place patients at the heart of the healthcare system. Second, to help patients retain a degree of quality of life (particularly through better integration into their social environment). Third, to optimize hospital bed allocation.

Having investigated the conditions under which the experiment may diffuse more widely, Barcet et al. see this innovation as heralding the emergence of a new model of service production – one that seems perfectly suited to some of the specificities of hospitals and healthcare provision. The new model is, after all, an appropriate one for dealing with the problems facing a universal service, in which a wide range of different professions work in collaboration with self-governing institutions. It is also likely to encourage the development of greater responsibility and collaboration amongst independent professionals. It provides a basis for efficient management of the random flows of singular events that characterize a universal health service while at the same time minimizing coordination costs (economies of networking). Finally, the model is conducive to combining market principles, on the one hand, and public sector and charitable/voluntary principles, on the other.

Implementation of the combinatory principle at the inter-organizational level is illustrated by a number of other examples of public and private sector cooperation in healthcare. The Nord-Pas-de-Calais region seems to be particularly active in this regard with several 'healthcare consortia' set up there. It was in Lens that the first healthcare consortium in the region was established, bringing together a public hospital specializing in heart surgery and a large private hospital specializing in cardiology. This consortium has been undeniably successful, with more than 400 operations carried out each year, and has considerably helped reduce what had been long waiting lists in the region.

Another example is the healthcare consortium which brings together the Lille teaching hospital and a private hospital that specializes in hand surgery. Following the establishment of this consortium, the teaching hospital's hand surgery unit has been relocated to the private hospital. This unit has ten public and ten private beds, and a single surgical team made up of public and private sector surgeons who specialize in hand surgery and microsurgery.

The Agence Régionale Hospitalière[3] (ARH) in Nord-Pas-de-Calais presents yet another example. It encourages the pooling of interventional cardiology services, both diagnostic and therapeutic, in four public–private centres. The first was in Valenciennes, followed by Lens, Boulogne-sur-Mer and then Roubaix. Using the same technical facilities, public and private-sector doctors treat patients requiring interventional cardiology procedures. Procedures are carried out day and night, Saturdays and Sundays included. According to professional standards, a doctor must perform at least 100 angioplasty dilatations per year in order to be considered competent, while an angioplasty centre has to carry out at least 400 procedures per year. This is impossible for individual doctors, but feasible if the technical facilities are shared. Since the establishment of these cooperations, local doctors have been able to develop excellent competences in this procedure.

7.4   CONCLUSION

The hospital is a complex service organization, providing a broad and open range of services that accompany and influence the quality of the care. It is a 'multi-service' system which brings together and coordinates medical and non-medical services. One can even view the hospital as being composed of multi-product companies in which different services are carried out by different producers (Mougeot, 1994).

The forms and modes of innovation are very diverse within such an organization. Our assumption is that medical innovation is not synonymous with hospital innovation. In other words, hospital innovation is a much broader category than medical innovation. It is thus necessary for the hospital actors, for the public authorities, but also for research in social sciences to take into account the various locations of innovation and their actors and to examine their interactions (their reciprocal effects, their conflicts).

The perspective of innovation as a technical system is fundamental. Indeed, this perspective needs to be developed, particularly with resepct to areas where this is neglected, such as logistics, catering and cleaning. It is not our intention to devalue the role of the doctors. Rather, the point is not to neglect any source or form of innovation, or any actor promoting innovation that contributes to better quality services, to improved economic efficiency and to improved hospital performance more generally. Thus, in addition to new MRI scanners and other medical devices, we need to take into account improvements in the reception of patients, the introduction of new organizational forms and new services in the non-medical sectors, the development of new types of cooperations, innovative network structures and so on.

In this chapter we have tried to provide a structured and systematic analytical framework of hospital innovation. The theoretical framework is based on the results of services economics and evolutionary economics of innovation. It allows us to grasp the diversity of the forms and actors of innovation in a hospital at different levels. One can use it to study the hospital as a whole, to study some of its components or the analysis of the hospital as one element in a network of care.

The relatively flexible framework that we have proposed allows us to draw up a cartography (satisfactory, if not exhaustive) of the locations of hospital innovation (in its various dimensions). The aim is to provide a theoretical basis for the construction of questionnaires devoted to innovation within hospitals. Such questionnaires would enable one to statistically validate the relevance of the categories suggested. From a more dynamic, strategic and prospective point of view, they would allow managers to consider the innovation trajectories that are possible (or desirable) in a hospital and in the health system more generally.

NOTES

1. This trajectory is also relational.
2. Resource Use Groups for the dependent elderly.
3. Regional Hospitals Agency.

REFERENCES

Argacha, J.P. (1991), 'Borne interactive de communication', *Gestions Hospitalières*, **311**, 910–12.
Arras, J.D. (ed.) (1995), *Bringing the Hospital Home*, Baltimore, MD: Johns Hopkins University Press.

Barcet, A., J. Bonamy and M. Grojean (2002), 'Une innovation de service par la mise en réseau de services: réflexion sur une expérience dans les services de santé', presented at the 12th RESER Conference, Manchester, CRIC and PREST, 26–27 September.

Bentur, N. (2001), 'Hospital at home: what is its place in the health system?', *Health Policy*, **55**, 71–9.

Bernardy-Arbuz, M.-A. and M.-F. Bannier (1999), 'La démarche qualité au service des Trans'comm', *Gestions Hospitalières*, February, 98–101.

Bertrand, E., A. Escoutay and C. Paillat (1994), 'Unité de retour à domicile', *Gestions Hospitalières*, **334**(March), 223–4.

Bonhomme, D., M.-R. Astic, P. Anhoury, M.-C. Mazé and A. Mercatello (1994), 'Pour une dynamique de la gestion de la qualité et des risques à l'hôpital', *Gestions Hospitalières*, **334**(March), 208–12.

Borrel, C. (1996), 'Personnes âgées dépendantes: les définir, les compter, les décrire', *Solidarité-Santé*, **3**, 45–51.

Coffey, R.J., J.S. Richards, C.S. Remmert, S.S. Leroy, R.R. Schoville and P.J. Baldwin (1991), 'An introduction to critical paths', *Quality Management in Health Care*, **1**(1), 45–54.

Cubbin, J., S. Domberger and S. Meadowcroft (1987), 'Competition tendering and efficiency: the case of hospital cleaning', *Fiscal Studies*, **8**(3), 49–58.

Diebolt, J.M., A. Deloche and J. Willi (1995), 'La cellule "accueil étrangers" de l'hôpital Broussais', *Techniques Hospitalières*, **595**, 61–4.

Djellal, F. (2000), 'The rise of information technologies in "non-informational" services', *Vierteljahrshefte zur Wirtschaftsforschung*, **69**(4), 646–56.

Djellal, F. (2002), 'Le secteur du nettoyage face aux nouvelles technologies', *Formation Emploi*, **77**, 37–49.

Djellal, F. and F. Gallouj (2005), 'Mapping innovation dynamics in hospitals', *Research Policy*, **34**, 817–35.

Dubuisson, F. and P. Gardeur (2000), 'Amélioration de la qualité de vie en établissement d'hébergement pour personnes âgées dépendantes', *Echanges santé-social*, **99**, September, 41–8.

Gadrey, J. (1996), *L'économie des Services*, 2nd edn, Paris: La Découverte.

Gadrey, J. (2000), 'The characterization of goods and services: an alternative approach', *Review of Income and Wealth*, **46**(3), 369–87.

Gallouj, F. (2002), *Innovation in the Service Economy: The New Wealth of Nations*, Cheltenham, UK and Northampton, MA, USA: Edward Elgar.

Gallouj, F. and O. Weinstein (1997), 'Innovation in services', *Research Policy*, **26**, 537–56.

Gestions Hospitalières (1994), *Le Prix de L'innovation Hospitalière 1994*, **334**, 195–232.

Hill, T.P. (1977), 'On goods and services', *Review of Income and Wealth*, **23**(4), 315–38.

Hill, T.P. (1999), 'Tangibles, intangibles and services: a new taxonomy for the classification of output', *Canadian Journal of Economics*, **32**(2), 426–44.

Hoffman, P.A. (1993), 'Critical path method: an important tool for coordinating clinical care', *Joint Commission Journal on Quality Improvement*, **19**(7), 235–46.

Huteau, M. (1996), 'La créativité à l'hôpital', *Gestions Hopitalières*, supplement, **361**(December), 839–41.

Lebas, J. (1995), 'L'espace "Baudelaire" de l'hôpital Saint-Antoine (AP-HP)', *Techniques Hospitalières*, **595**(April), 58–61.

Lebas, J. and P. Chauvin (eds) (1998), *Précarité et Santé*, Paris: Flammarion.
Loriol, M. (2002), *L'impossible Politique de la Santé Publique en France*, Paris: Eres.
Lumsdon, K. and M. Hagland (1993), 'Mapping care', *Hospital and Health Networks*, October, 34–40.
Mougeot, M. (1994), *Systèmes de santé et concurrence*, Paris: Economica.
Nelson, R. and S. Winter (1982), *An Evolutionnary Theory of Economic Change*, Cambridge, MA and London: Belknap Harvard.
Planchon, G. (1996), 'Un véhicule multifonctionnel', *Gestions Hospitalières*, **361**, 842–4.
Ponchon, F. (1999), 'Des antennes dans les services de soins', *Gestions Hospitalières*, **383**, 96–8.
Ponchon, F., M. Boutly-Salon and D. Nicolas (1998), 'Une expérimentation de télé-travail en service administratif', *Revue Hospitalière de France*, **6**(November–December), 599–602.
Rabeharisoa, V. and M. Callon (1998), 'L'implication des malades dans les activités de recherche soutenues par l'association française contre les myopathies', *Sciences Sociales et Santé*, **16**(3), 41–64.
Sachot, E. (1989), 'La productique entre à l'hôpital', *Politique Industrielle*, Winter, 135–41.
Sasaki, L. (2003), 'Hospital offers unconventional services in hopes of attracting future patients', *Hospital Quarterly*, Spring, **6**(3), 85–6.
Storper, C. and H. Labrouve (1996), 'Une expérimentation logistique au CHU de Montpellier: évaluation d'un robot autonome', *Techniques Hospitalières*, **608**, 32–4.
Sundbo, J. (1996), 'Development of the service system in a manual service firm: a case study of the Danish ISS', *Advances in Services Marketing and Management*, **5**, 169–91.
Sundbo, J. (1998), *The Organisation of Innovation in Services*, Roskilde, Denmark: Roskilde University Press.
Swindley, D. and C. Thompson (1992), 'Hospital retailing', *Service Industries Journal*, **12**(2), 210–19.
Teboul, J. (1999), *Le Temps des Services*, Paris: Les Editions d'Organisation.

8. Patient-centred diabetes education in the UK

Paul Windrum

8.1 INTRODUCTION

This chapter analyses the birth, development and implementation of patient-centred diabetes education in the UK. It is a radical innovation within the UK National Health Service (NHS). The case study is of interest for four reasons. First, it is a pure public sector innovation. As such, it provides a clear counter-example to the suggestion that the public sector is not innovative in its own right but applies innovations developed in the private sector. The concept of patient-centred diabetes education is being driven by ongoing innovations in two areas: the public health sector and the public education sector. Second, the case study takes us beyond the usual descriptions of innovation, which overwhelmingly focus on product and process innovation in manufacturing. Patient-centred diabetes education involves innovation in multiple dimensions, simultaneously. It involves the development of a radically new concept, policy innovations and administrative/organizational innovations, as well as innovations in service and service delivery. As such, the case study highlights the expansiveness of innovation in public sector services. Third, it highlights the key role of innovation champions within the public sector. These are the counterparts to private sector entrepreneurs. These innovation champions drive the innovation process through their personal motivation, their ability to command financial and other resources, and by their networks of influence. Fourth, the case study is interesting for what it tells us about innovation in general. It forces us to reappraise what we (think we) know about innovation.

Diabetes is a chronic long-term condition for which there is, as yet, no cure. Education is a first, important, step in a longer programme of individual behaviour change. The particular programme that we analyse is the outcome of collaboration between the Salford PCT Diabetes Education Unit and a group of education specialists at Manchester Metropolitan University. Diabetes mellitus is a very common chronic disease. There are 1.4 million people with diagnosed diabetes in England, and its incidence is rising. This is a direct consequence of an ageing population – more than 10 per cent of people over 65 are diabetic – and an increasing incidence of obesity. The vast majority (85 per cent) of people living with the disease are diagnosed with type 2 diabetes. Patients with type 2 diabetes are able to produce some insulin but the levels are not sufficient to properly control their blood sugar levels.[1] It is estimated that 1 million people in the UK have the condition but are currently undiagnosed due to a lack of screening. Type 2 diabetes tends to run in families and is particularly common amongst people of African, Caribbean and Asian origin. At the moment, the average age for developing the disease is 52 years old. The average age is falling and some very overweight children are starting to become affected.

The complications associated with diabetes are very serious. They include blindness, heart disease and foot amputation. Through management of their lifestyle and daily care control, type 2 diabetes patients can control and reduce the impact of complications. The key aspects are a healthy food regime, regular physical activity, the monitoring of blood sugar levels and (if necessary) the use of drugs to control blood sugar levels. In practice, changing exercise patterns may be all but impossible for some individuals (that is, those who are badly overweight and suffering from arthritis), so the focus tends to fall on diet.

8.2 PATIENT-CENTRED EDUCATION

Patient-centred health is a radical conceptual innovation. Its introduction and development marks a major departure from the traditional healthcare model. The traditional model has proved highly effective for the treatment of acute illness. Health professionals are in overall charge of care, which includes diagnosis, treatment decisions and ensuring that treatment is carried out as prescribed. The person receiving treatment, meanwhile, is an entirely passive patient who accepts medical decisions, complies with instructions and is dependent on the healthcare professional. In the patient-centred health model the patient is the central focus of healthcare, and engages in a partnership with the healthcare professional.

In addition to the physical aspects of a condition, the knowledge and skills of the patient are important, as are their psychological, emotional and behavioural states. Within the patient–practitioner partnership, each brings their knowledge and experience to the table, engages in negotiations, and makes decisions about areas for improvement in the patient's self-care and daily choices. In the case of diabetes, the healthcare professional brings knowledge about the illness, treatment options, preventative strategies and prognosis. The diabetes patient brings their knowledge and personal experience of living with the condition, their values and beliefs, their social circumstances, habits and behaviour, and attitudes to risk taking (Coulter, 1999). The professional adopts a facilitating role, asking open questions, helping individual patients to look at alternatives and assisting in the setting of behaviour-based goals. It is argued that the patient-centred health model is more suitable than the traditional model for the treatment of chronic diseases such as diabetes (Hampson et al., 1990; Funnell et al., 1991; World Health Organization, 1998; Ashton and Rogers, 2005). This is because diabetes patients need to self-manage their condition, that is, by self-testing blood glucose, taking medication, eating healthily, caring for their feet, and balancing medication against food intake and medical activity.

The idea of patient-centred diabetes education is one manifestation of this radical concept of patient-centred health. During the period discussed by this case study (2002–05) there was no clear sense of what patient-centred diabetes education actually looked like. Rather, there were a set of experiments (of which the Salford PCT programme described here was one) which were exploring content, design and delivery. Two policy agencies determine the minimum standards of care and targets for diabetes education services to be delivered by Primary Care Trusts (PCTs) in the UK: the National Institute for Clinical Excellence (NICE) and the National Service Framework (NSF). The NSF for diabetes contains nine standards, ranging from screening, to education and to the detection of complications. The set of NICE guidelines and NSF standards issued in 2002 were deliberately left vague in order to provide a window of opportunity for the development and evaluation of new, patient-centred education programmes. Following an evaluation of several different programmes, a new set of NICE guidelines and NSF standards were issued in 2006. Still, it would be fair to say that the new set of standards are not overly prescriptive, allowing for flexibility in content and delivery in order to meet the variety of patients' needs.

Those designing and delivering patient-centred diabetes education must address a set of critical issues and constraints. First, a set of interrelated concepts need to be operationalized: patient-centred health, consumerization and empowerment. Second is the need to deal with the fundamental dilemma facing all health service providers – the opposing forces of unlimited wants on the part of users, on the one hand, and scarce and costly resources on the other.

Turning to the first of these issues, the concept of patient-centred education is strongly related to the concepts of patient empowerment and consumerization. The goal of patient-centred education is the development of empowered, self-motivated patients. This goal is framed within a political and media discourse (for example, Cumbo, 2001; Department of Health,

2004) which proposes that users of healthcare services are now highly sophisticated and demanding. They are 'customers', rather than 'patients', who are likely to litigate when errors are made. The change is said to be driven by a number of factors. The first is a shift in attitude, partly driven by the influence of the USA, where litigation is now common practice. The second is the growth of the internet as a source of medical information. The reason for the internet's popularity is easy to appreciate. Here is an opportunity for people to go beyond their GP and gain information about conditions and treatments when they want, and from many sources.

Closely linked to consumerization is the notion of individual empowerment, where the customer wishes to take responsibility for the management of their condition. Consecutive governments in the UK have been keen to place greater emphasis on the responsibility of individual 'health service consumers' to take greater care of their own health. The shift from 'passive patient' to 'empowered customer' is illustrated by the proposal, put forward in the late 1990s, that smokers should be refused cancer treatment if they failed to quit smoking (the public outcry that ensued meant that this proposal was never actually put into practice). As yet, there is no political consensus in the UK about the appropriate balance between societal and individual responsibility. However, the Labour government withdrew the 'Patient's Charter for England' – a list of rights and entitlements drawn up by the previous Conservative administration in 1991 – and replaced it with a new document, 'Your Guide to the NHS', which emphasizes patients' responsibility to look after themselves.

Turning to the issue of constraints, any education programme must deal with the fundamental dilemma that faces healthcare providers (public and private). On the one hand, there is the goal of maximizing service quality. On the other hand, public service providers need to minimize the use of highly expensive, extremely scarce resources. This fundamental dilemma pervades all discussions within the NHS, as it does for all other health service providers. The stated aim of NICE/NSF is to develop patient-centred education in order to address NHS costs by reducing (or at the very least warding off for as long as possible) diabetes-related complications of heart disease, amputations and liver damage. At the local level the PCTs delivering diabetes education need to provide a high quality service within tight budgets.

The design of patient-centred diabetes education programmes needs to negotiate these issues. Programmes that treat the trade-off differently will appear very different. Further, the success of alternative education programmes will to a large extent depend on how the trade-off between effectiveness and efficacy is addressed. Designers of a patient-centred education programme also need to address the significant problems faced by both healthcare professionals and patients in shifting to this new conceptual paradigm. For professionals, patient-centred education requires a radically different set of skills and knowledge bases to be developed in order to deliver patient-centred health. Skills and knowledge, developed over years of formulating and delivering directive education programmes (where information is imparted to passive patients), become redundant. Patient-centred diabetes education requires a very different set of skills and knowledge of how to support self-motivated patient learning and patient empowerment. This helps explain the findings of Roisin et al. (1999). They found that practitioners had extreme difficulties changing their mode of interaction with type 2 diabetes patients, and continually fell back on directive education methods and practices where 'experts' engage with 'passive patients' in a one-way discourse to impart a maximum amount of information. People with diabetes may equally find it difficult to change their behaviour and to buy in to the new paradigm. Not only do they typically lack the necessary skills and knowledge to be self-motivated, independent managers of their own disease, but the concept is often alien to them. Their previous experience of interaction with professionals is invariably under the traditional medical model. Indeed, they continue to experience the traditional model during such occasions as visits to hospitals for annual check ups, visits to foot specialists and surgery.

8.3 CONTEXT OF INNOVATION WITHIN THE NHS

It is important to understand the innovation process within its wider environment. This is more than mere contextualization. As we shall see, changes that have occurred in the NHS have directly shaped the design of the patient-centred education programme developed in Salford. They have informed the rationale, objectives and constraints of the programme's design.

A set of radical conceptual and organizational innovations have occurred within the NHS. The objective is the creation of a 'primary care led NHS' that is responsive to 'local needs'. The stated aim of the new structure is to facilitate the implementation of central government policies that reduce variations in quality and access to services, and to reduce health inequalities while ensuring that the structure of the NHS and the delivery of services focuses on making the service more patient-friendly while tackling the causes of illness with prevention strategies.

There has been a radical rethink about the management of chronic diseases within the NHS. First, local (regional) Primary Care Trusts were established to coordinate and manage resources. PCTs are umbrella bodies responsible for managing health services locally and all practitioners offering primary care services (for example, GPs, dentists and opticians).

The rationale for creating PCTs lies in the current government's belief that these institutions are best placed to understand local needs and, hence, ensure that these needs are met. PCTs control the allocation of funds awarded annually by the Department of Health, and now receive some 75 per cent of the total NHS budget. In addition to the organization of primary care services, PCTs are also responsible for secondary care organizations (that is, hospitals, mental health services and ambulance services). This is a radical change. Under this newly reformed system, secondary care organizations are no longer responsible for their own budget allocations but are dependent on their local PCT. For example, Salford PCT, the focus of this case study, is responsible for the allocation of funds for all primary care services in Salford. The PCT comprises 140 family doctors in 68 practices. Salford PCT contains a district hospital, Salford Hope Hospital.

Second, there has been a reallocation of activities between secondary trusts (hospitals) and PCTs. This includes responsibility for type 2 diabetes.[2] A key factor behind this reallocation is cost reduction. Service costs in secondary trusts are much higher than in PCTs. Following this reform, Hope Hospital is no longer charged with the care of type 2 diabetes patients.

Finally, the NSF was created in 1995 and NICE in 1999 in order to set standards of care to be consistently delivered across PCTs. In order to do this, there has been a process of evaluating needs, setting and enforcing standards of care. Within these standards the development of patient-centred diabetes education services is identified as a priority. NICE guidelines were defined to achieve more cost-effective, higher quality and standardized care and management for diabetes patients. This is a radical organizational innovation. Previously diabetes education was entirely conducted within hospitals and tended to be unstructured. The quality of education varied enormously, as it depended on the knowledge of specialists and nurses in particular hospitals, on their skills as educators and more pragmatically on their workload. In addition, the knowledge imparted tended to depend on what healthcare staff thought was necessary for patients.

The new structure embodies a major shift in power within the NHS. On the one hand, decision making, funding allocation and responsibility for service delivery have been devolved to the local level through the creation of PCTs. On the other hand, there has been a significant shift in power towards the centre, notably in the specification of NHS-wide standards by NICE and the NSF, and their implementation and enforcement under the Government's Modernisation Agency.

The system of policy learning developed by NSF/NICE in diabetes education deserves closer analysis. The NSF/NICE initiatives have greatly evolved since their creation through a cyclical growth and review process. It is a system of policy learning that deals with the principal–agent problem.

There is an asymmetry of information between those setting quality stand-ards (NSF/NICE) and the healthcare professionals who are able to develop innovative education services, and therefore establish what the standards should be. The 'solution' that was developed involved creating a pseudo market for innovation, encouraging local experiments in PCTs (some cen-trally funded, others self-funded by PCTs), evaluating the results of these local experiments over a three-year period and then introducing a tight set of standards.

This is a circular process of policy learning. The process can be character-ized in the following way. A top-down induced opportunity for radical inno-vation (a window of opportunity) was created at the NSF and NICE policy level. An initial set of loosely set of standards was deliberately introduced, providing a space for local initiatives. At the local level, highly innovative pro-grammes were experimented with. Important differences existed between the programmes as different groups explored what a patient-orientated educa-tion programme actually is, what it looks like and how effective it can be compared to more traditional, directive education programmes. These local experiments provided the learning inputs for effective standards setting. Once the evaluation process had taken place, the next part of the process involves the introduction of a more specific and prescriptive set of guidelines issued to PCTs, and a clear set of formal standards and targets that need to be met. The process is represented in Figure 8.1.

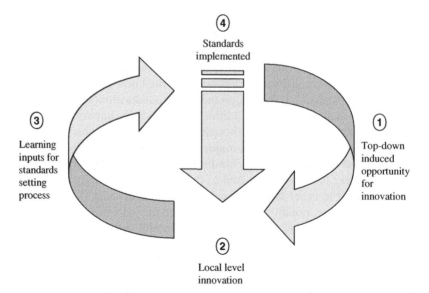

Figure 8.1   Circular policy learning

8.4 THE SALFORD EDUCATION PROGRAMME

8.4.1 Critical Events and Local Innovation Champions

Let us now examine the process that led to the development of a patient-centred education programme innovation in Salford PCT. A number of critical events facilitated the development of the programme. Some of these events were precipitated by national level changes occurring across the NHS as a whole. The Salford education innovation was a local initiative by two public sector institutions: the Salford PCT Community Diabetes Team (hereafter 'SCDT') and a group of education experts from Manchester Metropolitan University (hereafter 'MMU'). Hence, this was a purely public sector innovation project, driven by a team of public sector experts in education and medicine interested in experimenting with new models of diabetes education. Following a number of initial meetings it was agreed that the teams would work together in order to review and develop a new programme for diabetes education. Two separate applications were drawn up and sent to the Salford and Trafford Local Research Ethics Committee (LREC) in order to gain permission to conduct research in Salford PCT. The author was a member of the innovation team, enabling him to gain intimate access to the innovation process.

Another critical event, which occurred a few years prior to the commencement of the project, was the setting up of the SCDT. The SCDT was one of the first dedicated PCT education units in the UK. Its creation was prompted by a short-term payment to GPs for taking on diabetes patients (this is no longer paid). A key figure was Dr Robert Young of Salford Hope Hospital. A leading UK national expert in diabetes care and research, Dr Young instigated the idea of pooling together GP payments to set up a dedicated education unit. The future of the SCDT was subsequently secured when Dr Young successfully bid for long-term funding from the Department of Health. The creation of the SCDT means that there is a single institution within Salford that is responsible for the design and implementation of innovation within type 2 diabetes education. This confers the SCDT with a degree of autonomy from the other primary care institutions within the PCT.

A third critical event was the successful application of the MMU team for external funding for research into public sector innovation. This was used to fund a full-time Senior Research Fellow for 12 months. The Research Fellow is a recognized expert in 'learning sets', a method of facilitated group learning. Dr Eileen Fairhurst, the Chairperson of Salford PCT, put the MMU team in contact with Dr Young, who in turn put the team in contact with Mrs Jackie Steadman, the Manager of the SCDT. This was the starting point of the SCDT–MMU collaboration. The aim of the project was to develop a practical, workable patient-orientated education programme that is effective and viable, given the tight financial and other resource constraints of the SCDT.

There were a set of local 'innovation champions' in these public sector institutions who played a key role in making the innovation possible. These local champions are respected experts in their field and hold positions of authority and influence at the local and national level. They recognized and had the wherewithal and will to exploit a particular opportunity when it arose. A key figure is Jackie Steadman, Manager of the SCDT. She is well known to the staff at Salford Hope Hospital, having been trained there, and is a close colleague of Dr Young, a nationally recognized advocate for diabetes health. Mrs Steadman has successfully built a team of highly competent specialists that include two specialist diabetes nurses, two dieticians and two podiatrists. The SCDT team is critically aware of its own performance, continually seeking to improve the quality of education delivered, and is extremely open minded with regards to experimenting with alternative educational practices from other fields. Indeed, prior to the new programme, the SCDT had revamped its teaching methods and content on a number of occasions. Another key figure was the head of the MMU team. He recognized the opportunity to use research monies to put together a team of education to work with the SCDT in order to develop a patient-orientated education programme, and to subsequently evaluate the programme.

8.4.2   Education and Resource Objectives

Let us now consider the set of objectives that the designers of the new programme addressed. As noted earlier, these were directly informed by the changes going on across the NHS. The original education programme delivered by the SCDT was highly directive. It involved members of the SCDT delivering two presentations (in the style of a lecture), each presentation lasting two hours.

The SCDT was unhappy with aspects of the directive programme it had been delivering, and wished to improve both the quality of material and the delivery mode. As one member of the SCDT put it, 'there was a distinct feeling that we were more concerned with ticking boxes than actually delivering "real" education'. Importantly, the members of the team are extremely open minded with regards to learning about and using new teaching methods and materials. There are, however, major constraints that affect their degree of freedom. Notably, these are extremely tight constraints on staff time and resources, the availability of local sites in which to deliver the courses and the organizational overheads involved in arranging meetings with patients. These practical constraints are common across the NHS.

In initial discussions, the SCDT–MMU team identified a set of six objectives for the new patient-centred programme. The patient-centred education programme should:

1. Improve the learning experience of patients
2. Support patient self-empowerment
3. Provide timely information, as and when users require it
4. Improve efficiency in delivery, and
5. Shorten the time between initial diagnosis and the first education session.

In addition, the programme must:

6. Be feasible, that is, be delivered using existing staff and the physical resources that are locally available.

There are many different ways in which the first five objectives can be addressed. In particular, there is the matter of how one understands, defines and translates into practice the related concepts of patient-centred health, consumerization and patient empowerment discussed in Section 8.2. Alternative understandings of these concepts leads to the development of very different types of education programme, not only in terms of content but also in forms of delivery. This explains the very different types of programmes that were developed by other groups across the UK in this time period.

In order to give greater focus to the project, the original set of objectives were translated into a set of more specific design questions:

• How to build self-confidence and independence?
• How to design content that imparts key messages?
• How to effectively deliver a large amount of material in a short time period?
• How to deal with a diversity of clients' needs, great diversity in their educational background and in their self-motivation or ability to 'be' empowered?
• How to identify appropriate modes to deliver the material?
• How to provide materials that support further reading and promote self-reliance and continuing self-education?

An additional aspect of the design brief concerned attendance and drop-out rates of patients attending the education programme. Poor attendance rates (particularly amongst males) and high drop-out rates were both of concern for SCDT staff under the old directive programme. Hence the design aspect also addressed the question of how to increase the number of people attending the course.

8.4.3 Scoping Exercise

Having identified a set of objectives and design questions, the MMU team members engaged in an extensive scoping exercise lasting three months. This included detailed primary and secondary research. Secondary research comprised a thorough literature review, focusing on academic research into principles of adult education, and on previous research on patient-centred education for other chronic illnesses. Non-scientific publications (in national newspapers and magazines and on the internet) were examined in order to assess the style and content of general information on diabetes in the UK. In addition, government documents and other key secondary sources were examined. These included government White Papers on reforming the NHS, on diabetes and diabetes care, NHS publications, the NHS Direct website, the NICE website and NICE guidelines, the NSF website and NSF publications, and the Diabetes UK[3] website. Other, lesser well known sources were used, such as internet user groups dedicated to diabetes patients and carers, and national websites based in Canada, New Zealand and France. Finally, material from the two other diabetes education programmes were examined.

Detailed primary research involved the MMU team members conducting 11 face-to-face interviews with patients who had attended SCDT education sessions during the previous 12 months.[4] In addition to these interviews, the MMU team attended and observed three sessions of the existing (directive) programme given by the SCDT. A number of pilot interviews were also carried out in Gorton, another district of Greater Manchester with similar demographics to Salford. These included three GPs, two nurses involved in diabetes care at GP surgeries and five people living with type 2 diabetes. Together, this primary research enabled the MMU team to appreciate the particular issues faced by patients and educators in the Salford area, and provided the basis for an assessment of the strengths and weaknesses of the existing programme. This was the starting point for the collaborative development of a radically new, patient-centred programme.

8.4.4 Meeting the Design Objectives

Meeting the design objectives required product, process and organizational innovation. These went hand-in-hand in the development of the new programme.

8.4.4.1 Mediated learning: building patient self-confidence and independence

The new patient-orientated programme is based on a new starting premise: patient-mediated learning. It is an adaptation of the 'moderated learning sets' approach, which itself is an important innovation developed in public sector education over the last decade.

Rather than 'teaching' patients, members of the SCDT mediate discussions between patients on key areas of diabetes health. This strongly supports the development of critical, self-empowered learners. Patients learn how to use and critically appraise information on diabetes, how to translate this information to their own individual circumstances and learn about the multiple potential benefits of interacting with other diabetes patients. The latter ranges from contacts that can help find additional sources of information to gaining alternative opinions about new information. When this experience is repeated over a number of sessions patients build confidence in their own abilities to discover and discuss information, both from written literature and from other people (that is, experts and other people with diabetes), and learn how to ask questions and engage in useful discussion with medical experts.

8.4.4.2 Education pack: imparting content and key messages

A second innovation was the development of a specially designed education pack. This was tailored to support patient-mediated learning within the new education programme. The pack comprises a number of sections of education material. Each section of the pack relates to a different topic area covered by the course. Prior to an education session patients are given the supporting material as a handout. This provides patients with the material they will discuss in the next education session. The course requires that patients read the relevant section of material before attending each session. In this way key content and messages are imparted, through a combination of prior reading and discussion amongst fellow patients in the education sessions. As the patient proceeds through the course, so the material in the education pack is built up. The material is held in a specially designed folder. The folder and all materials are provided to patients free of charge.

Developing the pack allowed for specialization across all materials. These could now be tailored to the needs of the education team delivering the sessions. By integrating home-based learning materials and formal, mediated sessions, patients have more opportunity to process and learn the material. Further, specialization of sessions and the provision of different levels of material in the pack (that is, basic introductory information and more advanced information) increases the chances of keeping the interest of younger, better educated and more independent patients.

Second, standardizing the material ensures that patients from all Salford GP practices receive the same information early on. In the scoping exercise it became clear (from interviews with patients and practitioners) that there exist enormous differences in what patients are told by local practices and the quality of the information that is disseminated.

The use of visual images and basic material in the pack was honed to impart key messages. These key messages form the backbone for more extensive learning. For example, understanding the role of insulin in the body is a key message because this is a basic building block for understanding what happens when not enough insulin is produced by the pancreas.

Various mechanisms are used to reinforce the key messages. These take three forms. One form is a quiz. These follow each major section in the pack. A second form is the self-evaluation exercise. This involves patients applying the new knowledge to their own situations, and asking them to consider how they can improve things by changing or altering their own behaviour. For example, after learning about different food groups and their impact on blood sugar levels, patients are asked to complete an exercise listing everything they eat that day. Thereafter, patients are asked to consider whether their diet is healthy in general, and whether the levels of carbohydrates, protein, sugar and fat in their diets are correct. The third mechanism that is used is an open section, placed at the end of each learning unit, in which patients are asked to list a set of questions and/or queries on the material they have read. These are brought to the next education session. Having worked through the learning materials, and formulated a set of questions and issues to be addressed, the discussions at the education session are 'moderated' by the SCDT.

In addition to the material that is handed out during the course, patients are provided with a second set of more detailed material at the end of the course. This includes material on each of the key areas covered in the programme. A list of key resources, from local groups to useful websites, is also provided. The idea is to stimulate further reading, promote self-reliance and continuing self-education after the course has finished.

8.4.4.3 Appropriate modes to deliver material

In the early days of the collaboration it was thought that the internet could be usefully employed in order to deliver one or more web-based components. However, the scoping exercise made it clear that the demographics of patients in Salford – that is, age, education and income – together with a lack of computer and internet access amongst the sample, meant that this would not be an effective use of resources. The MMU–SCDT team instead turned to more traditional paper-based resources as these were more appropriate in this case.

The scoping exercise highlighted the use of images as an important learning format. It was found that patients, sometimes with poor reading abilities (due to a combination of age and education), are more likely to access, understand and remember information that is presented through clearly structured images. Clear images were found to have greatest impact when combined with short, concise written messages. Generally, information communicated in detailed and long texts were not found to be effective. Having said this, there were a minority of patients interviewed who were comfortable with extensive texts, and also desired that these would be available. Consequently, an effective programme would need to take on board the preferences and needs of this minority group as well as those of the majority within the user group population of Salford.

8.4.4.4 Multiple sessions: effectively delivering material

The third innovation involved a reorganization of resources in delivery. Under the old directive programme, four members of the SCDT would deliver all material over two one-hour long sessions. Under the new programme material is delivered over three one-hour sessions. This addressed an important criticism of the old programme identified in the scoping exercise. The old programme had attempted to deliver too much material within too short a time period. While the SCDT members felt that they had 'ticked the box' and 'delivered' information, interviews with patients indicated a very different story; that of information overload with little or no long-term retention by patients.

A novel solution was needed to increase the number of 'learning points'. Breaking the material up and delivering it across three sessions would, it was believed, help address the information overload problem. This reorganization of delivery had a number of positive and negative implications for SCDT resources. Together, the education sessions and the learning material containing in the education pack provide six learning points. This compares with just two separate learning points (the two one-hour sessions) in the old education programme. Figure 8.2 highlights the increased number of learning points under the new programme, and places this within the context of an ongoing process of education and treatment.

Effectively supporting the three education sessions placed a great onus on the quality of the education material. Handout materials were used in the original directive programme. These were leaflets and other printed materials published by the NHS, Diabetes UK and other sources. It was recognized that they would not suffice for the patient-orientated programme, however. This required tailored material that directly supported the content and the teaching style of the new programme. The development

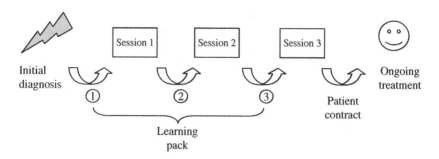

Figure 8.2   Learning path of new education programme

of this supporting education pack was resource intensive. The development work was led and managed by the MMU team members.

As noted, the education pack comprises three separate sections, indicated as (1), (2) and (3) in Figure 8.2. Each provides patients with all the material and information needed to support the session that follows it – that is, this is the key resource for the mediated learning conducted in each of the three education sessions. The first section provides a general introduction to the new programme; it introduces patients to what diabetes is, how it can be recognized and the medical complications that can arise. The second section provides extensive coverage of different issues in diet and exercise. The third section addresses medication and provides in-depth information on specialist issues, such as maintaining healthy feet and eye care.

The process does not end with the third education session. Patients return to their local GPs/diabetes nurses where they continue along their diabetes pathway. Through a patient contract titled 'My Action Plan', drawn up between the SCDT and the patient, a link is made between the education programme and the local GP practice. The contract is, in part, a certificate of achievement for having attended the course and, in part, an agreement (of good intentions) on diet, exercise and so on that the patient takes back to their local GP.

8.4.4.5   Addressing the diverse needs of local users

Salford is predominantly a white, working-class area, where the average educational background is low compared to the national average. However, interviews with Salford patients during the scoping exercise revealed a diversity of educational backgrounds and needs. A patient-centred education programme must take this heterogeneity into account. The interviews also indicated the need to deal with the changing needs of individuals over the course of their illness pathway.

In order to deal with this diversity it was decided that all the learning material would be delivered at two levels. Level 1 material is provided in a simple format with an extensive use of visual images. According to most of the patients interviewed, this was the best way of introducing the subject matter and making it memorable. Level 2 material provides much more detailed, extensive textual information and does not use illustrative images. This caters for the demands of better educated patients and for patients who wish to delve more deeply into their condition later in their illness pathway. Better educated patients stated that, while they were happy to initially read introductory material, they would later want to access more detailed information. They had found this very hard to find through their own searches (for example, over the internet). While this type of patient was fewer in number, they still made up a significant proportion of the patients interviewed.

8.4.4.6 Improving attendance rates
The SCDT was concerned that only a low percentage of patients contacted were actually attending the directive programme. It was particularly felt that attendance rates amongst men were low. As one member of the SCDT put it, 'women seem quite happy to come along for a chat, but men aren't'.

On the old programme, patients were sent a letter stating that they had been referred to the education programme by their local GP. The letter did not contain detailed information on the content of the programme or its method of delivery.

In order to stimulate initial attendance on the patient-centred programme, the first section of the new education pack was posted along with a new introductory letter. The letter explained the structure of the course, and the first pages of the learning material explained in detail the basis of the course and the need to read the material and carry out the written exercises before attending the first session. The idea was to engage patients about the course, its content and the commitment required from them in order to complete the course. In this way the importance and standing of the course were emphasized. It was hoped that this would improve attendance rates, particularly amongst men.

There were, however, fears that increasing the number of sessions on the new programme would lead to an increase in drop-out rates. This would be mitigated, however, if patients were committed to the programme.

8.4.4.7 Reducing the time between initial diagnosis and education
Another advantage of sending out the first section of the pack prior to the commencement of the education programme is that it reduces the time between the diagnosis of illness and the start of the patient's learning process.

178   *Case studies*

8.4.4.8   Feasibility of new programme using existing staff and local resources

The resources available for the new programme are the same as for the old programme. The SCDT comprises 12 staff members, 11 are medical practitioners (podiatrists, dieticians and specialist diabetes nurses) and there is one full-time administrator. They deliver the education programme in a number of locations within Salford, typically GP practices and local public libraries to which patients have easy access.

Increasing the number of education sessions, from two to three, has implications for organization costs. On the positive side, the move to three sessions reduced the number of staff needed to attend each session, providing an efficiency gain in staff time. Under the old programme staff from each of the four specialist areas attended two sessions. Specialization of topic areas in the new programme means that only one or two members of staff need to attend a particular session, according to the particular specialist area that are dealt with. Hence, per session staff costs are reduced. On the negative side, the increased number of sessions that had to be arranged led to a rise in overhead costs for back-office staff. It also placed further demands on local libraries and GP surgeries where the education sessions are held. These do not charge the SCDT for the use of their premises. Nevertheless, there are real costs associated with organizing more education sessions. There is also additional postage costs involved in sending out the first section of learning materials from the education pack.

8.5   EVALUATING THE PROGRAMME

The ultimate goal of the patient-centred programme is to improve patients' daily control of their type 2 diabetes through diet and exercise. Diabetes education, however, is a necessary precondition for a change in an individual's lifestyle. It does not guarantee that an individual will actually change their diet and exercise regime. We know from evidence on cigarette smoking that an individual knowing something is bad for their health does not automatically lead them to change their behaviour. Similarly, knowledge about what diabetes is, its complications and the need to control it through changes in lifestyle is a precondition for behavioural change. It does not guarantee that a behavioural change will occur. By making education more patient-centred and empowering, the hope is that individuals will take more responsibility for their own condition, and that this will affect the likelihood of a change in personal behaviour occurring.

With these goals in mind, the programme was evaluated in two areas. The first is programme attendance and completion. This is essential if good quality diabetes education is be imparted. The second area is the impact of the programme on daily lifestyle. The best medical indicator of a patient's control of their diabetes is the HbA1c blood test that is conducted every two to three months by the patient's local GP.

8.5.1   Setting up Control and Trial Groups

The impact of the patient-centred programme was evaluated by setting up a trial group of patients receiving the new programme, and comparing data collected on them with a control group receiving the original directive programme.

Patients entering the two programmes are drawn from six GP practices in Salford. This ensures that the control and experiment sample share a common socio-economic background and receive a common set of GP patient services. Logistically it was not possible for the SCDT to run both programmes concurrently. Hence, sample groups were randomly drawn according to referral by their GP practices in two different time periods. GP referrals in the period 6 October 2003 to 1 March 2004 formed the control group. It was estimated that this period of time would be sufficient to ensure that the control group contained at least 100 patients who had completed the course. The new education programme was then rolled out. GP referrals in the period 9 March 2004 to 26 July 2004 were entered on the new, patient-centred education programme. The trial period for this group ended when 100 patients completed the programme. In this way, a control and an experiment sample contain a randomly drawn set of patients that share the same socio-economic background and receive a common set of local GP services.

8.5.2   Programme Attendance and Completion Rates

Tables 8.1 and 8.2 provide data on the attendance, completion and drop-out rates for the control group (directive programme) and experiment group (patient-centred programme).

From the data we see that the experiment group has a far higher initial attendance rate than the control group, 63 per cent compared with 49 per cent. These findings are important. They indicate that the content and the delivery of the patient-centred programme has a significant effect on attendance rates. This is achieved through the introductory letter and by sending patients the first section of training material in the education pack prior to the first session taking place. The intention is to engage patients and promote a strong interest in the education by providing information on the type of education to be provided (that is, patient-centred) as well as to start the process of education prior to the first session. By contrast, patients

Table 8.1   Attendance, completion and drop-out rates for diabetes control group

	Total	Men	Women
No. patients contacted with appointment	244	141	103
No. patients who attend 1st session	119 (119/244 = 49%)	65 (65/141 = 46%)	54 (54/103 = 52%)
No. patients who complete the course	95 (95/119 = 80%)	48 (48/65 = 74%)	47 (47/54 = 87%)
Drop-out rate	20%	26%	13%

Table 8.2   Attendance, completion and drop-out rates for diabetes experiment group

	Total	Men	Women
No. patients contacted with appointment	184	88	96
No. patients who attend 1st session	116 (116/184) = 63%)	52 (52/88 = 59%)	64 (64/96 = 67%)
No. patients who complete the course	111 (111/116 = 96%)	50 (50/52 = 96%)	61 (61/64 = 95%)
Drop-out rate	4%	4%	5%

attending the directive course were not sent training materials, only a standard letter inviting them to attend an education course with details of the date, time and place that the first session would be held.

A second striking finding is the improvement in attendance amongst men. Fifty-nine per cent of men contacted by the patient-centred programme (experiment group) attended the first session compared to just 46 per cent of men contacted by the directive programme (control group), a difference of 13 per cent. One of the goals of the innovation was to raise attendance amongst men. Sending out more detailed information on the course contents and delivery appears to have helped achieve this. What is also interesting is the fact that the improvement in attendance rates amongst women is even higher still. Attendance rates of women are 15 per cent higher on the patient-centred programme, that is, 67 per cent compared with 52 per cent on the directive programme.

The drop-out rate for the experiment group is also far better than for the control group – 4 per cent compared with 21 per cent. The drop-out rates are better across the board, but are particularly significant amongst men.

The drop-out rate for men in the experiment group is just 4 per cent compared with a very high drop-out rate of 26 per cent in the control group. These findings are extremely important. Despite the higher number of education sessions – three on the patient-centred programme versus two on the directive programme and the associated additional costs in time, effort and money (that is, travel costs) for patients to attend an additional session – the vastly improved retention rates are a very strong indicator that patients are more engaged by the patient-centred programme. This is highly significant for effective diabetes education.

8.5.3 Impact of Programme on Diabetes Control

The HbA1c blood test is the best biomedical indicator of whether patients have changed their lifestyles and brought their diabetes under control. It is the main test for diabetes control in the UK. The HbA1c test is conducted every two to three months by a patient's GP. The blood score should be below 7 per cent. We are fortunate in that Salford PCT holds these data on a central information system and we were able to access the HbA1c blood test data for patients in the experiment and control groups.

Data was collected on patients' HbA1c scores at two time points. The first recorded score is for the blood test immediately following the education programme (labelled 'Month 1'). The second recorded score is for the blood test conducted approximately 12 months after patients received the education programme (labelled 'Month 12'). Together, these scores give us a good indication of how well patients in the experiment and control groups are controlling their diabetes, and the scores of each group can be statistically compared.

We have complete data for 108 of the 120 patients in the control group and data for 94 of the 116 patients in the experiment group (80 per cent and 81 per cent samples, respectively). Missing data is explained by the patients having passed away, relocating away from the area or local GPs not recording data on the central information system.

The average mean scores of the control and experiment groups are almost identical in Month 1, that is, 7.7 in the control group and 7.8 in the experiment group. This indicates that patients in both groups are starting from the same base. The average mean blood scores for the control and experiment groups differ notably in Month 12. The average blood score in the control group is 7.2 but the average score in the experiment group is 6.8.

We are interested to assess whether statistical differences exist between individual rates of improvement in HbA1c scores for all patients in the two groups over the 12 month period. The independent samples t-test procedure is used in order to substantiate the observation that the distributions of

Table 8.3   Statistical data on HbA1c scores for Month 1 and Month 12

	Group	N	Mean	Std deviation	Std error mean
HbA1c score Month1	Control	109	7.739	1.6165	0.1534
	Trial	94	7.745	1.6193	0.1661
HbA1c score Month12	Control	108	7.172	1.0099	0.0972
	Trial	94	6.838	0.8599	0.0887

HbA1c scores for patients in the two groups were statistically the same in Month 1 but differed in Month 12. Table 8.3 provides information on sample size, mean, standard deviation and standard error for the HbA1c of the control group and experiment group in Month 1 and in Month 12.

Table 8.4 reports Levene's test for equality of variances, and both pooled and separate variance t-tests for equality of means.

For Month 1 HbA1c scores, the significance level of the estimated Levine statistic is 0.574. This is above the significance value of 0.10 and so we assume that these two distributions have equal variance. The test value for 2-tailed significance with equal variance is 0.977. This is greater than 0.05, that is, it is outside the 95 per cent confidence level. Hence, we conclude that the mean difference of -0.0065 between the experiment and control groups is not statistically significant.

The significance level of the estimated Levine statistic for Month 12 HbA1c scores is 0.097. This is below the significance value of 0.10 and so we assume that these two distributions do not have equal variance. The test value for 2-tailed significance with equal variance not assumed is 0.012. This is less than 0.05, that is, it is within the 95 per cent confidence level. We therefore conclude that the mean difference of 0.3339 between the experiment and control groups is statistically significant.

The HbA1c blood data clearly indicates that patients who attended the patient-centred education programme had far better control of their diabetes than patients who attended the directive education programme.

8.6   CONCLUSIONS

This chapter has analysed the birth, development and implementation of patient-centred diabetes education in the UK at two levels – at national policy making level within the NHS and at the local level where practitioners develop and deliver innovative education programmes. Both are important in order to see the web of interconnected forces and drivers that are shaping innovation in diabetes education in the UK.

Table 8.4 Independent samples test for Month 1 and Month 12 HbA1c scores

		Levene's test for equality of variances		t-test for equality of means					95% confidence interval of the difference	
		F	Sig.	T	df	Sig. (2-tailed)	Mean difference	Std. error difference	Lower	Upper
HbA1c score Month1	Equal variances assumed	0.317	0.574	−0.029	200	0.977	−0.0065	0.2261	−0.4524	0.4393
	Equal variances not assumed			−0.029	199.014	0.977	−0.0065	0.2261	−0.4525	0.4394
HbA1c score Month12	Equal variances assumed	2.780	0.097	2.510	200	0.013	0.3339	0.1330	0.0716	0.5963
	Equal variances not assumed			2.538	199.910	0.012	0.3339	0.1316	0.0745	0.5934

The case study captures four important facets of innovation. First, this is a purely public sector innovation built on previous innovations that have occurred in the public health sector and public education sector in the UK. The case study is important because it dispels the myth that the public sector is not innovative and relies on the private sector to develop innovations that public sector institutions can subsequently adopt. Far from being innovation laggards, public health and education professionals are leading the development of new ideas and innovative practices in diabetes education in the UK.

A second point of interest is the scope of the innovation process. The development of patient-centred diabetes education has required a set of radical, interconnected innovations to occur at both the level of national policy making and in local delivery. The idea of locally delivered patient-centred health is a radical conceptual innovation that breaks the traditional healthcare model. Realizing it has required a set of radical reforms to organization structure and delivery models of diabetes education. Type 2 diabetes care has been moved from hospitals to GPs, NHS standard-making institutions (NICE and NSF) have been established, and these agencies have set up a circular process of policy making that encourages experimentation and innovation amongst practitioners as part of the policy learning process. Each of these conceptual, policy, administrative/organizational and service delivery changes are a major innovation in their own right. Together, they have radically transformed the content and delivery of NHS care.

The third point of interest has been the role played by a number of innovation champions in driving forward the design and implementation of patient-centred education in Salford. These public sector champions are the counterparts to entrepreneurs in the private sector. They drive the innovation process through their personal drive, their ability to command financial and other resources, and by their networks of influence.

The final point of interest is what the case study tells us about innovation in general. It forces us to reappraise what (we think) we know, and what we do not know, about innovation. The case study highlights how radical conceptual, organizational and policy innovations in the NHS directly informed the design of the patient-centred education programme in Salford; its rationale, its objectives and the financial and resource constraints. This takes us far away from conventional descriptions of innovation that are found in the innovation literature. Conventional, largely manufacturing-based, studies privilege product and process innovation at the expense of other forms of innovation. Studies of private sector services innovation have drawn attention to other dimensions, such as organizational, market and input innovation (Drejer, 2004). Hopefully, this case study makes clear that service level innovations in the public sector cannot be understood in isolation from the wider conceptual, organizational and policy innovations that inform and shape them. This may also be true for innovations, or particular classes of innovations, in the private sector. Indeed, by conducting more studies of public sector innovations we may identify hitherto ignored dimensions and perhaps need to re-evaluate the set of explanatory factors that are thought to explain innovation in the private sector as well as in the public sector.

NOTES

1. Type 1 diabetes patients are dependent on insulin injections.
2. By contrast, the provision of type 1 diabetes services remains in hospitals. Type 1 diabetes is currently classed as an acute illness in the UK while type 2 diabetes is not.
3. Diabetes UK is a registered charity and the largest organization in the UK working for people with diabetes, funding research, campaigning and helping people live with the condition.
4. In the UK all research involving patients must have prior approval by a Local Research Ethics Committee. Two successful applications were made to the Salford and Trafford Research Ethics Committee for this project.

REFERENCES

Ashton, H. and J. Rogers (2005), 'A health promoting empowerment approach to diabetes nursing', in A. Scriven (ed.), *Health Promoting Practice: The Contribution of Nurses and Allied Health Professionals*, Basingstoke: Palgrave Macmillan, pp. 45–56.

Coulter, A. (1999), 'Paternalism or partnership?', *British Medical Journal*, **319**, 719–20.

Cumbo, J. (2001), 'Better-informed patients question bedside manners', *Financial Times*, 21 February 2001.

Department of Health (2004), *Choosing Health: Making Healthier Choices Easier*, London: Stationary Office.

Drejer, I. (2004), 'Identifying innovation in surveys of services: a Schumpeterian perspective', *Research Policy*, **33**(3), 551–62.

Funnell, M.M., R.M. Anderson, M.S. Arnold, P.A. Barr, M.B. Donnelly, P.D. Johnson, D. Taylor-Moon and N.H. White (1991), 'Empowerment: an idea whose time has come in diabetes education', *Diabetes Educator*, **17**, 37–41.

Hampson, S.E., R. Glasgow and D.J. Toobert (1990), 'Personal models of diabetes and their relations to self-care activities', *Health Psychology*, **9**, 632–46.

Roisin, P., M.E. Rees, N. Stott and S.R. Rollnkick (1999), 'Can nurses learn to let go? Issues arising from an intervention designed to improve patients' involvement in their own care', *Journal of Advanced Nursing*, **29**, 1492–9.

World Health Organization (1998), *Health Promotion Glossary*, Geneva: WHO.

9. Providing care to the elderly: political advocacy, innovation models and entrepreneurship in Oslo

Helge Godø

9.1 INTRODUCTION

This chapter presents a case study of public care service provision for the elderly in a local Oslo city district. The case study suggests that political advocacy and related entrepreneurship play an essential role in innovation dynamics. It calls into question the current scope of innovation theory, indicating that this needs to be broadened to include political perspectives. In addition to its theoretical implications, the case study raises important questions for innovation policy learning.

The Oslo case study presented in this chapter suggests that a number of different innovation patterns, designs or, more aptly, innovation models exist that can stimulate creativity and novelty in care services for the elderly. This variety and heterogeneity, in terms of innovation processes and innovation models, can in part be explained by contextual factors, such as a national policy of giving political autonomy to local authorities and politicians for designing and implementing local care services to the elderly living in their districts. However, other factors, such as political advocacy, communitarianism and ideological factors are also important. Within this, which may be termed a selection environment, a wide range of entrepreneurship was also observed. At one extreme, technocratic entrepreneurship was observed. This was seen in public sector managers and personnel, who design and promote novel management systems, processes and methods which they believe will boost efficiency and productivity of public service provision to the elderly. At the opposite extreme the study observed local community activists and zealots with a burning sense of mission and ingenuity for 'doing something good' instantly, for the benefit of elderly or other disadvantaged people in their community. In between these extremes other types of entrepreneurship were observed – and interesting political alliances and configurations between various types of entrepreneurships and advocacies. Most of these entrepreneurs share a motivation based on some type of political, normative or ideological conviction and agenda – although these may diverge and conflict in terms of rationales, aims and strategies.

These observations from the Oslo district case study, that is, the variety and scope of innovation models, political-normative advocacy as a dynamic factor, and the variety of entrepreneurship aligned with these, suggest that innovation policy learning should recognize and convert these insights into innovation policy measures. One contribution in this direction would be from future innovation research, which should reorient the research agenda towards obtaining a better understanding of the political dynamics involved in public innovation processes. These topics will be further explored and discussed in the last part of this chapter. In the first part of this chapter some of the empirical material for the Oslo city district case study will be presented. The presentation will focus on two different innovation processes in order to illustrate the variety found in the case study. The chapter will then present and analyse the innovation models that emerged in the analysis of the Oslo material and some aspects related to innovation theory will be discussed. Finally, the chapter will suggest some policy and strategic implications in an innovation perspective.

9.2　CONTEXTUAL FACTORS FOR INNOVATIONS: NATIONAL AND LOCAL

9.2.1　The National Action Plan for the Elderly in Norway[1]

Norway's current policy for elderly people was sanctioned by the Storting, Norway's parliament, in the mid-1990s. It emerged after a prolonged public debate following a number of incidents and outrages that the media aptly termed the 'revolt of the elderly'. One of the policy goals in the national action plan was that public services, as far as possible, should enable elderly people to continue living in their own homes or to live 'normally' on their own in special care homes designed for the elderly. This goal and others that were intended to raise the capability and quality of care services to the elderly were spelled out in a 'national action plan for the elderly' in 1997.

In the national action plan one of the goals was that all local municipalities should build up a 24-hour service providing coverage for 25 per cent of the population aged 80 years and above, either in nursing homes, homes for the elderly or care homes. From 1997 to 2005, the total public investment in the action plan has been about NOK 32 billion (approximately

€4.1 billion), and the running expenses increased from NOK 500 million in 1997 to NOK 3.7 billion in 2001.[2] The number of employees working with care provision for the elderly has increased by 12 000 'man-years' since 1997. Providing care services to the elderly in their homes was given high priority in the national action plan. The total number of those receiving home-based services in Norway in 2002 was just above 162 000, an increase of approximately 20 000 people in ten years. Although elderly people constitute the largest group of recipients of home-based services there are also other disadvantaged groups receiving these services and included in these figures (for example, physically disabled young people, mentally ill and so on). In short, the national action plan for the elderly has contributed to a substantial increase in public spending on care services and related infrastructure for the elderly. However, the population of elderly people has also increased during this period.

In the national action plan, municipalities were given the freedom to design and organize elderly services in ways they considered appropriate for achieving the service goals. In the 2006 national budget proposal the Ministry of Health and Care Services reaffirmed this policy by stating that it will '. . . provide municipalities with increased freedom in designing good care services based on local conditions and demand'.[3] The responsibility of providing services to the elderly was also placed at the local authority level, in municipalities or, in the larger cities, in districts. This explains the variety of solutions and models that exist in terms of service provision to the elderly in Norway and why a space for innovation activities and entrepreneurship has emerged. In this environment broad top-down national policy measures mix with decentralized, local design and implementation, that is, various types of bottom-up initiatives and processes. Within this framework the context of Oslo should be briefly explained.

9.2.2 City of Oslo

Although Oslo traditionally has had (and still has) a large system of service provision to the elderly run by public organizations and employees, Oslo is distinct from the rest of Norway because some non-governmental organizations (NGOs) also play an important role in the provision of welfare and care. These NGOs own and run hospitals, homes for the elderly, clinics, all kinds of day care centres, homes for the destitute, alcoholics, addicts and prostitutes, orphanages, employment training schemes and so on. In terms of funding these activities, the NGOs receive significant support from public sources, there being a longstanding belief that NGO services are beneficial for the Oslo community, that is, the NGOs provide services that are perceived as public obligations. However, this has changed with the influx of New Public Management (NPM) ideologies because the current right-wing city government of Oslo would like to introduce competition among its service providers. In this process the NGOs have been classified as private firms, and they have been forced to submit tenders for their services just like any other for-profit company. Partly as a response to this, NGOs and public service organizations have become more innovations oriented. One reason for this is, of course, to increase economic efficiency. In addition, developing unique innovations will hopefully contribute both to the long-term sustainability of the organizations and increase their ability to provide people in need with new care services.

9.3   INNOVATIONS IN HOME-BASED SERVICES FOR THE ELDERLY IN OSLO

In Oslo a number of different actors provide or are involved with different aspects related to the provision of healthcare and welfare services to the elderly living at home. Although the NGOs are important in this, the main responsibility for the elderly rests with the districts of Oslo, that is, the public administration of the districts and their employees. In analysing the data, a salient result seems to be the variety of innovations and innovation processes; however, they are created within different systems, processes and contexts. The case study was undertaken in the local district of Østensjø in Oslo. Østensjø district is one of 15 local districts in the city of Oslo. In the case study a number of different innovations were found. Two somewhat contrasting innovations from the case study of Østensjø are presented below. The first is managerial and organizational innovations created by the introduction and implementation of NPM in the provision of home-based services to the elderly. The second is policy innovations that define the standards of welfare for the elderly.

9.3.1   Managerial and Organizational Innovations

In 1999 the former district of Manglerud in Oslo (Manglerud was merged with two neighbouring districts in 2004 and is now part of the new Østensjø district) introduced a 'purchaser–provider' model. A few years later, in 2002–03, the district also reorganized its service provision for home-based services for the elderly by introducing a new 'roster scheme' and 'SmartWalk'. Simultaneously, it started development of what may be translated as an 'achievement-based financing model' for the budgetary management of its service provision. All these measures were innovative because they were novel in the management and administration of the district. The driving force for introducing these novelties was the implementation of NPM, that is, innovative responses to a new policy (NPM) introduced/ imposed by the commissioner in the city hall responsible for care and welfare, a right-wing politician.

9.3.1.1 Purchaser-provider model

The basic principle in this model is to divide the organization of the district administration related to service provision in two. One part has the role of purchaser, the other part has the role of provider. The purchaser part allocates services to eligible clients (dependent elderly) based on requests and applications. The services are specified (that is, what kind and how much) in requests (orders) to a provider unit, that is, a contractual relationship is established. Afterwards the purchaser controls if and how the service has been performed (quality assurance) – and pays the provider for services rendered. Traditionally, the provider role was 'bundled' into the organization of the district administration. Introduction of the purchaser–provider model enabled the administration to 'unbundle' itself, thus opening up market competition in service provision.

Prior to the introduction of the purchaser–provider model, the providers of the home-based care services were themselves responsible for defining the needs of the elderly home care services, creating a problem of subjectivity when assigning the services. The demands or requests could come from hospitals sending elderly people back home from hospitals, from elderly people themselves or from concerned next of kin. One of the objectives of introducing the purchaser–provider model was to achieve a more systematic and just assessment and allocation of home-based services for the elderly, that is, compliance with the equality principle. Another was to shield the home-based service providers from the storm of demands and requests for services put forward by elderly users or their relatives. A third objective was to streamline and standardize the needs of the users. The policy goal of keeping the elderly in their own homes for as long as possible has also contributed to the increasing pressure for providing services to the elderly at home. Simultaneously, as budgets did not reflect this increase of pressure, this became an incentive for finding new, more efficient and effective ways of allocating resources for home-based care services. In this context the purchaser–provider model was introduced.

Development of the purchaser–provider based organization was achieved in a lengthy process. The work was carried out by a team of mid-level managers in the district administration, that is, administrative managers and professionals with managerial responsibilities (such as the head nurse) who worked on providing services to the elderly in the existing organization. Defining roles and criteria for allocation and services were important in this work. After introducing the new model, the criteria have been revised several times, making adjustments based on feedback from both the purchaser and the provider units. According to informants, one of the managers had an entrepreneurial role in the development. In addition to being energetic and creative, she was empowered by the top management of the district administration to develop and implement the new model.

9.3.1.2 Roster and SmartWalk

In 2002 the former district administration of Manglerud carried out a time study of service personnel in the home-based health and care services in their district. The goal was to explore new ways to increase the amount of time spent by service and care personnel in the homes of the users (elderly), this being defined as 'good practice'. The results of the time study gave a surprisingly diverse picture of home-based services. Although the providers of the home-based services felt that they worked very hard, one of the main findings of the time study was low efficiency in providing the home-based services, thus indicating organizational weakness. Subsequently, SmartWalk and a new roster were developed and introduced.

SmartWalk is a computer-based (spreadsheet) management support application developed by one of the entrepreneurial managers in the former district of Manglerud. SmartWalk links lists of service personnel (home nurses and home helpers) with lists of clients and lists specifying exactly what kind of services should be given. SmartWalk provides managers (for example, the head nurse) with a planning tool enabling them to optimize manpower resources needed for providing the required services.

After introducing SmartWalk the management decided to enrol most of its service personnel in a roster. Traditionally, home helpers had only been working during the daytime, while the home care workers, such as nurses, worked according to a roster on an around-the-clock basis. Introduction of the roster for all personnel provided more flexibility in the use of the various occupational groups. In introducing the roster, home helpers were given additional responsibilities for simple care tasks related to the elderly at home, not only household chores, such as cleaning, shopping and so on. Helping the elderly in and out of bed, with dressing, bathroom support, making breakfast and so on became new care tasks for home helpers.[4]

9.3.1.3 Achievement-based financing

In contrast to lump sum budgeting, in the concept of achievement-based financing a district or public institution receives remuneration for public services rendered on a piecemeal principle. Being the first district in Oslo to introduce the purchaser–provider model, the former district of Manglerud volunteered to become a pilot district for the development, introduction and implementation of achievement-based financing in Oslo. Representatives from the district of Manglerud participated in a national development project aimed at developing 'good practice', coordinated by KS – the Norwegian Association of Local and Regional Authorities. Named 'the Efficiency Network Project', the project had participants from several other Norwegian city districts and municipalities.

However, the city council of Oslo eventually rejected the proposal for introducing the achievement-based financing pilot in the former district of Manglerud. In spite of this, Manglerud continued its participation in the 'Efficiency Network Project'. According to informants, their knowledge and ideas contributed substantially to further development of this model in other municipalities. Oslo rejected the introduction of this model because it was perceived as incompatible with the policy of 'service guarantees', that is, a standard for the quality and cost level of each individual service offered to clients. The present status of the project is that the Østensjø district has been granted pilot city district status together with three other Oslo city districts.[5]

9.3.2 Policy Innovations Defining Standards of Welfare for the Elderly

The idea a 'security contract'[6] was conceived early in 2000 by local socialist politicians in the former district of Bøler (the district of Bøler was later merged with its neighbour Manglerud and is now part of the new, larger Østensjø district). As a policy initiative, the idea of a 'security contract' was launched as an alternative to the NPM-inspired policy measures, which the ruling right-wing government of Oslo wanted to introduce. After winning the elections in September 2003, a majority, based on a coalition of socialist politicians from the Labour Party and the Socialist Left Party in the new Østensjø District Council, decided to develop this further and implement the 'security contract' as a policy measure. Designed to guarantee welfare for the increasing number of elderly citizens living in the Østensjø district, the contract describes four levels of public commitment and obligation in providing care services in response to the individual needs of each elderly citizen.

1. Level 1: For the healthy and self-reliant elderly – access to senior citizen service centres and provision of contact and security services, such as security alarms and regular telephone calls to enquire about health and wellbeing.
2. Level 2: For the elderly in need of some help, but still capable of living in their own homes – home-based care services.
3. Level 3: For the elderly who are frail or physically impaired and incapable of living in their own homes, but still able to manage most of their

daily routines alone – 'care homes', that is, apartments in small communities specially designed, often close to other health and social service centres.

4. Level 4: For the elderly in need of nursing care to cope with daily routines or the elderly who are incapable of taking care of themselves in spite of services provided at level 3 – nursing homes; that is, traditional institution-based care, and medical treatment for physically and mentally disabled elderly people.

According to the socialist politicians who drafted the 'security contract', the four levels constitute a comprehensive chain of measures and initiatives based on fundamental values embedded in the socialist democratic legacy of Norwegian society. The goal of the system is to enable elderly citizens to stay on the lowest possible level for as long as possible. The basic assumption is that the welfare and dignity of the elderly is best served by enabling them to live as long as possible in their own homes. In contrast, providing care to the elderly in institutions is not only very expensive (that is, a heavy burden on public finances), but gives the elderly little autonomy in their own lives.

The socialist coalition's electoral victory was interpreted by them as a 'request from citizens to implement a socialist policy in the Østensjø district', that is, development of welfare services, the local community and protection of the local environment. These policy goals were spelled out in a 'Statement of Østensjø' after the election, formally constituting the ruling coalition of socialists. The statement also signalled a countermove to privatization of social care services advocated by the right-wing government of Oslo, at least within the jurisdiction of the district of Østensjø. The provision of public healthcare and social services to the elderly was one of the top priority items on the agenda.

The majority of socialists in the city district of Østensjø also recognized the need for reforms in the traditional public health and social care services. For this reason, they retained the purchaser–provider model that had been introduced in the city district of Manglerud as early as 1999, in spite of its non-socialist origin. The socialists also recognized the need to make radical organizational changes in service provision, specifically in nursing homes. Their basic belief was that public service provision, if managed optimally and under proper working conditions, is superior and serves the needs of society in the best way. Private sector companies and NGOs are not necessarily more efficient and better in providing public services than public service agencies. In these and other types of service provision, the socialist politicians initiated comprehensive organizational development projects designed simultaneously to increase the quality of service provision and the quality of working life for employees. One of the aims of these measures was to reduce turnover rates and employee sick leave, while encouraging them to become more professionally qualified through enrolment in educational training programmes. Some of the socialist politicians who initiated and followed up these reforms had long experience with organizational development from private sector industry and large public corporations. These experiences made them experts in initiating and managing changes and reforms, but within a socialist rationale and as an alternative to the liberalistic interpretations of NPM professed by the right-wing government of Oslo.

The reorganization of one of the nursing homes in the area, the Langerudhjemmet, was given as a good example of the innovation potential of the public sector. The employees were actively involved in the reorganization, and developed ideas about new job descriptions, new work concepts, career planning and so on in cooperation with the politicians. The nursing home established an internal educational scheme for educating low-skilled attendants to become licensed practical nurses. This programme has significantly lowered the turnover rate of the personnel, decreased the job stress and level of sick leave, and increased job satisfaction. The beneficiaries of these measures were the elderly people living in the nursing home.

9.4   TYPOLOGIES AND MODELS OF INNOVATION IN THE PUBLIC SECTOR

In a broader analysis of the case study material, it is possible to discern at least five different innovation models insofar as they (mostly) represent policy-driven solutions (or prescriptions) that will alter existing ways of providing welfare and care services to the elderly. If implemented, these models will introduce novelties as existing or traditional public systems of service provision and the services themselves are changed. Implementation of these models requires political power and skills; simultaneously, the models represent ideological and normative positions in the shaping of civic society. The five models that were identified are:

- The corporative welfare provision model
- The market oriented welfare provision model
- The communitarian welfare provision model
- The family oriented welfare provision model
- The ICT oriented welfare provision model.

These models are discussed below. They are based on empirical material collected in a case study during 2004, mainly in Oslo.[7] As models, they are analytical constructs, that is, based on interpretation and systematization of the empirical material. The innovation models are not cognitive categories perceived by the actors who work in the field. However, many of the elements that make each model distinct are articulated by informants as political and normative identities and advocacy, that is, in terms of characteristics that they believe make them different from others.

The corporative welfare provision model is supported by labour unions and some socialist politicians,[8] who support the continuing public provision of services. This model is based on analysis of one of the innovations presented above in Section 9.3.2 on 'policy innovations defining standards of welfare for the elderly'. It consists of two essential elements. The first is 'elderly people's basic rights'. This provides a rudimentary specification of a standard related to what types of services and how much, should be provided, and is derived from mottos, such as 'the right to feel secure'. The second is the service provision organization reform. This is based on the introduction and development of novel ways of providing services, and is apparently inspired by industrial models of 'democracy and the quality of working life', for example, the establishment of autonomous working groups, career development schemes, providing empowerment and flexibility to individual workers, non-hierarchical, 'flat' organizational structures and so on.[9] Cooperation with voluntary local community NGOs in providing services to the elderly is an element in this model, justified by paroles such as 'solidarity'.

The market oriented welfare provision model is now being implemented by the right-wing city government of Oslo. This model closely resembles NPM. However, it is different in two basic ways. First, is 'user choice'. Each senior citizen (also interchangeably called 'customer' or 'user') has a right to choose (within economic limits set by a public authority) the type of service they need and who should provide it, and preferably from a private sector service provider market. The second element is competition among service providers. This is supposed to ensure the 'best quality at the lowest price', that is, economic efficiency and consumer benefit. In this model the main role of the public is to ensure or enable the private sector to deliver services, that is, to stimulate the establishment of a market for service provision. Service provision should not be provided by public organizations because they are rigid and tend to develop agendas that are not in the interests of users, or 'our customers' as some politicians are fond of calling their constituency.

The communitarian welfare provision model is based on ideologies or religious beliefs that have compassion and offer help to fellow human beings as an important *raison d'être*. Protagonists for these models are NGOs affiliated with Christian congregations, labour unions, humanitarian charity organizations such as the Red Cross, but also special interest movements representing a specific ailment (for example, dementia). Two elements are basic to this model. First, is the 'sacredness of humanity'. People in need are eligible for help, regardless of who they are and what caused their misery – because they are human. Second, is compassion and conviction. The provision of services to the dependent is an obligation that is best served by people who have conviction and compassion. Because of a strong sense of mission, proponents contend that volunteers, and personal sacrifice by dedicated individuals, will provide the best help. They are also more perceptive in identifying new types of misery (for example, drug addicts suffering from AIDS) and have more empathy in providing creative solutions.

The family oriented welfare provision model is based on the belief that the family as a unit and institution is best suited to provide help for members of the family that are dependent, that is, infants, the elderly, disabled people and so on. The two elements that are basic to this model are quality and concerns, and the economic viability of the family. The family provides the best context for high quality care and attention for the dependent; the sanctity of the family and associated traditional female cultural values (that is, a 'housewife' as a legitimate social person) should be maintained or reintroduced in modern society, not only because this makes economic sense, but because this institution is the basic element in society – civil society will degenerate if the family dissolves. To enable the family (and by extension to next of kin) to take care of its own members they (usually wife, mother, adult daughter) should receive economic remuneration from the public coffers for the care they provide to the dependent, because this saves the public considerable expense and because the viability of modern families requires dual incomes – which is not compatible with this model.

The ICT-oriented welfare provision model is a technological or technocratic model. Compared with the other models, it is 'agnostic' or non-normative. However, its focus is on efficiency of service provision and related logistical and organizational aspects, almost regardless of what type of service is provided. As the model assumes that service provision will benefit greatly in terms of efficiency by the introduction and implementation of ICT, it implies that current service provision is not efficient – and a moral concern for people (for example, the dependent elderly) who are not given help because of public poverty and bureaucratic inefficiency. The two basic elements of this model are total ICT penetration and organizational reengineering through the introduction of ICT. With regards to total ICT penetration, all people involved in the provision of care services must be connected to ICT systems (for example, by mobile communications and so on) and must become ICT literate and proficient, in addition to the development of relevant, user-friendly ICT applications. Organizational reengineering proposes that, by converting existing management and bureaucracies into automated ICT systems, large public resources will be liberated. Simultaneously, different, possibly more autonomous, service provision models will be supported, such as increased quality and democracy of working life, and the latter will also boost efficiency. These benefits will enable the system to provide more and better services – or save costs, that is, cut or limit growth in public expenditure.

Table 9.1 provides an overview of these five innovation models. Needless to say, these models are based on interpretations of empirical data, which have been stylized in order to make them into distinct types. In empirical reality, which is more fluid and rich in detail, the categories are not so clear cut – many hybrid varieties exist. The five models are not exhaustive because other models have also been observed. These, however, were not significant in the case study.

Some models are more flexible or agile than others in terms of discourse and rhetoric – the 'burden of proof' is external to the model. This is particularly evident in the market oriented welfare provision model. The commissioner for social welfare (a right-wing politician) in Oslo was asked to comment[10] why private service providers that run homes for the elderly, funded by the City of Oslo on contract, are more expensive than homes run by public organizations. She replied that competition from private firms had made the latter more efficient, that is, contestability spurs efficiency. While she now states that her approach is 'pragmatic' in terms of who should provide services, she and other right-wing politicians had earlier advocated that private sector firms 'by nature' are more efficient and better than public entities, and that, anyway, market competition and user choice are fundamental principles for how society should be organized. These principles are incompatible with a public service model.[11] In contrast, the family oriented welfare model, with its strong rationale related to the value and sanctity of the family, is less flexible. Many consider its agenda anachronistic, even repulsive and reactionary. They believe it will push women 'back into the kitchen', that is, reverse the trend towards gender equality, emancipation and development of modern female roles and identities. Adherents of the market oriented welfare model have sympathy with this model because it is compatible with their notion of user choice and freedom, that is, if people want to take care of their beloved ones at home they should be allowed to do so – that is their choice. In addition, the model is compatible with sectors of the economy where the basic productive unit is the family-based firm, such as in farming and small-scale fishing, but for different reasons than liberalistic ideologies. Thus, there is a close connection between innovation models and political positions – within this landscape of innovation models alliances are established while others are

Table 9.1 Typologies and models of innovation in welfare service provision

Type	Framework	Innovation focus	Networks and cooperation	Bottlenecks	Public measures	Technological aspects
Corporative welfare provision model (socialist)	Strong role of public entities in provision of welfare services – legacy of welfare society	Inherent belief in the creativity and commitment of workers	Autonomous working groups empowered to solve goals set by political system	Conservatism of groups with vested interests in existing systems (for example, labour unions) and commitment of management	New type of 'social contract' that will give legitimacy to the capability of public service provision	New technology should be developed in close cooperation with workers – training and education just as important as technology
Market oriented welfare provision model (right-wing, NPM)	Strong belief in the creativity and efficiency of markets, amplified by giving users right to choose	Clear roles related to provider–customer relationships; belief in efficiency of markets in providing welfare	Contractual and formalized with clear interfaces – delivery of services or goods most important criteria	Structural conflict of markets and hierarchies; contractual rigidities versus political malleability	Deregulation and liberalization of regulatory and legal barriers, focus on budgets	Accounting and standards enabling comparison, ICT based legal applications

Communitarian welfare provision model (NGOs)	Clemency coupled with ideals of civil society; communitarianism	Inherent belief in the creativity of altruism and idealism; idealism spurs search for innovative solutions	Based on common values and outlooks on providing charity and clemency	Exclusion and selection based on moralism ('pauvre honnête') capriciousness of voluntary culture	Recognition of the legitimacy of NGOs; financial aid to NGOs – donations and charity foundations	Publicity to community (media, PR), ICT for mobilizing volunteers
Family oriented welfare provision model	Ideal of household as the complete unit; private solutions provided by family members (that is, women – wives, mothers, and so on)	Basically non-innovation as an innovation, that is, reinventing the family through preservation and reinterpretation	Internal to the family, close and multiplex, rich modes of interaction – ego-dependent	Anachronism; values that are antithetical to modern values, in particular modern gender roles	Subsidies to families that provide care to elderly, disabled and so on	Few, related to rebuilding homes for elderly and disabled (wheelchairs and soon)
ICT oriented welfare provision model	Conventional bureaucratic model transposed to ICT systems	Engineers outside create innovations	Computer and mobile communications, 'user-friendliness'	Instrumentalism in approaching care	Infrastructure and investments in ICT development	Essential

199

incompatible with each other. Political advocacy, moral-normative interests and innovation models are closely aligned in ideas as to how provision
of public goods should be made and developed.

9.5   NOVELTY OF THE INNOVATION MODELS

The concept of innovation implies the successful introduction and diffusion
of 'something' new – a novelty, which usually means a new product or a
process, but may encompass just about any artificial phenomenon, object,
concept or idea. This broad definition may be qualified by characterizations
such as 'incremental', as in fashion (extremely minor and transient adjustments) or 'radical', as in the successful introduction of a digital mobile telephone system, such as GSM, which was truly 'new to the world'. Contrary
to innovations in the private sector, the novelty aspects in the public innovation models reviewed earlier are not as distinct. One reason for this is
institutional, that is, there is little or no patentability of the innovations, and
hence a lack of appropriability. This aspect was also reflected in the case
study. Few of the informants related their activities to the concept of innovation; many informants said that they did not understand the relevance of
this concept for their activities. Apart from one of the models reviewed
above there is little focus on technology; policy and organizational issues
are core elements in most of the innovation models. All the models seem to
be based on the following common set of perceptions:

1.   Present systems for providing care to the elderly are considered inade-
     quate or in crisis (many depict these as 'scandalous').
2.   Anticipation of a dramatic increase in demand for care services
     because of the demographic development of a large segment of the
     elderly in the population.
3.   A compelling need for developing new models for providing care to
     dependent people.

The models also have in common an obligation 'to do something', that
is, a sense of mission. For this reason, the innovation models may be characterized as basically strategic and policy oriented. If implemented they
imply innovations with variable degrees of novelty. None of the innovations implied by the models have a high degree of originality ('new to the
world'). Apart from the ICT-based reengineering model,[12] they may
perhaps more adequately be described as 'reinventions' or, more aptly, as
'reconfigurations', 'reinnovations' or 'reintroductions', because all have
predecessors and antecedents, that is, represent solutions that already exist

or have been implemented elsewhere. The market oriented welfare provision model has antecedents and predecessors dating back for many centuries, at least in Norway, where a system of competitive bidding was used in rural communities for providing shelter, food and care for poor and disabled community members (*legd*, the Norwegian word for 'parish'). More generally, this model assumes that private sector models are intrinsically superior to public, and hence private sector models should be adopted by the public sector. Similarly, the communitarian welfare provision model has clear historical antecedents, evident in the role of monastic orders such as the Franciscans and charity foundations going back to the twelfth century in Oslo, as in many other European cities. The corporative welfare provision model is also old in the sense that many elements of this model have antecedents going back to the early stages of industrial welfare systems.

In spite of these precedents that represent continuity with the past, and hence a low degree of originality, in the present context the models represent something new, that is, they are innovations or potential innovations. This interpretation may be justified by the fact that if the models are implemented they represent discontinuities with the present system of welfare service provision. They also reflect renewal or change in the rationale for shaping and providing these care related services. Thus, the policy aspect, or normative positions they represent, are articulated in these models, providing a qualitatively different rationale compared with innovation models that depict for-profit innovation processes.

9.6 THEORETICAL IMPLICATIONS

The main focus of innovation theory has until recently been on technological and economic aspects, that is, on explaining the emergence of new technology and innovations in the private sectors of the economy, such as in firms, industry or the nation – or as outcomes of entrepreneurial activities in these sectors. In approaches that attempt to explain innovations as a systemic phenomenon, a more complex set of factors may enter into the analyses, as evident in the conceptual framework of the national systems of innovations (NSI) (Lundvall, 1988, 1993; Nelson and Rosenberg, 1993). Complementary to the NSI approach, the conceptual framework of sectoral systems of innovation (SSI) (Pavitt, 1984; Breschi and Malerba, 1997; Malerba, 2004) maintains that each sector of a society differs in terms of how innovations emerge because each sector has distinct technological regimes and innovation regimes (Godø, 2000). Hence, there has been little focus on public sector innovations in traditional approaches to innovations.

In the analysis of the innovation models presented earlier, political advocacy and entrepreneurship are important aspects in the dynamics of these models. Although the models as analytical constructs are stylized and simplified representations, they nevertheless represent empirical reality, that is, the models reflect the ideas that creative individuals and various organizations (such as NGOs) expend much time and energy in order to materialize. In the pursuit of this, they become in some way or other entrepreneurial (Broch et al., 2005; Zerbinati and Souitaris, 2005). The political advocacy and interests embedded in these models cover a broad range of issues and goals; in some contexts they are very explicit – in others they are more obscure.

The immediate theoretical inference is, of course, that these innovation models represent the distinctiveness of the public sector, that is, that political advocacy and the type of entrepreneurship this entails is sector specific. This interpretation accords well with assumptions that the public and private sectors represent different worlds. However, one may plausibly suggest that some of the basic factors that motivate entrepreneurs in the public sector, such as idealism and political agency, may also be important factors in the private sector. Hence, one may suggest that awareness of this possible interpretation may be obscured in part because of the hegemony of economic explanations in innovation models of the private sector – and in part because non-economic factors are more elusive to research and somewhat incompatible with the assumptions of *homo economicus*. Although entrepreneurship in the private and public sectors have much in common in terms of the dynamics that encourage it at the level of the individual, each sector has unique systemic characteristics that make them distinct. This may explain why entrepreneurship in the private sector appears to be different from public sector entrepreneurship. In policy perspective this has challenging implications. Should measures be developed in policy that encourage entrepreneurship in the public sector – just as in the private sector? This question will be discussed in the next section.

In the analysis of innovations the concept of source or sources of innovations commands a special status. In a research perspective a focus on this may be considered strategic for a number of reasons.

1. 'Ownership' – aspects covering a broad range of topics from IPR related issues (for example, legal aspects, such as patents) to recognition and acknowledgement of fame and honour related to originality and priority (who discovered something first and so on). Because ownership invariably implies an owner, the bias of this approach, as with ownership in general in our cultures, is towards the individual, whether a person, a firm or (more rarely) an organization.

2. Motivation – basically answering the questions related to why an innovation emerged, that is, construction of a plausible reason or chain of reasons as to why a novel idea emerged in the first place and why a particular solution or implementation was developed. In some approaches this aspect is closely intertwined with ownership because ownership explains motivation.
3. Method or heuristic for mapping – the chain or network of people, events and objects (for example, technology) that were involved during the development of the innovation and the subsequent diffusion phase. The idea in this may be termed genetic; the source of innovation will provide crucial information about the subsequent innovation and its diffusion.

Empirically, the sources of innovation, just as society, are complex. Most theorists seem to acknowledge a broad range of sources. The ambition of innovation research is to provide general explanations of why and how innovations emerge, that is, construct explanations that are able to encompass a broad range of innovations. More specifically, the focus is on finding patterns, causes or dynamics that are identical or significantly similar in most, if not all, innovations. Needless to say, if successful this will provide theory with predictive capabilities, making it possible to provide sound advice for innovation policy and strategy.

Following von Hippel (1988), analysis of the case study material should focus on who benefits from the innovation activities, that is, who expects to harvest an innovation related profit or benefit. In the Oslo case study, this primarily points to the elderly because they are beneficiaries of the innovation activities. However, it is clear from the material that the elderly are not sources of innovations. Generally, the elderly are dependents. Thus, an application of von Hippel's approach is not very fruitful unless the question of 'who' is asked on a more general level, that is, not as individuals or groups, but as a more general, diffuse category of interests or particular worldviews in which the elderly have a position. This reinterpretation, however, requires a much broader definition of 'profit' and 'benefits'.

In an institutional approach one could possibly interpret entrepreneurial activities of some public organizations and NGOs that are active in new service concept development as seekers of an innovation profit that will incur a benefit to the organizations. Some of the informants suggested that their motives were also related to a concern for the long-term sustainability of their organization. Thus, motives are not clear cut and 'pure'; they are mixed. The theoretical implication of this is significant. In society, innovation activities in some non-private sectors are initiated by expectations that are altruistic and normative – or generally communitarian (Etzioni, 1998).

In these activities, results may be termed innovation related 'benefits' or 'profits' insofar as their effects increase quality, scope or quantity of welfare and care services. But mercenary terms such as 'profits' are misleading because they connote a tangible, monetary private benefit. Apart from a few firms that have been encouraged to provide services for the elderly,[13] private profit expectation is not an important dynamic in the innovation activities targeted towards the elderly. Furthermore, identifying the recipient of a benefit is a poor predictor of the source of the innovation.

Instead of economic, profit-oriented explanatory factors, political interests, goals and visions related to provision of public goods and the development of civil society may be more fertile for explaining innovations in services to the elderly. In this perspective the various innovation models may be interpreted as an articulation of political projects designed to implement ideals and interests of various protagonists. Organized as groups these protagonists constitute highly heterogeneous interests. Some have considerable power and influence because they currently hold office, and control the executive branch of the Norwegian government at local (Oslo) and state levels. Hence, they have been able to introduce and implement NPM. Others have different arenas and modus operandi, pursuing other strategies and opportunities, as evident in the variety of innovation models found in the Oslo case study.

9.7 POLICY AND STRATEGIC IMPLICATIONS IN AN INNOVATION PERSPECTIVE

As shown above, the innovation activities in the field are politicized within the context of a democratic, civil society. In this context a number of different innovation models exist; these articulate – as potential political projects or projects under implementation – the goals and missions of the interests and stakeholders they represent. Because the models in themselves represent political goals and aspirations it does not seem appropriate to indicate policy implications. After all, the policy implications are precisely the goals, and the goals and the interests they represent have legitimacy within the democratic space of most modern societies. Thus, the introduction of NPM is a legitimate political project, even if the model may be criticized by opponents, for a number of reasons, in terms of the solutions that its implementation may cause.

However, irrespective of political goals and missions, the Oslo case study indicates the existence of environments that are more conducive than others to stimulating creativity and entrepreneurship. Whereas the bureaucratic system that rolls out NPM in public care service provision seems to be populated by people with a technocratic mindset, other organizations, in particular NGOs, seem more capable of providing space for individual initiatives and entrepreneurship for creative employees, that is, communitarian zealots with special projects and a strong sense of mission. These observations, if valid, make NGOs similar to the type of creativity, enthusiasm and flexible, experimental approaches that are found in innovative, small firms in the private sector. No matter what the political interests and agendas, fostering these types of innovative environments should be encouraged because, in the long run, society's interests are best served by a continuous flow of innovative ideas and solutions. In other words, creating a political environment that encourages and rewards people – and civil society – to experiment and compete in terms of creating innovations is beneficial. Although this may be messy from a technocratic, top-down perspective, creating measures or instruments that will encourage public sector entrepreneurship should be designed. Needless to say, making a successful design for this type of policy measure would be an innovation in itself. For this reason the simple solution would be to encourage – and reward – civil society and democratic processes at the local level by giving them autonomy in the implementation of various policy goals. This may possibly be the safest strategy for creating a climate or environment favourable to innovation activities.

For innovation theory and research, understanding and explaining how and why political, ideological and normative factors influence and shape innovation dynamics represents a promising new path away from the *homo economicus* assumption that has dominated innovation theory for a long time. Future innovation research needs to recognize the importance of these and other non-economic factors in research agendas. This is important, not only in public sector innovation research, but more generally for the development of a more comprehensive, general innovation theory, which may also be fertile and improve private sector innovation studies.

NOTES

1. This and the following section is based on the PUBLIN case study report from Norway (Godø et al., 2005).
2. Figures for the following years (2002–05) are not available because the Norwegian state introduced a new system of lump sum allocations for all types of care services. The idea was that municipalities should themselves decide their own priorities.
3. St. prp. no. 1 (2005–06), Helse-og omsorgsdepartementet, p. 207 – quote translated from Norwegian by author.
4. The home helpers were paid extra to work in the afternoon and evenings.
5. The future of the project is still not clarified, but the mandate of the working group of the pilot city districts is to develop an achievement-based financing model particularly adopting the specific framework conditions which apply to the city of Oslo and its governing and financing structures.

6. Translated from the Norwegian '*Trygghetsavtale*'.
7. The interviews were carried out by a NIFU STEP team consisting of Marianne Broch, Rannveig Røste and Helge Godø during 2004. The core research consists of interviews with 24 organizations and entities that in some way or other are relevant to the question of providing help to the elderly, with a special focus on dependent elderly living at home – and innovation activities related to them. In addition, the models were constructed using secondary information sources such as the internet, newspaper articles and so on.
8. The Norwegian Labour Party is ambivalent towards NPM; some parts of the Party (in particular high-level technocrat members) are sympathetic to NPM and have advocated for its introduction. In this way, they have sympathies with the market oriented welfare provision model. Others, with close ties to labour unions representing public employees, are critical and opposed to NPM.
9. This is congruent with the notion of 'democracy at work', that is, the Scandinavian quality of work model (Emery et al., 1969), which professes flexible, 'flat' hierarchies and a high degree for empowerment for employees, combined with training and educational programmes.
10. See *Aftenposten* (Norway's largest newspaper), afternoon edn, 27 November 2004, article 'Skulle spare, privatisering ble dyrere' [Intention of saving, but privatization became more expensive].
11. An evaluation undertaken by the consulting firm Asplan Viak AS (see *Asplan Analyse*, October 2003) and commissioned by KS (a Norwegian acronym for the Norwegian Association of Local and Regional Authorities), compared privatization of care services in Oslo and Trondheim with public service provision. They reported no differences in the quality of services. Although privatization resulted on some initial public savings, the evaluation also referred to the fact that private service providing firms involved did not make any profit and were accumulating high deficits. The interpretation of this was that the firms miscalculated the costs of providing the services in their tenders and that, in the long run, their level of cost would be similar to those of public providers. A year later, Norway's largest newspaper (liberal-conservative) *Aftenposten* (afternoon edn, 27 November 2004) published an article 'Skulle spare, privatisering ble dyrere' [Intention of saving, privatization became more expensive] in which a number of other evaluations were presented and interpreted. According to the article, private service providing firms are more costly than public organizations. Some of the private firms are now bankrupt.
12. This model is comparatively new because it is based on technologies and software that have become widespread during the 1990s.
13. Few if any firms entering into this market have been profitable; in fact, some of the firms have gone bankrupt or withdrawn.

REFERENCES

Breschi, S. and F. Malerba (1997), 'Sectoral innovation systems: technological regimes, Schumpeterian dynamics and spatial boundaries', in C. Edquist (ed.), *Systems of Innovations*, London: Pinter Press, pp. 130–55.

Broch, M., H. Godø and R. Røste (2005), 'Entrepreneurship in innovation of home based care for elderly in Norway, a case study', paper presented at Innovation in the Public Sector Conference, Cork, Ireland, 22–23 September.

Emery, F.E., E. Thorsrud and E. Trist (1969), *Form and Content in Industrial Democracy: Some Experiences from Norway and Other European Countries*, London: Tavistock.

Etzioni, A. (1998), 'The responsive communitarian platform: rights and responsibilities', in A. Etzioni (ed.), *The Essential Communitarian Reader*, pp. xxv–xxxix, Lanham, MD: Rowman and Littlefield.

Godø, H. (2000), 'Innovation regimes, RandD and radical innovations in telecommunications', *Research Policy*, **29**, 1003–46.

Godø, H., R. Røste and M. Broch (2005), *Case Study Report Norway: Innovation in Home Based Services for Elderly*, Oslo: NIFU STEP.

Hippel von, E. (1988), *The Sources of Innovation*, Oxford: Oxford University Press.

Lundvall, B.-Å. (1988), 'Innovation as an interactive process: from user–producer interaction to the national system of innovation', in G. Dosi et al. (eds), *Technical Change and Economic Theory*, London: Pinter Publications, pp. 277–300.

Lundvall, B.-Å. (1993), 'User-producer relationships, national systems of innovation and internationalization', in D. Foray and C. Freeman (eds), *Technology and the Wealth of the Nations – The Dynamics of Constructed Advantage*, London: Pinter Publishers, pp. 349–69.

Malerba, F. (2004), 'Sectoral systems of innovation: basic concepts', in F. Malerba (ed.), *Sectoral Systems of Innovation*, Cambridge: Cambridge University Press, pp. 9–35.

Nelson, R.R. and N. Rosenberg (1993), 'Technical innovation and national systems', in R.R. Nelson (ed.), *National Innovation Systems – A Comparative Analysis*, New York and Oxford: Oxford University Press, pp. 3–21.

Pavitt, K. (1984), 'Sectoral patterns of technical change: towards a taxonomy and a theory', *Research Policy*, **13**, 343–73.

Zerbinati, S. and V. Souitaris (2005), 'Entrepreneurship in the public sector: a framework of analysis in European local governments', *Entrepreneurship and Regional Development*, **17**, 43–64.

10. Learning to innovate in a transition country: developing quality standards for elderly residential care in Slovakia

Katarina Staroňová and L'udmila Malíková

10.1 INTRODUCTION

This chapter focuses on understanding the nature of innovation processes in a transition country. The case study is taken from the area of social services provision, notably a residential home for the elderly in Slovakia. The transition from communism to a market oriented democracy brought about changes in the beliefs and the overall organization of a society that was based on a uniform bureaucratic model. Do these changes encourage entrepreneurship and innovative thinking? This chapter reflects on empirical material collected in Slovakia in 2004 in an organization providing direct services to its clients. The research methodology selected was to map the development of innovation within the context of the public sector, and to examine the factors that stimulate, drive, facilitate, resist and disseminate innovation in a case study taken from the area of social services.

Social policy and social care in Slovakia are undergoing transition simultaneously with reforms in the economic and political spheres. The original social protection system that functioned under the communist regime was challenged, and new welfare relations needed to be established. These included systemic changes in the provision of social services and the introduction of efficiency measures and new forms of financing. Decentralization processes affecting competencies, such as social services in general (including the care of the elderly) have meant a new distribution of responsibilities and more power for residential homes to participate in systemic changes from a bottom-up perspective. Within this environment, residential homes that we have studied have introduced innovative processes in the structure of their facilities to achieve higher standards of quality. These are driven by two factors. The first is the desire to individualize and humanize care (in contrast to the institutionalized care of the previous regime), and so influence the system of financing institutions in a way that reflects individualized care at policy level. The second factor is the change in demographics,[1] similar to those in other developed countries, that has necessitated a radical rethink of the provision and financing of social services by policy makers.

The context of residential homes for the elderly was selected following the overall changes in the legal framework mentioned above. These changes enabled greater diversity in the provision of social services for the elderly, and the combination of various types of services in one institution. Thus, a shift occurred from state care of an institutionalized nature to smaller and more service oriented institutions and family/community care. This trend will be intensified even further with the preparation of a draft Social Services Act that is currently being discussed (and influenced) by practitioners and service providers in the field of social assistance and care.

Residential homes have introduced innovative processes in the structure of their facilities in order to achieve higher quality in the services provided with two ultimate aims. First, to improve care for the elderly at the service level; and second, to influence the system for financing institutions in a way that would reflect individualized care at policy level. Thus, the innovation analysed reflects a combination of both shifts in the philosophy of service provision to the client (that is, changes in the belief system) that are a result of the overall context of transition, and a specific need to solve fiscal problems that arose in the transition period (both the reduction of finance flowing into social services and the increased demand for social services).

These experiences, and the newly piloted services, became part of the provisions in the law in 1998, with the introduction of quality standards at service level now being discussed as a benchmark for introducing quality standards at policy level (and thus at national level) in the new Social Services Act. The case study is based on a set of in-depth interviews conducted with ten directors of residential homes for the elderly in the Bratislava region (including both state institutions and newly established non-state institutions), ten interviews with policy makers at local and state levels, and interviews with non-profit sector representatives active in the field.

10.2   INNOVATION ENVIRONMENT: SOCIAL SERVICE REFORM IN SLOVAKIA AFTER 1990

The case study approach depends on the assumption that every innovation, whether at an operational level or a policy level, can be placed within an innovation environment or domain. Molina (1990) saw this innovation environment as containing socio-technical constituencies in which stakeholders work to develop specific innovations, and where factors such as policy regulation, trends, history, organizational capabilities and other contextual pressures shape the development of innovation.

Under the communist regime the public sector and the state were identical terms as the state dominated, and interfered in, all aspects of society. Consequently, at the beginning of the transformation period in the 1990s governments had to confront multiple internal challenges, such as distrust in the public sector, higher demands for public services and fiscal deficits simultaneously with economic, political and institutional transition (Elster et al., 1998). Reforms in the public sector were inspired by New Public Management (NPM) principles in both increasing management and financial efficiency, and in introducing diverse actors into the provision of social services, such as NGOs and the private sector. However, the reforms that were inspired by NPM were often introduced by copying Western models without governments realizing why or for what purpose.[2] What this meant in practice was, from the very beginning of the 1990s, the diversification of service providers and a search for efficiency in service provision. For example, service providers became independent legal units with freedom to decide, within set limits, on the direction and scope of service provision. This was an institutional change that took place without a coherent prior strategy on how effectively and efficiently to manage processes in the public sector.

From a functional and institutional point of view the dismantling of the old and the composition of the new social services was a process of functional differentiation at various levels of administration, paralleled by inter-governmental coordination at each level. In the period 1990–2004 the entire public sector had to be reorganized administratively, an entire new system of financing had to be introduced with different ways of social service provisions (Concept Paper 1996 and 2004). This had an immense impact on the overall philosophy, mechanics and quality of the organization and provision of public services, and the social services system in particular. Thus, two parallel processes were influencing the provision of social services:

1. Public administration reform, which introduced new local government authorities with the power to found and supervise institutions providing social services, with subsequent fiscal decentralization that changed the system for financing the institutions.
2. Transformation of the system of social services with the ultimate aim of increasing the responsibility of the citizen for their own social situation (Concept Paper, 1996 and 2004). Only in adverse circumstances would the state intervene, and offer assistance and services in order to sustain an adequate quality of life.

In public administration reform the ultimate aim of transition was to devolve power from the central state[3] to local government institutions, on the one hand (deconcentration and decentralization processes), and to private owners operating in a free market, on the other hand (privatization and restitution processes), as well as by creating civil society. The state administration was separated from the agenda of local (municipal and regional) government and a new division of responsibilities between municipality, region and state was created with the aim of achieving increased efficiency and improved quality of public services. From 1 July 2002, responsibility for providing social services was transferred to local government, which had to assess needs and then establish institutions providing appropriate services.

As a result, not only were alternative forms of service providers introduced (ranging from churches and not-for-profit organizations to the private sector),[4] but local municipalities and regional governments also gained increased autonomy. Functional and fiscal decentralization brought them powers and competencies which had formerly been exercised directly by state ministries or state territorial offices. From a functional and institutional point of view, the dismantling of the old and the creation of the new public sector was a process of functional differentiation at various levels of administration, paralleled by inter-governmental coordination at each level.

Besides the transfer of competencies, the reform processes also included changes in the field of public service financing. First, in 1998 the Social Assistance Act created the possibility for institutions providing social services to diversify their income in order to reduce dependency on national and local government finances.[5] Second, the so-called 'fiscal decentralization' changed the system of financing of institutions providing residential care for the elderly. The main objective of fiscal decentralization was to strengthen the financial autonomy of municipalities so that they could provide services in fields where competencies had been transferred to them, as well as increasing the stability of their income base, increasing the pressure for more efficient use of their own income, and linking the scope and quality of services provided by local government with the tax burden of the population. In this way market conditions were imitated in public service provision. However, fiscal decentralization (financial support for transferred competencies) lagged behind the decentralization of competencies and has only been implemented since 1 January 2005.[6] During the transition years of 2002–05 a 'decentralization subsidy' from the state was supposed to bridge the gap for individual local authorities. The decentralization subsidy was provided for a range of competencies (for example, social services, education and health) and its further redistribution among individual institutions providing services within a given field was carried out by local government. In the field of social services further redistribution was needed among institutions such as boarding houses for the elderly, children's homes and crisis centres. All providers (not only municipality run but also church and non-governmental institutions) are entitled to receive the decentralization subsidy. In theory this means that the regional state office bridged the difference between an institution's average expenditure and its income (initially up to 50 per cent and, after 2003, up to 100 per cent of the shortfall). The total amount is subsequently allocated according to the number of clients in the institution. Changes in 2004 amended this so that, instead of a percentage allocation, an exact minimum amount per person in care per year is specified.

In this way the transition years should have provided the basis for a more objective financing ratio between the state and local government. The financing system is based on the type of institution and the number of clients accommodated in the institution rather than on the type of services provided and the individual cases of service provision. Moreover, the division between the social services and health systems causes non-effective, non-flexible redistribution of finance and care as the individual client has to address two different systems. Finances were redistributed through local government (municipal or regional), and the amount depended on the need of individual providers of social services as perceived by the local government institutions, and on the number of clients that the institution accommodates. In practice, however, the institutions did not receive even the minimum amount corresponding to the number of clients in the institution and were facing serious financial problems.[7]

The inherent nature of philosophical change in the social system during the transition years is apparent from the names of the legal regulations. The main legal documents specifying the form and role of providers of social services (that is, under what conditions the state/municipal and alternative forms of providers can offer social services), their scope (that is, the range of social services provided) and the types of institutions providing social services are the Provision of Social Services Act of 1992, the Social Assistance Act of 1998 and the Social Services Act currently under preparation (Table 10.1).

10.3 INNOVATION PROCESS DYNAMICS IN A TRANSITION COUNTRY

Transition countries are primarily associated with overall changes in economic, political and social areas. The changes range from substantial systemic ones, to operational and functional changes, to smaller intra-organizational changes. Are these systemic, process and institutional

Table 10.1 Summary of changes influencing the innovation environment in social service provision in Slovakia

Period	Source of finances	Establisher	Provider
Until 1990	State	State	State
Since 1990	Line items in the budgets of the regional state offices or municipality budget (for example, Bratislava	State administration of Social Security Act of 1990	State
Since 1992	municipality utilizes finances from the Fund on Housing Development)	(deconcentrated power on lower levels plus existing state providers became independent legal entities in organizational form)	Non-state actors such as churches, nongovernmental organizations are introduced in the provisions of the Social Services Act of 1992
1998	In addition to the above, the Social Assistance Act of 1998 enables the providers to seek additional financing via grants, sponsorship, contributions and so on.		
Since 1 July 2002	Line items in the budgets of the regional state offices and transfers in the form of 'decentralization subsidy' to the budgets of individual local governments for social services as a block payment. Local government institutions redistribute decentralization subsidy to various providers of social services, including residential homes for the elderly	Local governments: municipal or regional (Competency Act of 2001 introduces gradual transfer of rights on self-government)	

Table 10.1   (continued)

Period	Source of finances	Establisher	Provider
2003–04	Decentralization subsidy from regional state offices via local governments to residential homes		
Since 1 January 2005	Formula from municipal taxes plus subsidy for institutions providing social services		

Source: Compilation by authors from existing legal framework.

changes innovations? How do they occur? Is it possible to trace input–output effects of the innovations?[8] This section tries to answer these questions.

The private sector is often viewed as the source of innovative ideas for the public sector. The technical-economic research on innovation in particular has focused on innovation as a market phenomenon. However, most public organizations do not function in a conventional market environment (Halvorse and Røste, 2003). Moreover, the first market elements only started to be introduced in transition countries after 1990, with the privatization and liberalization of the state run economy. Only a few respondents that we interviewed had direct or indirect experience with management in the private sector, and perceptions of the private sector varied from fear and distrust, to misperceptions about the way it functioned. Most of the respondents were thus unfamiliar with the private sector, had only a vague idea of how it operates, and, when asked directly, had not considered it as a source of innovative solutions. In spite of this, in the case study of residential homes for the elderly that we conducted, both policy and service level respondents saw the introduction and adherence to quality standards as a facilitator and driver for introducing market elements among institutions providing social assistance and services, which would enable them to improve the level of quality services provided and to improve their financial situation.

Nevertheless, many of the innovative solutions were indirectly inspired by the NPM movement outside the Slovak public sector. The legislation and service practice of other EU countries, and the Czech Republic in particular, inspire the introduction of innovation in Slovakia. Thus, an important source of innovative solutions at the service level are partner organizations at home and abroad. Stone (2004) argues that such partnerships and networking bring together representatives of various sectors (market, state and civil society), and create a framework for the exchange of information, debate, disagreement, persuasion and the search for solutions.

In our case study, quality standards, such as record keeping and managing the type of services provided for each client, have been adopted from foreign partner organizations, while the NGO Council for Advice on Social Work adopted several quality standards established in the Czech Republic.[9] The director of one of the homes that we studied is in contact with a German sister institution (via the network of the church founder). This was critical for the birth of the 'idea' of innovation itself. The director became inspired by an existing system of high quality service provision during her study trip, and her ideas were further developed thanks to contacts with the Council for Advice on Social Work. Their mutual interaction resulted in a pilot project on quality standards. Another important source of ideas and transfers are pilot projects initiated or enabled by donor organizations, such as the Council for Advice on Social Work's pilot project on quality standards, which was able to carry out research and pilot studies (including our case study of the St Anne's residential home for the elderly) on the quality of social services thanks to the international organization ASHOKA, which supports innovative ideas and environments. Some of the respondents at policy level, however, said that they refer to other countries for the purpose of negotiating and persuading, rather than using them as a source of inspiration.

The creation of quality standards in a residential home for the elderly is an innovation that reflects a shift in the philosophy of services provision (the belief system), and is also driven by a need to solve specific problems that arose during the period of national transition (that is, a reduction in the finances flowing into social services, combined with an increase in demand). The shift in philosophy – the orientation towards the client – became the centre of all innovative efforts that focused on the 'humanization' of the environment, the gradual deinstitutionalization of social care and the improvement in relations between the staff and institution and the client (or senior citizen).

In the context of transition this innovative approach, though common in developed countries, was reflected in a range of new features from the creation of alternative services, physical improvements in the institution, the introduction of new (personalized) services according to clients' needs and the provision of corresponding free time activities for senior citizens, to the introduction of quality standards and performance management to secure minimum standards in the services provided. At the same time, innovations focused on the efficiency and effectiveness of the resources used. Thus there was a perception at the service level of low levels of services provided to clients (with a focus on the provision of technical institutional care rather than individualized care) and processes within the organization (management efficiency, staff professionalization, expansion of services targeted towards client needs and so on) and there was a drive to improve the system of financial redistribution from local government to the care institutions. In the latter case, the system for redistributing the decentralization subsidy from the state, via the local government, to institutions was perceived as non-transparent and rigid as it was tied to the number of patients in the institution, regardless of what type and quality of services the institution provided. The institution director wanted to introduce a system that would take quality into consideration and make it the prime criterion for the redistribution of finances, as well as providing quality services attracting additional finance.

The orientation towards the client[10] became the centre of all innovative efforts, which focused on the 'humanization' of the environment and the improvement of relations between the institution's staff and the client (the senior citizen). This innovative approach was reflected in changes to the institution. At the same time, the second type of innovation dealing with processes of social services provision focused on the efficiency and effectiveness of the resources used, which would enable the institution to secure additional financing. Also, the process innovations looked at improving the working environment of the staff in order to simplify working procedures and increase the quality of services provided. The respondents in our interviews identified two types of innovations: those directed towards a client and those targeted at processes (within the organization or of the system). Innovations directed towards clients' needs were perceived to be more difficult to implement because they need a leader with a strong character and creative skills to introduce them.

It is important to note that the term 'innovation' is not used very often. Rather, policy level respondents equated innovations with structural reforms in social services, while service level respondents viewed innovations as structural reforms in the sector as a whole and as changes within their organization. Thus, innovations are associated with ongoing reforms and changes, although the respondents perceived that not all changes and reforms are necessarily innovative. In their view, innovations are only those reforms and changes that break with daily routine and tradition, that motivate and energize people, and bring positive results to all parties involved. The policy level respondents characterized this as 'change in the parameters of the system and increased efficiency (quantitative and qualitative) as defined by the implementer of the reforms', whereas the service level respondents viewed innovation as 'improvements directed towards client satisfaction'.

10.4   ROLE OF ENTREPRENEURS

In examining the factors that facilitate innovation, the role of agents or actors with entrepreneurship is critical (Roberts, 1992). In particular, the public management literature discusses the ability of public sector managers to foster entrepreneurial spirit and innovative thinking within their organizations. Mintrom (1997, p. 739) defines policy entrepreneurs as 'people who seek to initiate dynamic policy change' by engaging in a variety of strategies to win support for ideas, such as 'identifying problems, networking in policy circles, shaping the terms of policy debates and building coalitions'. Without these entrepreneurs, innovation would not be possible, although external top-down processes were necessary in order to create an innovative environment. One of the first steps in the reform was making individual social care institutions independent legal entities. In this way, directors became true public managers with freedom to reorganize their institution, to create a vision and mission, and to actually run the institution. This was an important prerequisite for any innovative thinking, and was stressed by all the directors interviewed as a crucial factor.

It is widely recognized that top management affects organizational innovativeness, particularly attitudes towards change by the staff, support for creativity and vision for the organization (Shoham et al., 2003). Our case study highlights the role played by the directors in developing and successfully implementing (vertically and horizontally) innovative ideas in the organization. Thus, the chief initiators of innovation are the directors, regardless of whether the ideas come from inside or outside the organization. In this sense, innovations at the service level are initiated in a top-down fashion, although the process of implementation flows in all kinds of directions. Feedback on practice, and additional ideas from the staff, follow a bottom-up pattern. Still, the overall implementation and management of innovation is based on the top-down approach, with feedback from the bottom and 'sides', such as fellow institutions and other institutions and stakeholders. The true 'entrepreneur' directors, together with their closest team, would not have successfully innovated without persistence and hard work, for example, in obtaining as much information as possible on existing ways to achieve high quality services standards, in gaining the approval of the church board and managing the innovation process itself. As one of the directors we contacted noted, 'it is possible to make fundamental changes of rules (laws) if one wants to' and 'literature or consensus will not tell us whether this is right or wrong; innovation, and the willingness to pursue it, is more about belief in ideology, philosophy, and certain principles . . . and persuading others of your truth'.

Internally it was important, in the words of this director, to create 'agents of change' among the employees who could motivate the rest of the staff and assist in overcoming internal resistance. These agents of change were selected from committed staff, who further disseminated their ideas among colleagues and tackled the potential resistance that arose. Another important aspect in influencing the innovation process was creating a climate supportive of creativity, particularly by encouraging learning from outside. As there is no system in place for lifelong learning and competence development, the director supported participation of staff in any relevant educational seminars, training sessions, conferences or workshops, which were mostly run by NGOs, and occasionally by the municipality or ministry.

The findings of our case study correspond to those of Grady (1992), who reported that the majority of public managers use professional development as an incentive for fostering innovativeness. The directors we studied had developed systems for improving internal communication of the experiences gained through professional development. For example, staff members in one institution, who return from a course, seminar or conference, are asked to make short presentations that give colleagues a summary of what they have learned through their training. The director of this institution stated that 'explaining to others makes the person themself understand better, and the rest of the staff gain some information too'. In this way a higher level of identification with the innovation was achieved as well as the staff members themselves experiencing what the possibilities might be if asked for alternative thinking. This illustrates Borins's (2001) argument that frontline public sector managers can overcome the public sector environment's traditional inhospitality towards innovation, most notably by taking a supportive role, setting priorities and articulating a vision.

As noted by Grady (1992), creating the right internal environment is necessary but not sufficient, and a manager must be able to communicate to external policy actors. In the Slovak case an important alliance exists between the municipality and other institutions. Regardless of whether the policy or service level is being observed, the innovation process is strongly influenced by the skills and abilities of the entrepreneurs, such as negotiating, lobbying and communicating with stakeholders, particularly politicians, the media, founders and establishers. One director of a residential home that we interviewed stressed that it is important to 'make members of the city council and institution board be interested and take part in solving the problem'. Thus, in order to successfully implement innovations (whether at the service or policy level), one has to be persistent and have managerial, negotiating and communication skills.

At the policy level, innovations associated with national transition have largely been initiated by the government, and thus are top-down in nature. But, again, a very important source of ideas is the legislation and practice of other countries and practice at service level. Once work on the new

Social Services Act had been initiated, input from the service level (a bottom-up response) was very much welcomed, although there was no system in place to facilitate such an approach. With regard to innovation at policy level, respondents added that the time it takes to implement innovations in the public sector is slowed down by the fact that 'while introducing innovations in the public sector, the continuity of service provision has to be preserved, although the reforms change the overall concept and philosophy, and thus an adjustment period is necessary' and 'the transition country has accumulated a number of problems that have to be dealt with simultaneously'. It was perceived that the inevitable adjustment period where old 'routine' and new 'innovative' elements are mixed on a large scale complicates the implementation process.

10.5   ROLE OF NON-GOVERNMENT ORGANIZATIONS (NGOs)

There is a lot evidence that innovations are related to a certain type of interaction and knowledge transfer, where innovations can be considered a 'new combination' of elements of existing and/or new knowledge (Edquist, 1997). These knowledge elements often originate from different actors and agents, and create relations that are characterized by interactivity, reciprocity and feedback mechanisms. The literature tends to be focused on lessons and knowledge transfers between nation states or private–public spheres. However, there can be transfer agents that occur between non-state actors or from multiple places of origin, leading to a hybrid combination of 'synthetic innovation' in order to best fit local conditions (Stone, 2004).

In the transition context, non-governmental organizations play a critical role at both service and policy levels in all stages of introducing and implementing innovation: development, dissemination and learning. First, they are small, active, flexible and, most importantly, mission driven for the particular purpose, be it the improvement of social services or capacity building among local government institutions. Second, in the transition period, civil society became, with the assistance of foreign donors, the fastest developing sector and on many occasions assumed the role of the state, local government or educational institutions, thus filling the vacuum created by the collapse of the previous system.[11] In this way, innovation processes are guided by advocacy, and very often these NGOs quickly assume the position of institutions that in developed countries are occupied by big organizations. In the case we studied, several NGOs assumed a critical role in the innovation process.

Networking patterns represent a major support mechanism (Edquist, 1997) and this was noted in the case study. Networking is essential for making alliances and partnerships, for obtaining information (for example, ideas and inspiration for alternatives, lateral thinking and creativity) and for negotiating – skills that are also essential for successful entrepreneurship. However, the problematic part is its dissemination into a broader network, and most importantly into the administrative (and legal) system. Although both policy and service level respondents regard networking and two-way communication from the bottom-up and top-down to be of huge importance, there is no system in place that would enhance networking. After the decentralization of competencies the information flow system collapsed, both horizontally and vertically. This unintended consequence of the reform cut the ministry off from what was happening in practice on the ground as the new establishers (municipalities and regional government) do not provide feedback, and it is difficult to gather data from the field when drafting new laws.

In interviews the respondents said that the NGOs assumed the role of facilitator in networking, with a focus on two functions: research and pilot testing of innovative ideas, and the diffusion of information and learning. In the first aspect of networking, the NGO Council for Advice on Social Work assumed the role of a research institution. The organization conducted an initial analysis of the problem (low quality in social services), published the results, prepared discussions where various quality indicators were discussed and started piloting quality standards in some of the service providers. In the latter facet of networking, NGOs sought to involve all stakeholders in generating and exchanging new ideas that would lead to new programmes and management initiatives and reports. NGOs were crucial in preparing and advocating the introduction of new university courses on social care and social work (including the care of senior citizens), which had not previously existed. NGOs collaborated with some of the active directors in developing a new course at university level that would meet the needs of those providing social services to the elderly. After its introduction, several institution directors started to study part-time, and encouraged their staff to study as well. One of the directors we contacted admitted that 'a lot of ideas come from my university studies as I try to apply theoretical knowledge and improve it'. Networking at the service level is important too, as conferences, conventions or meetings, whether mandatory or optional, yield possibilities for further learning and collaboration beneficial for service provision.

The successful diffusion of innovations at the policy level (for example, the incorporation of quality standards into draft law) was facilitated by NGOs and ad hoc networks. Vertical communication was based more on personal contacts and the supporting role of NGOs. Active institutional directors, together with the NGO Tabita (which facilitated these sessions), regularly visit municipalities, regional authorities and the ministry when they want to bring about policy level innovations, and networking is an integral part of their strategy. For example, the idea of introducing quality standards, and ways of using them, was diffused at both service and policy levels by NGOs. NGOs provided written material, helped in piloting and testing in institutions, and provided and supervised training in the area. NGOs are also part of a working group at the ministry that is drafting a new law in which minimum quality standards are to be included, and they form an essential bridge between local care institutions and policy makers.

The situation is similar at the service level. There is no formal body that could facilitate interaction among institutions providing social services for the elderly or between the institutions and policy makers. The interaction among directors of residential homes for the elderly was secured by the non-governmental Centre for Self-government Development, which facilitated discussions between the providers of services and local government. This interaction was crucial for the dissemination of innovation, and for brainstorming and training at the horizontal level. On the basis of this initiative, active and innovative directors of care institutions have created an informal network. This informal forum became critical for the sharing of experience and initial training that have inspired the directors to introduce innovation. This informal network has also served as a basis for competence building among the staff.

10.6 CONCLUSION

This chapter has focused on the processes and dynamics of innovation that surround the creation of quality standards in residential homes for the elderly in Slovakia. This case study makes an important contribution to our understanding of public entrepreneurship and innovation in transition countries. By examining the normative structures and the process of innovation we clearly see the extent to which the external administrative environment and system induces innovativeness, provided that sufficient operational freedom is given to local public sector managers. The devolution of power from the central state to local authorities, the decentralization of competencies to regional governments and to independent agents (new providers of social services, such as churches and non-governmental organizations), together with the introduction of a legal independence for institutions have created an environment where providers are formally enabled and motivated to introduce innovations.

The case study confirmed the central role of the public managers (the directors of care institutions) in fostering innovativeness by creating a supportive environment and establishing a network of contacts with internal

and external policy actors. An important and decisive part of implementing innovation was the belief of the entrepreneurs (directors), as reflected
in the mission of their institutions, in the humanization and individualiza-
tion of social services for the elderly. This vision translates into the provision of complex services (both social and medical) that are tailored to
specific needs, thereby abandoning the former system in which a strict division was made between social and medical care. The dearth of finance
available to the institutions further accelerated this process, despite the fact
that the field of social service provision is not yet competitive enough. The
case study has shown that, besides the directors of care institutions and
politicians, a crucial role is played by NGOs in the diffusion of innovation,
learning processes and transfer at the policy level. This is particularly true
in a transition country where the usual systems of information flow at the
horizontal and vertical levels have collapsed and new ones have yet to be
established. Thus NGOs fill the role of facilitator at policy and service
levels, as well as between institutions providing social services. Also, NGOs
are the main actors to have contact with external (foreign) bodies, and are
in a better position to transfer policy ideas.

To summarize, our case study portrays a complex picture of ongoing
transformation, the search for new innovative approaches, and an interaction between policy and service levels in a new environment in which the
relationships between the client, service provider, institution founder, institution establisher and the policy maker are yet to be clearly defined. This
study has highlighted the importance of the role and characteristics of
public sector managers in shaping, mediating and ensuring the successful
achievement and diffusion of public sector innovations. Our study of
public sector managerial entrepreneurship and creativity may be a starting
point, but it is important because it indicates the clear need for further
research on this most important of topics.

NOTES

1. In 2002 people aged 65 and over reached a historic peak of 11.6 per cent of the total
   population. This was a 6 per cent increase since 1995 (Government Office Slovakia,
   2002). Between 1995 and 2002 the number of economically active people dropped by
   12.8 per cent (Slovak Statistical Office, 2002).
2. EU institutional models were adapted by Central and Eastern Europe institutions and
   policies as part of the accession process, with very limited scope for negotiation. See the
   vast literature on the 'Europeanization' of the CEE countries and the discussion of EU
   influence in governance development in CEE countries, for example, Grabbe (2001);
   Goetz and Wollmann (2001).
3. The basic principle of state socialism in the public sector was unitary power, that is, state
   ownership meant political control over all spheres of social life. In 1990 the Municipal
   Establishment Act (re)introduced local self-government at the municipal level. The

administrative reorganization started in 1996 with the Territorial and Administrative System Act of the Slovak Republic, when new administrative divisions were created at regional level. The introduction of the 2001 Competence Act set out five phases (1 January 2002, 1 April 2002, 1 July 2002, 1 January 2003 and 1 January 2004) for the transfer of individual responsibilities/competencies from the national government to the local government for more than 400 types of public services. This meant radical change in the division of responsibilities between national and local government.

4. In 2002 there were 251 registered non-governmental institutions providing social services for 29 303 clients (Ministry of Labour, Social Affairs and Family, 2002). The majority of alternative providers primarily focus on the provision of basic care, advice and catering for the elderly. Only a few (30) provide residential homes with full social services (*Guide on Social Services in Slovak Regions*, 2003).

5. Today, the income of social services institutions comes from the following sources: state budget (via regional state offices), local government budgets (municipal and regional), grants, subsidies and client fees (Social Assistance Act 1998).

6. In the period 1990–2003 municipalities were mostly funded by transfers from the state budget through shares of state taxes and special purpose subsidies.

7. Interviewees in most of the institutions providing residential care and in regional government confirmed this practice. The reason, it was stated, was that the priorities lie in the different fields of social service providers, such as child care (Staroňová, 2004).

8. As one of the policy respondents stated, 'when one makes such fundamental changes to the system, institution and financing, it is almost impossible to discover the causality of particular components. All reforms take place at the same time (economic reform, tax reform, social system reform, etc.) so there is an element of unpredictability. However, it is very important to know WHY we are making all these reforms. We can assess the results of the reform only after a certain period of time when the reforms will be more settled' (Staroňová, 2004).

9. These were also published and distributed among institutions providing social assistance and services (Quality in Social Services, 2003).

10. Orientation towards clients (and the philosophical shift) is also reflected in language. For example, the term 'client' gradually replaced terms such as 'patient' or 'inhabitant', which were common during the communist regime.

11. There has been some research and discussion on the importance of NGOs in transition countries, where NGOs fulfil important functions in society, ranging from providing services to citizens in fields that are not yet or inadequately covered by the state, acting as watchdogs for state power and carrying out advocacy work, to preparing key legislation in all fields of social life.

REFERENCES

Borins, S. (2001), 'Encouraging innovation in the public sector', *Journal of Intellectual Capital*, **2**(3), 310–19.
Den Hertog, F. (2003), 'Doing case studies in PUBLIN', PUBLIN working paper.
Edquist, C. (1997), 'Introduction', in C. Edquist (ed.), *Systems of Innovation. Technologies, Institution and Organizations*, London: Pinter Publisher, pp. 1–35.
Elster, J., C. Offe and U.K. Preuss (1998), *Institutional Design in Post-Communist Societies: Rebuilding the Ship at Sea*, Cambridge: Cambridge University Press.
Frost, P.J. and C.P. Egri (1991), 'The political process of innovation', *Research in Organizational Behavior*, **13**, 229–95.
Goetz, K.H. and H. Wollmann (2001), 'Governmentalizing central executives in post-communist Europe: a four country comparison', *Journal of European Public Policy*, **8**(6), 867–87.

Grabbe, H. (2001), 'How does Europeanization affect CEE governance? Conditionality, diffusion and diversity', *Journal of European Public Policy*, **8**(6), 1013–31.
Grady, O.D. (1992), 'Promoting innovations in the public sector', *Public Productivity and Management Review*, **XVI**(2), 157–71.
Guide on Social Services in Slovak Regions (2003), Bratislava: S.P.A.C.E.
Halvorse, T. and R. Røste (2003), 'On the differences between public and private sector innovation', PUBLIN working paper.
Mintrom, M. (1997), 'Policy entrepreneurs and the diffusion of innovation', *American Journal of Political Science*, **41**(3), 738–70.
Molina, A.H. (1990), 'Transputers and transputer-based parallel computers: socio technical constituencies and the build up of British-European capabilities in information technology research', *Research Policy*, **19**, 309–33.
Mumford, M.D.,G.M. Scott, B. Gaddis and J.M. Strange (2002), 'Leading creative people: orchestrating expertise and relationships', *Leadership Quarterly*, **13**(6), 705–50.
Quality in Social Services [Kvalitné sociálne služby] (2003), Bratislava: Rada pre poradenstvo v sociálnej práci [Council for Advice in Social Work].
Roberts, N.C. (1992), 'Public entrepreneurship and innovation', *Public Productivity and Management Review*, **16** Winter, 137–40.
Shoham, A., A. Ruvio, E. Vigoda and N. Schwabsky (2003), 'Organizational innovativeness in the public sector: towards a nomological network', PUBLIN working paper.
Staroňová, K. (2004), 'Interview report from public sector senior managers: social services to seniors in residential institutions', PUBLIN working paper.
Stone, D. (2004), 'Transfer agents and global networks in the "transnationalization" of policy', *Journal of European Public Policy*, **11**(3), 545–66.

Government Publications

Competence Act – Act on Transfer of Competencies from State Administration to Municipalities and Higher Territorial Units (2001) (Slovakia) [Zákon č. 416/2001 Zb. o Prechode niektorých pôsobností z orgánov štátnej správy na obce a na vyššie územné celky].
Concept Paper for Transformation of the Social Sphere (1996) (Slovakia) [Koncepcia transformácie sociálnej sféry].
Concept Paper on Social and Long-term Care (2004) (Slovakia) [Koncepcia sociálnej a dlhodobej starostlivosti].
Government Office Slovakia (2002), *Report on Social Services 2002.*
Ministry of Labour, Social Affairs and Family (2002), *Report on Social Situation of Citizens of Slovakia*, accessed November, 2004 at www.employment.gov.sk/ statistika/soc_sprava_2002/sprava02.html.
Municipal Establishment Act (1990) (Slovakia) [Zákon č. 369/1990 Zb. o Obecnom zriadení].
Provision of Social Services by Legal and Physical Entities Act (1992) (Slovakia) [Zákon č. 135/1992 Zb. o Poskytovaní sociálnych služieb právnickými a fyzickými osobami].
Slovak Statistical Office (2002), *Report on Population Structure 2002.*
Social Assistance Act (1998) (Slovakia) [Zákon č. 195/1998 Zb. o Sociálnej pomoci].

Social Security Act (1988) (Slovakia) [Zákon č. 100/1988 Zb. o Sociálnom zabezpečení].
Social Services Act (Slovakia, unofficial draft) [Návrh zákona o Sociálnych službách].
State Administration of Social Security Act (1990) (Slovakia) [Zákon č. 543/1990 Zb. o Štátnej správe sociálneho zabezpečenia].
Territorial and Administrative System Act 1996 (Slovakia) [Zákon č. 221/1996 Zb. o Územnom a správnom usporiadaní].

APPENDIX: GLOSSARY OF TERMS[1]

Establisher (Zriad'ovatel') – Public administration entity (local government body at municipal level or regional level) with the power formally (and legally) to establish and/or terminate an institution providing social services.

Founder (Zakladatel') – Legal entity (regional government, church, non-profit organization) that runs an institution providing social services.

Material need (Hmotná núdza) – People are in material need when their net income is lower than the minimum income guaranteed by the government and who are not able to increase their income by any other means.

Medical care/health services (ošetrovatel'ské služby) – Health services are not part of the social system in Slovakia; they are regulated by a different set of regulations and cannot be provided by social service institutions.

Medical nurse (ošetrovatel') – Provides basic medical assistance.

Nursing, care services (Opatrovatel'ské služby) – Provided to those individuals whose health condition require basic everyday life assistance (care), assistance in looking after the household and assistance in social life. Nursing should be provided mostly in the home or residence of the client. Other clients eligible for nursing are listed in the Social Assistance Act, but are not relevant for the case study (for example, children, single mothers and so on).

Provider (Poskytovatel') – Institution providing social assistance/services.

Residential home for the elderly (Domovy dôchodcov) – Type of social service institution providing various kinds of institutionalized care for elderly, including accommodation, catering, laundry, social activities and basic medical services and so on; it is aimed for those elderly people whose state of health has deteriorated to such an extent that it is not possible to provide care in their home surroundings.

Residential nursing institution (Zariadenie opatrovatel'skej služby) – Type of social service institution providing care for those who are in need of basic everyday assistance which it is not possible to provide in their homes.

Sheltered accommodation (Domovy – Penzióny pre dôchodcov) – Type of social service institution providing various kinds of care, particularly accommodation, for senior citizens who are over 60 years of age and whose state of health does not require constant care by a third party.

Social assistance (Sociálna pomoc) – Combination of social prevention and a system for addressing the social needs of people with a disability; also provides compensation for the social consequences of disability.

Social care worker (opatrovateľ) – Provides personal help with dressing, bathing, toilet, feeding, physical help with acitivities, such as walking, practical help with meals, housework and shopping, other sorts of help, such as medication and so on.

Social need (Sociálna núdza) – People in social need are those who are not able to take care of themselves and their household; who are not able to exercise and fulfil their rights and interests because of their age, health condition or loss of job.

Social service homes (Domov sociálnych služieb) – Care in these institutions is provided for disabled persons and those suffering from mental health problems; care includes accommodation, catering, laundry and also therapy, free time activities and so on.

Social service institution (Zariadenia sociálnych služieb) – Care in these institutions is provided to those individuals whose social and material needs cannot be adequately covered by other types of social services.

Social services (Sociálne služby) – A set of specialized activities defined by the Social Assistance Act (1998) with the aim to tackle social or material need; these include nursing and care services, organization of common catering, transportation, care in social service institutions and social loans.

System of social care (Sociálne zabezpečenie) – Fundamental pillar of social policy; includes social insurance, system of social support and social assistance.

NOTE

1. Note that this glossary only provides a basic explanation of the terms used in this case study. It is not the intention of the authors to provide precise legal definitions, although the explanations are derived from the Social Assistance Act (1998).

11. Conclusions: public innovation and entrepreneurship

Paul Windrum

11.1 INTRODUCTION

The research presented in the preceding chapters represents a significant contribution to our understanding of public sector innovation. It has identified a set of key factors that stimulate and shape creativity and the development of new service innovations, and discussed the complex institutional environment, containing multiple public and private actors, that determine whether service innovations are taken up and diffused. The research has also highlighted the importance of public sector entrepreneurship and management in the generation and diffusion of these innovations.

This chapter has the challenging task of bringing together the various research findings and developing a general overview of their implications for our understanding of public sector innovation and entrepreneurship. This will be organized around the seven core research questions that were discussed in Chapter 1:

1. Do public services innovate?
2. If so, under what conditions do public service organizations innovate?
3. What form does this innovation take?
4. When and how does innovation occur?
5. What role does entrepreneurship and management reform play in the innovation process?
6. How does an evolving policy context influence innovation?
7. What is the link between public sector innovation and private sector innovation?

Section 11.2 will address questions (1) and (2), highlighting the overwhelming evidence of innovation in the public sector. Questions (3) and (4) are addressed in Section 11.3. The focus here is the empirical evidence provided on the different forms of innovation contained in the taxonomy of public sector innovation that was presented in Chapter 1. Section 11.4

evaluates the contribution the research makes to our understanding of the nature of public entrepreneurship, the motivations of public sector entrepreneurs and the entrepreneurial process. The research findings support Morris and Jones's model of the entrepreneurial process. Understanding how entrepreneurs operate is essential to understanding public entrepreneurship, and how public sector entrepreneurs create and manage successful innovations. Questions (6) and (7) are considered in Section 11.5 within a broad discussion of the interactions between the public and private sector, NGOs and consumers. Finally, Section 11.6 looks forward to the policy implications of the current research, and to future research in the field.

11.2 INNOVATION IN PUBLIC SERVICES

The answer to the question 'Do public services innovate?' is a resounding 'Yes'. The research has identified and discussed innovative activity at two levels. At the macro/meso level it has discussed the innovation dynamics of policy. At the micro level it has investigated specific service innovations.

The word 'innovation' is not commonly used by public sector practitioners. Rather, terms such as 'service reforms', 'service improvements', 'service reorganizations' and 'restructuring' are commonly used. Nevertheless, applying well established research definitions of innovation, the research presented in this book reveals that innovations are abundant within public sector services.[1]

The econometric analysis performed by Maroto and Rubalcaba in Chapter 3 examines taxation, spending and levels of service provision across the European Union. Testing the link between economic growth and the size and performance of the public sector, they find that an efficient public sector – one that promotes productive investment and innovation – is positively correlated with economic growth and social development. An inefficient public sector, which focuses on current spending levels and crowds out private and social sectors, is correlated with low economic growth. This is an important macro finding, and one that sets up the case studies of public sector innovations presented in the book. Rather than national size or the relative size of the public sector, the findings indicate that economic growth and social welfare depend on the quality of public sector services, the organization of public service providers, and the types of interactions that exist between public service providers, society and the private sector.

As well as dispelling the myth that public sector services do not innovate, the research dispels any suggestion that the public sector is merely a passive recipient/adopter of innovations initially developed in the private sector. For example, Windrum's diabetes case study (Chapter 8) is a wholly public sector innovation in which two public sector organizations came together to develop a radically new education programme for type 2 diabetes patients. Staroňová and Malíková's case study of innovation in elderly care services in Slovakia (Chapter 10) provides another clear example. Due to their history these public sector organizations have little or no direct experience of private sector managers or practices, and remain very suspicious of the private sector. Changes in the post-communist era have meant that they have had to learn how to locally organize and manage their resources, and how to innovate. The organization in this study took as its role model public sector organizations in other countries (notably near neighbours in the Czech Republic) and NGOs in Germany.

The second research question is 'Under what conditions do public service organizations innovate?'. The research has highlighted a number of important issues:

- the problem orientated nature of innovation
- bottom-up and top-down innovation
- incentive structures
- public sector entrepreneurs
- management of innovation.

The detailed case studies consistently highlight the fact that public sector innovation is problem driven. One recurring observation is that voters want ever better quality public services but are unwilling to pay more taxes for those services. This establishes an ongoing agenda for innovation – to address this fundamental dilemma of the minimalist state paradigm (discussed in Chapters 1, 3 and 4). There are general trends that place great stress on public sector services, such as health and social services. Notably changing demographics mean ageing populations are placing greater demands on health and social services while a smaller proportion of working people are being required to finance the additional expenditure. At the service level, García Goñi's case study (Chapter 5) discusses the role played by bottlenecks in focusing attention on particular areas for innovation. The need to identify solutions to bottlenecks leads service level entrepreneurs to develop their own novel solutions or to take up and adapt new ideas, medical technologies and organizational practices being developed outside their own organization.

As well as discussing the problem orientated nature of innovation, the chapters amply demonstrate how the initial impetus for innovation can come from politicians (often in response to a perceived problem or 'crisis') as well as from local service providers. The former has been referred to as 'top-down innovation' initiated by political entrepreneurs while the latter has been referred to as 'bottom-up innovation' initiated by service level entrepreneurs. This different initial impetus can result in differences in the level, shape and direction of innovation.

The research has raised the issue of conflict between political and service entrepreneurs. In part, these conflicts reflect the differing viewpoints and perspectives of people who operate at different hierarchal levels. The case studies indicate that political entrepreneurs are keen to promote efficiency gains, through organizational restructuring, while raising standards through NPM. Service entrepreneurs tend to focus on service level innovations that improve service quality while taking efficiency into account. Additionally, there is a principal–agent issue. The setting of 'targets' by politicians (the principal) is a means of establishing greater control over the activities of service entrepreneurs (the agent) while at the same time passing responsibility for meeting those targets to service entrepreneurs.

Different types of innovations are developed and diffuse in alternative incentive structures and in alternative selection environments. Godø's study of health and welfare care services for home-based elderly patients (Chapter 9) explicitly deals with the existence of multiple possible solutions. Which of the alternatives is developed depends on the political-philosophical–social selection environment in which innovators operate. Godø identifies five different, and competing, 'models' of welfare provision operating within the Oslo region. Each contains a different set of political-philosophical–social perspectives and beliefs: the corporative model, the market oriented model, the communitarian model, the family oriented model and the ICT oriented model.

The discussion of alternative selection environments ties in with Maroto and Rubalcaba's discussion (Chapter 3) of heterogeneous welfare state models within Europe and their effect on innovation. Their econometric study identifies significant heterogeneity across the welfare state models in Europe, and the very different approaches and methods that have been used to modernize public services. The findings indicate that, while there is a tendency towards convergence across the EU states since the early 1980s, significant national and regional differences still persist. The discussion provides an interesting counterpoint to Windrum's discussion (Chapter 8) of heterogeneity arising from the design choices of different innovators. Linking the discussions suggests that innovative ideas are filtered by selection on (at least) two levels: by the innovator and by the selection environment in which the innovator operates.

Path dependency means that the reorganization of an organization's activities fundamentally affects its future innovative potential and scope.

Further, the adoption of market principles places consumer satisfaction at the centre of quality and cost-efficiency indicators and, hence, at the centre of innovation as well. Linking budgets and expenditures to measurable performance outputs led to a major reorientation of the internal organization and management of public health and social services. Relationships are reconfigured within a set of contracts. Within provider organizations financial rewards are elevated (rather than non-financial remuneration) as incentives are linked to individual performance measures.

The search for greater efficiency with public sector health provision by national governments has led to the introduction of new tiers of managers who are set targets by politicians, new management practices and styles, and institution-wide restructuring of public sector agencies. NPM, it should be remembered, is one particular style of management (as made clear in Godø's study). NPM is widely viewed as part and parcel of a fundamental shift in the nature of the relationship between politicians and service organizations – from a trust-based relationship in which a high degree of autonomy was given to service professionals, to a low-trust principal–agent relationship.

Political entrepreneurs are critical of 'professional resistance' to new policy initiatives and highlight ways in which a lack of dialogue between different professional groups inhibits innovation and its diffusion. For instance, public health systems comprise a number of distinct professional groups that have their own communities of practice, rationales and perspectives. It is claimed that these groups exhibit 'silo mentalities', each maintaining its own organizational norms, beliefs and practices, with little or no cross-group communication. Hence, it is argued, there is a need for greater control by the centre in order to ensure progress. Interestingly, one of the proposals of the new Labour government under Prime Minister Gordon Brown is to allow greater local flexibility in the future. It is argued that central control was initially necessary in order to ensure that large increases in funding were directed to improvements of core services, but that this can now be relaxed.

The diabetes case study presented in Chapter 8 provides a glimpse of an alternative. The setting of minimum standards – a prerequisite for NPM benchmarking – requires good information on appropriate medical options, their costs and their benefits. In the case of diabetes in the UK, the standards setting bodies of the NSF and NICE dealt with the principal–agent problem by creating 'pseudo markets for innovation', encouraging local experiments (some centrally funded, others self-funded) and evaluating the results. On this basis a tight set of standards were defined and enforced. This circular process of policy learning is a novel means of stimulating innovation. The process is neither top-down nor bottom-up. Rather, there is a top-down 'inducement' for innovation to be conducted at the local level. It is important to note that this system was short lived and was followed by a conventional NPM type arrangement. However, it offers the prospect of a less adversarial long-term alternative for promoting innovation.

11.3 FORMS OF INNOVATION

With regard to the form(s) that public sector innovation takes, the case studies consistently identify the six types of innovation contained in the taxonomy presented in Chapter 1. Moreover, the case studies highlight interconnectivity between these different forms of innovation:

1. service innovation
2. service delivery innovation
3. administrative and organizational innovation
4. conceptual innovation
5. policy innovation
6. systemic innovation.

The creation of new and/or improved services invariably goes hand-in-hand with service delivery innovations. Further, the research identifies a tight correlation between service, delivery and organizational innovations. This is pointedly remarked upon in the micro studies of hospital innovations conducted in France and in Spain by Djellal and Gallouj, and by García Goñi, respectively. The connections are also highlighted in Staroňová and Malíková's study of residential home services.

García Goñi's case study (Chapter 5) explores the interaction between service, delivery and organizational innovations by taking two rather different examples, digital radiology and ambulatory surgery, and the factors that have influenced the adoption and diffusion of these innovations within one particular hospital in Spain. In each case he finds evidence to support the reverse services lifecycle hypothesis. The initial focus was on efficiency improvements, the focus later changing to the development of new, improved services within the hospital.

In Chapter 7, Djellal and Gallouj view the hospital as a 'package' that combines a wide range of constituent services. This draws our attention to the diversity of potential sources of innovation within a hospital, and to the interactions between these different sources. The aim is to develop a general, integrative framework in which one can understand innovation in hospitals in all its diversity. This theorizing is empirically grounded but, rather than drawing on one particular innovation, it draws on a set of

extended interviews conducted in several hospitals and their health authorities in France, and on empirical material found in the specialist literature.

The wider research frame used in the case studies of Mina and
Ramlogan, Godø and Windrum enables them to additionally explore the
links between conceptual, policy and systemic innovation. The research
indicates that an innovation, is 'radical' when it is underpinned by a conceptual innovation, that is, it involves the development of new visions of
how services and organizations can function, and the development and
implementation of new service characteristics that lead to a significant
(rather than marginal) improvement in welfare. Fundamental conceptual
innovation therefore impacts upon, and requires changes in, service level
organizations and the policy level, necessitating change and innovation at
these different hierarchal levels. It may even require systemic innovation,
that is, the development of new knowledge bases, and new or improved
ways of interacting with other organizations.

Two examples of radical, wide ranging and interconnected innovations
are discussed in detail in the book. One is the shift to NPM-based services
in Western Europe during the 1980s and 1990s. The other is the transition
to market economies by Central and Eastern European countries. Each of
these movements required a new definition of the role of the public sector
and radically new forms of public service provision.

Holt and Hall (Chapter 2) provide an in-depth examination of the historical development of NPM and its impact on innovation. It offers a critical analysis of theory and practice through a case study of project sponsors
involved in public construction projects. The chapter highlights the importance of entrepreneurs ('project sponsors') who are able to successfully
engage a range of public and private sector groups within the innovation
process. This draws attention to the range of skills and knowledge required
for consensus formation. Importantly, the research finds that benchmarking
tools succeed when they support, and are part of, the innovation process.
They tend to fail when they are simply a means of external scrutiny.

Interactions between service, delivery and organizational innovation at the
micro level, and conceptual, policy and systemic innovation at the macro
level mean that multiple types of interconnected innovations may need to be
implemented in order for change to occur. Mina and Ramlogan's study of the
development of coronary angioplasty (Chapter 6) stresses the importance of
interconnected organizations within the wider innovation process. The interaction between public hospitals, private firms and regulatory agencies can
itself be a fundamental source of innovation. The case study highlights the
significance of the mechanisms through which medical knowledge emerges,
grows and transforms itself at the interface between biomedical research, the
manufacturing of drugs and devices, and the delivery of clinical services.

The interconnection and simultaneity of different forms of innovation within the public sector has important implications for policy makers and for our understanding of innovation in general. It is a common practice within the innovation literature to simplify the analysis by focusing on one particular form of innovation, notably product innovation, in isolation of process innovation, organizational innovation and changes in the wider policy environment. This axiomatic assumption of independence between different forms of innovation may (or may not) be a legitimate simplifying strategy for research on private sector manufacturing and services. What is clear, from the research presented in this book, is that it is definitely not appropriate for the study of public sector innovation. Not only do strong interconnections exist between the multiple forms of innovation discussed in the taxonomy of Chapter 1, but one or more tend to occur simultaneously. Interconnectivity and mutual feedbacks mean that each of the six types of innovation must be considered to ensure the drives and outcomes of the innovation process are correctly understood.

11.4 ENTREPRENEURSHIP

Addressing the fifth core research question, entrepreneurship and innovation management are found to play a central role in the innovation process. The chapters in this book consistently highlight the importance of entrepreneurship, creativity and innovation management within the public sector. They overturn the Weberian view of public sector organizations as highly conservative bureaucracies in which new ideas and change are stifled. Understanding how entrepreneurs operate is essential to understanding how public sector entrepreneurs create and manage successful innovations. As noted in Chapter 1, studies of entrepreneurship now go beyond small and medium size enterprises (SMEs). The focus is now on the process of entrepreneurship rather than the domain (see Shane and Venkataraman, 2000). This has opened up studies of large firm entrepreneurship. Our research contributes to the budding discussion of entrepreneurship in public sector organizations.

The research shows that public sector entrepreneurs share much in common with their private sector cousins. Notably, their search for entrepreneurial opportunities and risk taking behaviour. Public sector entrepreneurs have an ability to spot opportunities and to act on them. Without entrepreneurial opportunities there can be no entrepreneurship. Entrepreneurship is a creative process that thrives on uncertainty. As the research has emphasized, entrepreneurship is concerned with identifying opportunities, creatively breaking patterns, taking and managing risk, and organizing and coordinating resources. Entrepreneurs take neglected or underutilized resources and find new ways to use them: ways that satisfy unmet or unrecognized needs. Entrepreneurship integrates vision and action – it is about turning vision into a reality. Of course, the different environment in which public entrepreneurs operate means that there is an emphasis on social responsibility and accountability. Still, the research has shown that public and private sector entrepreneurs share much in common.

Two types of entrepreneurs have been extensively discussed: political entrepreneurs and service entrepreneurs. Political entrepreneurs are policy advocates who are willing to invest their resources – time, energy, reputation, money – to promote a policy in return for anticipated future gain.[2] Political entrepreneurs are constantly searching for new windows of opportunity to push their policies. Political entrepreneurs are driven by material rewards, power, status, reputation and social recognition. They are often highly committed to improving social welfare or achieving particular outcomes from public services. Political entrepreneurs seek to realize a particular vision of how society should work. This includes, for example, notions of when and how public services should be helping people achieve their aspirations and secure their quality of life. This is why political entrepreneurs champion major public innovations and sometimes are the original source of radical innovations. Far from being risk averse, some public sector managers believe that politicians are prone to promoting overly radical changes in public services as a way of making their mark.

Service entrepreneurs are the second type of entrepreneur that have been examined in depth. The research has noted the high level of professional expertise amongst public sector management and staff. They also exhibit a high capacity for creativity and problem solving. This provides a fertile ground for the development and adoption of innovations. This is frequently demonstrated by the presence of entrepreneurs or 'innovation champions' who drive forward the process of innovation and its implementation and diffusion. The service entrepreneur can also be a public manager who aspires to a higher position. Service level entrepreneurs are not always the originators of an innovative idea, they are also gatekeepers who interface with the outside world. They bring in, and then manage, the application of new ideas, technologies and organizational practices. This applied, incremental innovation may still involve radical changes to the services offered and the functioning of the organization itself.

Medical and social service professionals are generally driven by a strong desire to improve the wellbeing and quality of life of people in their care. This can prompt the search for new, service level solutions and approaches. Their close interaction with clients tends to place the emphasis on improvements in the quality of the final service. It is very likely that service entrepreneurs are present in other public sector services. Leadbeater (1997), for example, has found service entrepreneurs in various non-profit and voluntary sectors.

The research conducted in this book suggests that service entrepreneurs are strongly motivated by self-satisfaction, often related to their professional status and identity. There are other motivations. Manager entrepreneurs are interested in advancing their career opportunities, and some enjoy high status within their professional bodies and amongst politicians. Hence status, policy success and social recognition are additional motivations – motivations that coincide with policy entrepreneurs.

In addition to the search for entrepreneurial opportunities and risk taking behaviour, the research has drawn attention to the importance of financial capital and social capital. Successful public entrepreneurs are able to draw on, and exploit, their personal networks. These networks can contain a highly diverse range of people and public–private resources. It requires a particular ability to develop and manage organizations flexibly. The policy entrepreneurs that have been studied have taken advantage of their social networks in order to implement their own ideas. The ability to convince other strategic actors is perhaps an obvious essential quality for politicians. But the research shows it is equally essential for service entrepreneurs. Uncertain environments, devolution of power and the reallocation of resource ownership to unit management level are preconditions for service entrepreneurship. The findings are very much in line with the literature on the importance of social capital and networks for successful entrepreneurship in the private sector (see, for example, Granovetter, 1985; Birley, 1985; Aldrich and Zimmer, 1986).

The research strongly supports Morris and Jones's model of the entrepreneurial process in the public sector (Morris and Jones, 1999). This contains five steps:

1. opportunity identification
2. concept development
3. assessment of required resources
4. acquisition of resources
5. managing and harvesting the venture.

The model is a translation to the public sector of Stevenson's model of private sector entrepreneurship (Stevenson et al., 1989; Stevenson, 1997). Morris and Jones did not empirically test the applicability of the model within the public sector, although there were some casual suggestions that it can be applied to a public university. The research presented in this book is therefore of particular interest because it supports the process described in each stage of the Morris–Jones model.

The first step is opportunity identification. As discussed, entrepreneurship is synonymous with seeking entrepreneurial opportunities. These can be related to new policies, new services, new ideas/concepts, new forms of service delivery, organizational change or the forging of connections with new actors or new knowledge bases.

The second step is concept development. The ability to exploit an opportunity tends to occur within a very short time frame. Hence, the individual entrepreneur must be willing to commit themself to developing the concept at short notice. This requires strong bursts of creativity and imagination, as well as personal commitment. The generation of ideas and project proposals requires financial and social capital to build teams and political connections. Public entrepreneurs must therefore have strong, pre-existing social networks.

The third step is assessment of required resources. This involves identifying and putting in place the human and financial resources needed to implement a project. A set of specialized skills are required. These include the ability to define and implement project ideas, skills in bidding for funds, political support, partnerships and perhaps the ability to raise internal matching funding.

The control or acquisition of resources is the fourth step in the entrepreneurial process. Entrepreneurs learn to use other people's resources and to decide over time what resources they need to acquire. The research identified a range of necessary resources that organizations acquire for innovative projects: skilled professionals and external consultants may need to be employed, existing staff may require retraining, partnerships created and matching funding put in place.

Given the 'fundamental dilemma' of the minimalist state paradigm, that is, the demand for ever higher quality services by citizens unwilling to pay higher taxes – public entrepreneurs seek to maximize welfare while minimizing the level of resources being committed.

Managing and harvesting the venture is the fifth and final step. The ability to manage and successfully deliver the promised services and other outputs is essential. Measurable success increases an entrepreneur's reputation and social capital within their network. It sets up a virtuous circle of financial and social capital, increasing the probability of acquiring and successfully completing future projects.

11.5   INTERACTIONS WITH THE PRIVATE SECTOR, NGOs AND CONSUMERS

Let us now consider the implications of the research for our understanding of the interactions between the public sector, the private sector, NGOs and final consumers. Public sector innovation cannot be understood in isolation from its social and economic environment. This environment includes important interactions with private sector firms, NGOs and the consumers of public services. Equally, the relationship between the public and private sectors, and between public sector and NGOs, is two-way.

To understand public–private interactions and their impact on economic growth and social welfare, we need to go beyond discussions of the impact of public policy, regulation and procurement on the private sector and on private sector innovation. Much of the technological innovation that is taking place in the private sector is rooted in the interactions between public and private organizations. This is especially clear in the health sector case studies. New equipment is often developed as a result of a dialogue between specialists in hospitals and manufacturing companies. The pharmaceutical industry interacts closely with universities and research hospitals in the development of new medicines and treatments. This is more than a client–provider relationship. There is a circular flow of knowledge and expertise between public and private sector organizations.

Mina and Ramlogan's study of coronary angioplasty in Chapter 6 provides a perfect illustration of innovation in its widest setting. Innovation networks contain public and private entrepreneurs and other key actors who are distributed across time and space, and operate in different organizational domains. The authors argue that interactions between public hospitals, private firms and regulatory agencies were themselves a fundamental source of innovation, and highlight the significance of the mechanisms through which medical knowledge emerges, grows and transforms itself at the interface between biomedical research, the manufacturing of drugs and devices, and the delivery of clinical services.

This distribution of public–private networks raises a particular set of issues for management, creativity and entrepreneurship. Successful innovation requires the development of mechanisms that facilitate the development of co-related knowledge about the nature of the problem being tackled and its potential solution(s). Interactions between dispersed groups of practitioners need to be systematized through various communication channels, and incentive structures must be put in place that reward individuals without compromising the innovation process.

This book has highlighted the important role played by NGOs as sources of innovation, entrepreneurship and funding. NGOs have the political power and skills needed to negotiate the ideological and normative positions that shape civic society. They can provide an internal space (a protective environment) that encourages experimentation with new ideas and new initiatives. While NGOs are not necessarily 'representative', they do represent the interests of some, and are highly committed to public causes.

Godø suggests that NGOs can provide a similar function to new technology start-up firms: they are an agile and flexible vehicle for developing and testing new ideas and innovations. NGOs have networks of dedicated people who are rich potential sources of knowledge, skills and creativity. Staroňová and Malíková identified NGOs as a key source of learning for public sector organizations. In their case study the Slovak organizations learned how to manage innovation from foreign NGOs rather than local private sector organizations.

NGOs can also be important sources of additional financial resources necessary for research, evaluation and the piloting of an innovation. This was highlighted in the case of transition countries, such as Slovakia, by Staroňová and Malíková. Equally, Godø found that private charitable funds (old family fortunes) were an important source of venture capital in Norway.

The other key actor that has been discussed is the citizen – the 'consumer' of public sector services. Chapters 1, 2 and 8 have discussed the rationale and development of consumerization in some detail. Is it really motivated by the search for greater democratization in public services and for greater accountability of public sector professionals, as has been suggested? Alternatively, is it part of an ongoing principal–agent struggle between politicians and public service professionals? If it is the latter, then it is part and parcel of a process in which politicians seek to gain greater control over the behaviour and actions of service professionals.

Three key issues associated with consumerization have been discussed. The first is the rights and responsibilities of citizens, and the relationship between citizens and the state. These are very different to the relationship between providers and customers. There is an urgent need for a debate, not yet begun, on the implications of consumerization for civil society, individual responsibility, and the relationship between the individual, society and the state. As we have seen, confusion on the issue of societal and individual responsibility pervades current health and social service policies across Europe.

The second issue is the applicability and limits of consumer sovereignty. The concept of consumer sovereignty in markets makes some particularly strong assumptions about the conditions under which decisions are made. Notably, it is assumed that good quality information about products is available, and that consumers possess the knowledge necessary to translate that information into meaningful, informed choices. Over the last 15 years economists have debated whether these assumptions hold in many private sector markets. For knowledge-intensive services, such as health, for example, it is not obvious that individuals will possess the information and knowledge necessary to make informed diagnoses of their illness and, hence, informed and independent choices between the alternative treatments. Just as politicians face problems of sufficient information and knowledge, so too do patients. Are patients really expected to handle the often complex (and, through new knowledge, changing) medical information on illnesses, the alternative treatments and their side effects? To what extent is this socially responsible? This opens up important issues regarding individual and social responsibility and accountability.

The third issue is the important but unstated assumption that individuals 'want' to become empowered consumers. The idea is that informed, empowered customers will take greater responsibility for their own actions and, hence, place less strain on public services. For example, more environmentally aware consumers will be concerned about pollution. They will create a smaller carbon footprint and will recycle more, reducing demands on public refuse collection and processing, and landfill. Empowered health consumers will take greater care of their own health, reducing demands on the public health system.

Do a sufficient number of individuals really wish to take on these responsibilities? This is an empirical question that will be answered in the near future. But there is a potential sting in the tail. 'Consumers' may turn to their national governments, as 'service providers' to whom they pay taxes, and demand that the state take responsibility for solving customers' problems. If this occurs, consumerization will not lessen the burden on the state but increase it still further.

11.6   FORWARD LOOK

Let us finally look forwards to the policy implications of the current research and to future research in the field. There is a need to reappraise what (we think) we know about innovation. Our existing knowledge has largely been developed through studies of manufacturing. This has recently been challenged, and in part revised, by research on private sector services innovation. A far larger challenge is likely to arise from the study of public sector innovation, and of public–private sector innovation. This is not just of importance to academics. It is essential for policy makers. Deficiencies in our understanding of the drivers and dynamics of innovation have significant implications for effective policy making.

Effective policy requires an understanding of the relationship between public sector performance and overall economic performance. It represents a new perspective on the role of the public sector in the economy; one which sees the public sector as an integrated part of the economy and an important element of its development. Take, for example, the EU Lisbon Agenda.

Meeting the Lisbon Agenda crucially depends on understanding how to make the most of public and private services, their interactions and the essential role of innovation in public–private networks. A key role is to be played by policy and by policy makers. Different policies may be required in different sectors and at different stages of an innovation life cycle. Policy makers must understand how the institutional arrangements found in different nations and regions affect the development of life cycles, and their differential impact on economic performance and social welfare. They must also understand how public–private organizations interact within innovation networks, and identify the conditions under which these work best. This is essential for maximizing policy impact on growth, employment and welfare.

This is the ambitious agenda that is being mapped for future research. The research presented in this book has contributed to the beginnings of a new agenda by identifying a set of key drivers and facilitators of innovation within the public sector, and opening up a debate about the nature and drivers of public sector entrepreneurs. It is hoped that the reader has been stimulated by the book. Its contents may have caused the reader to pause and to reconsider their own experiences and understandings of public sector innovation and public sector entrepreneurship. Hopefully, the book will even inspire some readers to make their own contributions to the new agenda in the near future!

NOTES

1. It is worth noting that the word 'innovation' is not universally used in the private sector either. It is commonly used by manufacturing firms in the USA and the UK, usually tied to R&D, but its usage is far less common amongst private sector service firms where alternative words are used. Also, there is national variation in the use of the word. It is less commonly used outside the USA and the UK. In some Continental European countries, such as France and Germany, the word is hardly ever used. This has led to well known problems in accounting for innovation in the Community Innovation Survey, for instance.
2. The findings correspond with the previous findings of Kingdon (1984) and Boyett (1997), and with the work of Morris and Jones (1999).

REFERENCES

Aldrich, H. and C. Zimmer (1986), 'Entrepreneurship through social networks', in D.L. Sexton and R.W. Smilor (eds), *The Art and Science of Entrepreneurship*, Cambridge, MA: Ballinger, pp. 3–23.
Birley, S. (1985), 'The role of networks in the entrepreneurial process', *Journal of Business Venturing*, **1**, 107–17.
Boyett, I. (1997), 'The public sector entrepreneur – a definition', *International Journal of Entrepreneurial Behaviour and Research*, 3(2), 77–92.

Granovetter, M.S. (1985), 'Economic action and social structure: the problem of embeddedness', *American Journal of Sociology*, **91**, 81–150.

Kingdon, J. (1984), *Agenda, Alternatives, and Public Policies*, Boston, MA: Little, Brown.

Leadbeater, C. (1997), *The Rise of the Social Entrepreneur*, London: Demos.

Morris, M.H. and F.F. Jones (1999), 'Entrepreneurship in established organizations: the case of the public sector', *Entrepreneurship Theory and Practice*, **24**(1) (Fall), 71–91.

Shane, S. and S. Venkataraman (2000), 'The promise of entrepreneurship as a field of research', *Academy of Management Review*, **25**(1), 217–26.

Stevenson, H.H. (1997), 'The six dimensions of entrepreneurship', in S. Birley and D.F. Muzyka (eds), *Mastering Enterprise*, London: Financial Times Pitman.

Stevenson, H.H., M.J. Roberts and H.I. Grousbeck (1989), *Business Ventures and the Entrepreneur*, Homewood, IL: Irwin.

Index

Printed and bound by CPI Group (UK) Ltd, Croydon, CR0 4YY

23/04/2025

14660956-0008